THE UNSCRUPULOUS
*Scams, Cons, Fakes, & Frauds
that Poison the Fine Arts*

NICK JAMES MILETI

BORDIGHERA PRESS

Library of Congress Control Number: 2009905784

Printed in the United States.

Published by
BORDIGHERA PRESS
John D. Calandra Italian American Institute
25 West 43rd Street, 17th Floor
New York, NY 10036

VIA FOLIOS 56
ISBN 978–1–59954–003–0

AUTHOR'S NOTE

While it is naïve and without historic foundation
to expect members of the intelligentsia to behave
in a more scrupulous and humane fashion
than those who do not lead the life of the mind,
there has nonetheless been a persistent expectation
that they will do so.

— Jonathan Petropoulos

The renowned English critic, poet, and artist John Ruskin (1819–1900) wrote, "Great nations write their autobiographies in three manuscripts; the book of their deeds, the book of their words and the book of their art. Not one of these books can be understood unless we read the two others, but of the three, the only trustworthy one is the last." An Old Sicilian Saying is another way to put it. "If you have two coins, buy a bread with one and art with the other. The bread gives you life and the art a reason for living." There is one caveat, of course. Everything about art must be legitimate.

In the early 1960s, as Prosecutor and Assistant Law Director of the City of Lakewood, Ohio, I dealt with all crime committed in the city. It was my job to bring the perpetrators to justice. The cons and scams particularly fascinated me because they require a certain amount of intelligence, finesse, ingenuity, and, yes, charm. Why would people with these attributes go into a life of crime? Along the way I became intrigued by the specific subject of art fraud. What triggered the interest was a short film named *Day of the Painter*. That's right, a film. And a short one at that.

In the early 1960s, if you lived in the Western suburbs of Cleveland and wanted to see a foreign film, you had to drive across town to the East suburbs. I resented that, so I organized something I called The Classic Film Club of Lakewood. I found a distributor in Chicago, made-up a schedule of films from its catalogue of 35 mm films (remember, this is before cable, tapes, and discs), and sold the package, at cost, to friends, neighbors and appreciative film buffs who heard about the caper. I hired a school kid to run the projector and showed a short film and a feature foreign film in Lakewood Library (and later Lakewood High School) every Friday night in the winter. The program was so successful it ran in Lakewood for about six years (I forget exactly how many), and several summers in the further west suburb of Bay Village, which I organized at their request.

Day of the Painter, which won an Oscar in 1960 in the category Short Subject, Live Action, opened one of the movie nights. I'll tell you about the short if you absolutely promise to take into account I haven't seen the film in over 40 years. (I've tried to find it, but to no avail). The details escape me, but I remember the basics perfectly:

Not a word is spoken in the entire film.

The sun comes up on a little island. A man awakens in a dingy shack. After throwing on his clothes he goes outside to a decrepit pier. He takes a large piece of wood that was on the pier and lays it flat. He then uncovers several cans of paint (I forget how many). He takes the first can (let's say red) and swooshes it across the wooden square. He follows that with the can of green, then blue, then white (I forget the colors and the order.)

He then starts up a chain saw and begins to cut the big block of wood into about a dozen (I forget how many) smaller pieces. The chain saw noise segues into the sound of an approaching motorboat. The man (we now know he's an artist) props the pieces up for display just before the motorboat rounds a corner and approaches the pier.

The two men acknowledge each other; they obviously have done this on a regular basis. The man from the motorboat (we can tell he's an art dealer) points to several of the pieces and pays the artist.

The artist puts the sold paintings in the motorboat and the dealer leaves. When the boat rounds the corner of the small island and is out of sight, the artist tosses the unsold pieces of wood into the water. The End.

I have presented the stories that tamper with the souls of nations in logical order, as much as that is possible. One of the hardest tasks was slotting each rascal, as their cons and scams almost always overlap catagories. Although some scholars differentiate between fakes and forgeries, I use the terms interchangeably, as do most observers. Ditto scams and cons.

The facts presented in the book were obtained over a five-year period from various sources, including interviews, visits, books, newspapers, and periodical articles. Every item has been checked to insure accuracy and to satisfy my own conscience. If I couldn't confirm a fact or statement with double and triple checking, it wasn't used. If there are any mistakes (and there will be) they are honest mistakes, and like the conclusions, they belong only to me.

While this book is heavy with villains (hence the title) there are a number of heroes. Archaeologist Oscar White Muscarella and connoisseur Federico Zeri leap to mind. However, it is the courageous reporters, and their bosses, who deserve special mention. Virtually every art scandal, con, and scam has been exposed over the ages because of an alert press. Without their dedication, for example, the major scandals at the Getty and the Smithsonian (to name only two), would never have come to light.

Special mention is due Christopher Knight, Ralph Frammolino, and Jason Felch of the *Los Angeles Times*; James Grimaldi and Jacqueline Trescott of the *Washington Post*; Geoff Edgers of the *Boston Globe*; and Mike McGraw and Steve Paul of the *Kansas City Star*. The entire civilized world is indebted to them and their fellow journalists.

No matter how unscrupulous the people in this book may be, I am confident you will be fascinated by their stories, all of which are true.

No one could make this stuff up.

NJM

PREFACE

Art fraud is everywhere. As long as man has created something truly original, forgers have copied it, and the con men and scammers sell it as an original. Because the subject is so vast, it eventually became clear that it was necessary to pick one or two aspects of the problem and focus on them.

I originally intended to limit this book to fake paintings, the artists who create the works and the people who handle them. Why? Because paintings are the branch of the fine arts that command the most visceral attention from the public. If the average person is going to invest any money in the art market, no matter how little, he or she will almost always buy a painting or a reproduction.

My research led me to the dramatic work of the Italian government regarding the looting, smuggling and selling of their patrimony. This forced me to broaden my thinking to include fake sculpture and the handling of plundered artifacts and antiquities. Why? Because I learned that when museums or collectors buy real or fake statues, funeral wreaths or reliquaries (for example), they are cutting out a piece of a nation's heart. The context is lost, and so is the opportunity to learn about the culture from which the plundered item was wrenched.

The subject of fakes is so vast the reader needs to look elsewhere to read about forgeries of:

Books,	Engravings,	Money,
Book bindings,	Fiscal stamps,	Music,
Candlesticks,	Food,	Paperweights,
Carpets,	Furniture,	Porcelain,
Ceramics,	Glass,	Postage Stamps,
Chalices,	Icons,	Rings,
Clock cases,	Ivories,	Signatures,
Coins,	Lace,	Stock Certificates
Costumes,	Letters,	Seals,
Currency,	Locks,	Snuff boxes,
Custom stamps,	Manuscripts,	Watches,
Diaries,	Metalwork,	Weapons,
Documents,	Miniatures,	Wine,

and anything else man is capable of selling for more than it takes to create.

As Horace said 2,000 years ago, "He who knows a thousand works of art, knows a thousand frauds." Even though the subject of art theft is of monumental importance (more than 12,000 pieces of art are stolen from Italy and France each year; in a ten-year period, over 6,000 grave sites were looted in Italy, which, coincidentally, is the same number that have been examined by archeologists), the reader will have to look elsewhere for an in-depth study of the subject. In addition, since it's easier to move art around the world than it is to move money, financial crime (including money laundering) is rampant in the art market. That is also a subject for its own book.

TABLE OF CONTENTS

CHAPTER ONE
ATTRIBUTION OR AUTHENTICATION.
WHATEVER YOU CALL IT, IT'S A BEAR

I am prepared to admit that it is a pardonable mistake
to be taken in by a forgery, if the forgery is well done;
but when it is a case of a genuine work of art,
then there should be no mistake about it,
and I cannot excuse the man who declares it to be false.
It can only be bad faith or ignorance on his part.
— Icilio Federico Joni

The difference between the right artwork and almost the right artwork
is the difference between lightning and the lightning bug.
— Old Sicilian Saying

If I like it, I say it's mine. If I don't, I say it's a fake.
— Pablo Picasso,
when asked about fakes of his work

Anyone who has seen a painting or other work of art will tell you that, at best, distinguishing between the real and the fake is difficult. Why? Art is imponderable, incapable of being evaluated with exactness. This is one of the forger's greatest advantages because this inexactness is the basic reason for the inconsistency of the experts regarding authentication. Moreover, the quality of the forgery adds to the level of inconsistency in spotting fakes; the better the fake, the harder it is to uncover. In the case of the Old Masters, there is little, if any, information available to help the connoisseur. Adding to the confusion, if a fake hangs on a wall long enough, it becomes right in the eyes of the experts, and future paintings by that artist are judged to be authentic based on the fake. Sadly, attributing mediocre works to leading masters is often market driven, which is a major reason there is so much acrimony in the matter of attribution.

But, doesn't scientific analysis solve all questions about who painted or sculpted what? Nope. Even though there are abundant ways in which paintings and other artworks can be scientifically tested for authenticity, that doesn't solve the problem.

Scientific methods range from neutron activation analysis (analyzing the composition of the elements) to computers; from fingerprint analysis to digital image processing; from X-ray to infrared and ultra-violet photography (detecting underlying earlier paintings and later repairs); from carbon dating (measuring age) to polarized light microscopy (pigment analysis); from chemical analysis (decomposing paint into its constituent elements) to dendrochronology (to determine the age of wood used.) And the list goes on. New scientific methods are regularly being brought to bear on the issue of authentication.

Why doesn't science tell us what's a fake and what isn't? First, scientific analysis is not infallible. Mistakes occur. Moreover, it is limited. Scientific investigation can, to a large degree, disclose that the component parts of a work of art are anachronistic, such as proving that paint or paper used in the work being examined wasn't invented or discovered until years after the artwork was claimed to have been created. That sort of thing.

Scientific analysis also has a fairly good record in determining the time period in which a painting was created. This gives the expert a leg up in his determination of whether a piece is authentic or a fake. This is science's greatest contribution, but a major problem remains. While scientific examination may tell us that the work is not by a certain artist, scientific examination cannot tell us who produced the work. For these reasons, the eye of the connoisseur is critical to authentication. If someone repeatedly examines an artist's work, like a handwriting expert, that person begins to know the idiosyncrasies of the individual artist.

If that's true, why is there still confusion over attribution? Several reasons. For one thing, aesthetic judgments are subjective. Most experts, fearful of a crippling lawsuit, are afraid to stick their necks out, so they bob and weave. They say things like, "I found nothing that was incompatible with the painting being an X." The problem is, this statement does not say the painting is by X. Or (the one I like best) "I have never seen an X like this."

The problem of accuracy is acute in France, where experts are held legally responsible for their authentications and mistakes can lead to heavy, career-ending damage awards. The person who is the reigning expert on an artist at any given time can also pose a problem. That is, a person who is stricter in interpretation might be replaced by a more liberal expert. And vice versa.

Adding to the confusion, a catalogue raisonné (a collection of an artist's work, which most people consider the definitive word on whether a work is authentic or a fake) historically prompts as many questions as answers. For example, when there is more than one catalogue raisonné of an artist's oeuvre, it is not unusual for authors of the catalogues (which require an inordinate amount of time and money) to have different opinions about the authenticity of certain works. Also, sometimes a painting that was originally listed as authentic is dropped in a later edition. And vice versa.

The history of workshops in days gone by makes it harder for the experts to authenticate artworks and easier for forgers to create and sell them. There are numerous examples of great workshops, most notably that of Rembrandt van Rijn (1606–1669). The Wallace Collection in London once displayed and labeled twelve paintings as true Rembrandts. Today, the red-faced museum displays only one of those paintings as a Rembrandt, and even that one is suspect. (While its number of Rembrandt fakes was startling, the Wallace was in good company. The number of Rembrandts in London's National Gallery shrank from 15 to 10, and even in the Rembrandt collection of Queen Elizabeth II, the number dropped from seven to four.)

The most interesting workshop, however, is that of Peter Paul Rubens (1577–1640) because of the all star cast he attracted, including Jacob Jordaens (1593–1678) David Teniers the Elder (1582–1649), and the incomparable Anthony Van Dyke (1599–1641), to name a few who worked for Rubens. To complicate authentication matters further, the practice was that whenever a workshop artist excelled at a subject (say flowers or animals) he would paint that part of the piece and the boss would tie it all together, if he had the time.

Experts agree that the lack of in-depth knowledge of the huge Cuban, Mexican and Latin American art markets (unlike that of, say, America or England) make it impossible to police them. Reputable experts, exhibition histories, and scholarly records are scarce. The same problem of massive amounts of new money combined with the lack of expertise plagues the Russian art market. According to a 1997 *Time* magazine article, after Russia opened up, many Russian art experts became capitalists overnight, selling their certificates of authenticity for tens of thousands of dollars. The forgers have become more clever, no longer just making up artworks, they make up artists as well, creating whole biographies. Here's a funny line from an expert in the field: "If you burned all the fakes of Russian avant-garde now hanging in galleries and private collections around the world, the West would obtain a valuable source of energy." There are so many fakes coming out of Russia that experts now consider every Russian painting to be a fake until it is proven to be authentic.

There are numerous cases where an artist has authenticated fakes as his own work, and, believe it or not, artists have sometimes even called their own works fakes. Maurice de Vlaminck (1876–1958) would sometimes refuse to authorize his own works because he didn't like them anymore; he was once charged and fined for rejecting one of his own paintings as a fake.

Bowdoin University art history professor Clifton Olds tells a wonderful story about Henri Matisse (1869–1954) giving an art dealer 20 drawings. After a time, the dealer had a chance to sell the works so he asked Matisse to sign them. Matisse signed 14 and said the other six were fakes. The dealer could hardly contain himself, pointing out to Matisse that he (Matisse) had given him all 20 of the drawings at the same time. Unconvinced, Matisse left the gallery. Later that day, however, Matisse returned, studied the other six drawings, and, without a word, signed them. Yes, artists are not only complex creatures, they certainly complicate the process of authentication.

The following story perfectly encapsulates the difficulty (and emotion) of authentication. The renowned English art historian John Richardson, and Douglas Cooper, English art critic and expert on cubism and Fernand Leger (1881–1955), were close friends for many years. One day, while examining photographs of two paintings by Leger, Richardson said to Cooper, "They're fakes."

Cooper yelled in return, "How dare you pontificate to me about Leger? These paintings are absolutely authentic. Get out. Get out."

Richardson continues the story. "And [then] he took another look at the photos of the paintings and I realized he realized I was right and he was wrong. Things would never be the same [between us]."

Wow!

CHAPTER TWO
THE CRÉME DE LA CRÉME
THREE ART CONS THAT WILL PROBABLY NEVER BE TOPPED

THE MONA LISA

The Background

Marques Eduardo de Valfierno, born about 1850 into a moneyed family in Buenos Aires, began selling fake art early in life. Since the debonair, good looking man had automatic access to the rich and famous, scamming them was a breeze for the socially adept con man de Valfierno.

At the turn of the nineteenth century, the brilliant artist and restorer Yves Chaudron was also living in Buenos Aires. The artist hooked up with de Valfierno and began grinding out fake Bartolome Murillo (1618–1682) paintings to order. The paintings were of such high quality de Valfierno had no trouble selling them.

About 1908, de Valfierno decided he needed new challenges and to expand his horizons, so he moved to Paris, the center of the world's art action at the time. The artist, Yves Chaudron, missed his native France (and the money from de Valfierno) so he joined the dealer in Paris.

The Scheme

Sometime between 1908 and 1910, de Valfierno decided to execute the biggest con of his life. De Valfierno planned to sell fake copies of the world's most famous painting, the Mona Lisa by Leonardo da Vinci (1452–1519), to six unsuspecting marks. Why would anyone (much less six knowledgeable collectors) purchase a fake Mona Lisa when the masterpiece was known by one and all to be hanging in the Louvre Museum in Paris? That's the beauty of the scam.

De Valfierno planned to have the Mona Lisa stolen from the Louvre and then, under cover of what he knew would be an intense media spotlight of the theft, he would sell the fake paintings to six pre-selected marks. The claim to each of the suckers would be that they (and they alone) were going to be offered the original Mona Lisa painting that de Valfierno was arranging to have pilfered from the Louvre.

Assembling the Team

Confident that his old co-conspirator was up to the task, de Valfierno talked Chaudron into painting six forgeries of the Mona Lisa. How good was Yves Chaudron? Chaudron was described by journalist Karl Decker as "a pale wisp of a Frenchman, almost a skeleton," whose skill as a forger was of the "uncanny sort that breaks the heart of the collector."

In late 1910, Chaudron and de Valfierno visited the Louvre to inspect the new glass coverings that the museum had installed over paintings to prevent vandalism. The protective glass coverings gave de Valifiero his "Eureka" moment; he knew instinctively who should be his designated thief. After checking around town, de Valfierno eventually found the man he was looking for to pull off the heist. He was an Italian living in Paris named Vincenzo Perugia (c. 1881–1947).

De Valfierno recruited Perugia (and two associates) because the short stocky carpenter, with the black hair and imposing mustache, had worked in the Louvre constructing the controversial shadow boxes. How perfect was this choice? Vincenzo Perugia knew the layout of the museum, the habits of the security and cleaning personnel, and the rhythms and schedules of both.

The Execution, Part One

Yves Chaudron went to the Louvre and painted a copy of the Mona Lisa from the original. (This practice was popular by students and young artists at the time and raised no eyebrows.) Then, working out of a tiny studio in Montmartre, Chaudron copied the most famous painting in the world five more times, using his first copy as the model. Chaudron then purchased aged wooden panels, attached his fakes, and duplicated the fine, hairline cracks (known as craquelure) all old master paintings eventually acquire.

The Set Up

De Valfierno then went to New York and established relationships with several American and English con men. The group fanned out across America and visited the carefully selected marks de Valfierno had identified. De Valfierno handled Brazil himself. Following the de Valfierno script, the con men suggested to the potential purchasers that there might be something spectacular coming down the pike, broadly hinting at its subject. Without hesitation, just as de Valfierno figured, the greedy and unscrupulous collector/victims all signed on to the pitch.

While this was going on, de Valfierno was shipping the Chaudron Mona Lisa fakes from France to New York. He personally collected the fakes at customs. There was no problem from the customs officials because de Valfierno declared that the works were merely decorative copies, which, ironically, they were. In addition to stashing away five Mona Lisa fakes in New York, he forwarded the sixth to Brazil.

The Execution, Part Two

In 1911, the plan was put into action. On August 21, a Monday morning, Perugia and his accomplices, having hidden in a storeroom overnight, donned worker's tunics, removed the Mona Lisa from the wall and made their way to a service stairway. Safe from the eyes of the real workers who were busy cleaning the closed museum (as they did every Monday), Perugia cut the tape holding the wooden panel on which the masterpiece was painted. He then brazenly walked out of the poorly-secured museum with the Mona Lisa tucked under his tunic.

The deed was done in about one hour, but it took over 24 hours before anyone in the museum realized that the most famous painting in the world had been stolen from under their noses. (The workers who noticed the Mona Lisa was missing assumed that the masterpiece was being photographed, a practice that was prevalent at the Louvre at the time.)

The Reaction

The theft of the Mona Lisa caused the greatest press frenzy in the history of press frenzies. It was a worldwide free-for-all. Every police department in Europe and, predictably, considering the nature of the heist, every fortune teller, tarot-card reader, and spiritualist jumped on the case. In the course of the two-year investigation, even Pablo Picasso (1881–1973) and his friend, the poet Guilaume Apollinaire (1880–1918) were suspected. After being detained for over one week Apollinaire was released. Both men were eventually cleared. Heads all over France rolled, and new security rules were put into place at the Louvre.

The Aftermath

De Valfierno met with Perugia and his associates. After assuring himself that he was looking at the real Mona Lisa, true to his word he paid the thieves handsomely for a job well done. Yves Chaudron, the self-effacing, timid faker, had already been paid well for his part of the scam so he was content to remain in the background for the remainder of the con.

The Payoff

De Valfierno went back to New York. He set up an office in a fancy hotel where he met his previously recruited colleagues. The con men fanned out once more and delivered Chaudron's fake paintings to the marks. Since the original was still missing, and every newspaper in the world had written endlessly about the theft, it was easy for de Valfierno and his crew to convince each of the six buyers that the Chaudron Mona Lisa fake they were offering them was the original Mona Lisa stolen from the Louvre. The team collected $300,000 for each fake (de Valfierno personally handled the Brazilian sale), raking in $1,800.000. In today's dollars, the take was worth approximately $50,000,000.

The Mistake

Since the caper had worked perfectly, de Valfierno felt no need to keep romancing his operatives. After all, he never wanted the Mona Lisa, he was only interested in the money from the scam. Two years after the heist, in 1913, Perugia (who had hidden the masterpiece in a false bottom of an old truck) still had not heard a word from de Valfierno. He became disillusioned, feeling he was being unfairly abandoned. The thief of the century (or any century) then turned bitter, then angry, then vindictive. Besides, Perugia was basically broke.

The Beginning of the End

Using the amusing pseudonym of Leonardo Vincenzo, Perugia took the masterwork, which he had been hiding in his tiny apartment in Paris, with him on a train ride to Florence. Perugia tried to sell his authentic Mona Lisa to Alfredo Geri, a dealer in Florence. After examining the masterpiece, the stunned but astute dealer contacted his friend, Giovanni

Poggi, the director of the Uffizi Gallery, who confirmed the authenticity of the painting. Instead of making a deal, Vincenzo Perugia was arrested.

The Italians agreed to return the Mona Lisa to France (after a triumphant tour of Italy), but would not release Vincenzo Perugia to the French. While being interrogated, the unschooled but street-wise carpenter came up with a brilliant story. Perugia claimed that he had stolen the Mona Lisa because he wanted to return the lady to her rightful home, which, naturally, was Italy.

The End

Vincenzo Perugia became a national hero, and his 1914 trial and sentence reflected this. Perugia, who had served seven months in jail during the investigation and trial, was given a seven month sentence and freed. The Marques Eduardo de Valfierno disappeared with a small fortune and died in New York in 1941. The cautious and mysterious copier Yves Chaudron took his fees and disappeared into the woodwork, living comfortably the rest of his life, basically retired, outside of Paris.

The purchasers of the six fake Mona Lisa paintings have never been identified, and Yves Chaudron's six fakes, undiscovered to this day, joined the hundreds of other Mona Lisa fakes scattered throughout the world. Incidentally, there was no need to blow off the suckers as is almost always necessary in long cons. The scam was so beautifully conceived and executed, each of the marks believed deep-down that he owned the authentic Mona Lisa that had been stolen from the Louvre.

ANTE TOPIC MIMARA

Ante Topic Mimara was an unscrupulous art dealer, painter, restorer, and forger. Throughout his life, Mimara changed his name and abode like mothers change diapers on their newborn babies. In fact, his entire life is surrounded in mystery, although he was probably born in 1898 in Split, Croatia and died in 1987.

Early in life Mimara figured out that art would be his passport to riches. In the mid-1920s, while still in his twenties, Mimara opened a gallery in Vienna, which he stocked with fakes he painted himself. He also hired artists to paint fakes to his specifications from photographs he had collected. When things got hot in Vienna, always one step ahead of the authorities, Mimara moved to Paris where he continued producing and selling fakes. Nothing unusual so far for an art dealer. But wait, it gets better. Much better.

Mimara served in the Yugoslav army with Josip Broz, who became world famous as Marshall Tito. Together they sacked the cathedral in Zagreb of its artistic treasures, which they sold to whomever would buy the looted artworks, including American museums.

In the run-up to World War II, Mimara positioned himself in Berlin because he correctly read the situation the world was in at the time; the Nazis were coming into power. He assiduously courted the hierarchy of the party, ingratiating himself as an art expert to Hermann Goering, among others. (Mimara always claimed he was buddies with Hitler, but this is unsubstantiated.) In any case, his connections with the Nazis gave him the opportunity to acquire, at rock bottom prices, artworks the Nazi's had plundered, mostly from the Jews.

When the German's surrendered in 1945, most people associated with the Nazis were distraught. Not Mimara. His first move was to contact his old army buddy Tito. His pitch to Tito was that he would represent the Yugoslavian government and reclaim its looted art treasures. Wink, wink.

Mimara explained that his target was the Central Collecting Point in Munich, which was established after the war. (In one of history's most intelligent and humane efforts, tens of thousands looted works of art were brought to the agency in Munich where they were researched and returned to their rightful owners.) Tito, with nothing to lose and everything to gain, readily agreed to the scam and appointed Mimara an officer in the Yugoslav army. The suave Ante Topic Mimara had all of the typical con man's attributes, including being well-groomed and generous with cash. With his slicked-back long black hair and black beard, he also looked smashing in his fake Yugoslav army uniform.

Mimara's first move was to become accredited by the Allied Control Council of Germany, which was the Big Four governing body that ran defeated Germany from 1945 to 1948. Once this critical accreditation was accomplished, Mimara put the second phase of his plan into effect. It was equally brilliant. Mimara romanced a young German art historian who worked in Munich (you guessed it) at the Central Collecting Point. His mark's name was Wiltrud Mersman, and she and the newly-minted Colonel became lovers. After that, it was (relatively) easy.

Thanks to Mersman, Mimira gained access to the agency's official card catalogues, which contained the complete list, including descriptions and measurements, of all of the unclaimed works of looted art in the agency's possession. While waiting for the most propitious moment to make his move, Mimara would send information on the pieces he wanted to home base. His contacts would then send official requests for restitution to Mimara in Munich.

In December, 1948, Mimara made his move. The ersatz Colonel presented himself to the Americans at the Central Collecting Point. As usual, his instincts about timing were impeccable: The work of the agency was almost over, so there was a great deal of confusion and urgency. "I am," he told the Americans, "the Yugoslav government's representative in charge of Restitution of Fine Arts and Monuments." He then submitted an impressive list of hundreds of paintings, tapestries, silver pieces, and various other art objects.

Within six months after investigating the claims, every one of the 166 claims Mimara had fabricated from the official card catalogues were turned over to him. The loot weighed several tons and included some 60 paintings, most of them important pieces. Mimara double-crossed his partners back home and siphoned off the cream-of-the-crop. He moved those pieces to Switzerland, which he later sold for his own benefit.

Mimara was able to continue his scamming for three more decades. How was Mimara able to continue his scam into the 1950s and '60s? The United States government would not admit it had been duped and had handed over millions of dollars of precious artwork to a con artist. Worse, they decided to lie and cover-up their horrific mistake. In 1952, when the US government was questioned by the rightful owners about their missing artworks (the pieces given to Mimara), the Americans said those pieces were lost. Mimara had one last scam up his sleeve.

In 1972, Mimara made a deal with the government of Croatia. He donated the items he scammed from the Central Collection Point that he couldn't sell, plus he included in his gift his vast collection of over 3,000 fake pieces. All to be housed in something called The Mimara Museum.

The building selected was a classic old schoolhouse, which the government would pay to rehab. Mimara also demanded (and received) substantial yearly annuities and living arrangements for him and his wife, Wiltrud, for the rest of their lives. (Wiltrud, you will remember, is the young art historian Mimara married in 1957.) Since Mimira had assured the government that the donated works were worth over $1,000,000,000, it's understandable that when the museum opened in 1987 it was touted as the "Zagreb Louvre."

There was, however, a surprise for the government officials. It was promptly determined that almost the entire collection consisted of fakes, and even the over-the-top aggressive attributions of the handful of authentic pieces have since been downgraded.

JOHN DREWE

When paintings don't look right, meaning, in art world double-speak, they look like fakes, the experts turn to the provenance of the work. Provenance is the history of a piece, the paper trail that traces ownership from the time it is created, through its sales and exhibitions, to the present. Art authenticators are trained to double-check their eye by going to the records. Where does the authenticator look? Anywhere and everywhere, particularly the archives of major museums.

What kind of evidence do the experts look for? Sales receipts, letters, stamps, catalogues, certificates of authenticity from painter's estates, any documentation that tells the researcher where the painting has been over the years. Generally speaking, experts don't have much faith in themselves, so if the evidence satisfies them that the painting is real, they inevitably stop doubting their eye and authenticate the item. There is one caveat. A gigantic one. The evidence uncovered must be real or the entire process is absolutely meaningless.

John Myatt, a facile English painter born about 1945, lived in Fair Oak, a small town in Staffordshire. In the mid-1980s Myatt's wife walked out on him and their two infant children. Barely making a living wage as an art teacher and desperately needing money, Myatt had a brainstorm. To earn money working part-time out of his home, Myatt placed an ad in an

English magazine called *Private Eye,* offering to paint legal copies of nine-teenth- and twentieth-century paintings for 250 pounds each.

In the late 1980s, an English con man named John Drewe (born c. 1941 as John Cockett) spotted the ad and contacted Myatt. Drewe commissioned the artist to begin painting fakes for him. At about the same time, Drewe came upon a neglected, archive of the Institute of Contemporary Arts (ICA) in London. The discovery of the treasure trove of over 50 boxes of exhibition catalogues, letters and various other documents detailing the works of some of the most influential painters of the twentieth century rang a bell in the head of the man who had been living on the fringe all of his life. (If you hold up the index finger on your right hand, you have "one." Drewe knew, however, that if you then hold up the index finger on your left hand and place it next to your raised index finger on the right hand, you get "eleven." Myatt, the painter was Drewe's "one," but the ICA archive gave Drewe "eleven.") Bingo.

Drewe went to work. While he had the artist Myatt painting fake Matisses, Paul Klees (1879-1940), Georges Bracques (1882-1963), Alberto Giacomettis (1901-1966), and others, he snuggled-up to the director of the ICA and gained access to the archives. During Drewe's unsupervised examinations, he stole Institute letterheads and correspondence and whatever else he felt he could use in his next step. The next step was the big one that set up what most observers call "the biggest contemporary art fraud of the century." It certainly was the most ingenious.

What Drewe did next was ingratiate himself (using donations of fake Myatt paintings) with the Victoria and Albert Museum (called the V & A) and the Tate Gallery in London, two of the most prestigious art institutions in the world. These simple acts gained him private access to the V & A's National Art Library, and the Tate's archives. Drewe understood perfectly what constitutes acceptable evidence to art connoisseurs and took great pains to get it right.

Once inside the hallowed inner halls of the museums, the unsupervised Drewe used an ordinary scalpel to cut and alter exhibition catalogues, substituting photographs he had taken of Myatt's forgeries for the original pages. He also reproduced receipts and planted them along with fake correspondence he had carefully created, using stolen and fake letterheads, old manual typewriters, aged paper, and old ink.

Drewe even had fake rubber stamps made up, which are impressive when used on fake documents. He used the names of unsuspecting old friends as previous owners of the fake paintings, and when necessary, he created fake owners as well. Drewe basically created entire fake catalogues and planted them in the V & A and the Tate. In a final coup, Drewe convinced the V & A to purchase the ICA archives, which were the very ones he had compromised. In other words, Drewe was able to integrate archives he had corrupted into archives he had corrupted.

Drewe was also smart in other ways. To be safe, he used old friends as runners, so that the buyers wouldn't tie him to all the fakes. Also, Drewe had Myatt fake only artists who were born in a short time period and had the artist use common household emulsion and lubricating jelly as paint which kept the need for aging to a minimum. This simplified Myatt's work.

Drewe was ready to unleash Myatt's fakes. (In John Myatt, Drewe had found the perfect accomplice for his scam because he asked no questions of Drewe.) When Myatt started reeling in money he was hooked.

Drewe charged relatively modest amounts so as not to arouse suspicion. To use a baseball analogy, Drewe was hitting singles and doubles instead of home runs, although one fake Ben Nicholson sold for $175,000. (Authorities later estimated that Drewe made over $5,000,000 from the scam while Myatt received something like $200,000 for his efforts. This was a totally unfair split, of course, but Myatt did better than most artists in the same situation.) The provenances Drewe created were impeccable. In fact, the fake provenances were so perfect and thorough, they made the success of the scam possible, fooling auction houses Christies and Sotheby's (which sold some 14 Myatt fakes) and top gallery owners around the world.

Even Sir Alan Bowness, Ben Nicholson's son-in-law and former head of the Tate, was fooled into authenticating up to half-a-dozen fake Nicholson's. Bowness didn't especially like the look of the paintings, but since the provenances were impeccable, like everyone else at the time, he bought into the scam. Remember, while authenticating the fakes, Bowness knew as much about Nicholson and his work as any person alive.

In 1996, police raided Drewe's home and confiscated hundreds of documents from the ICA, V & A, and the Tate. The following year Drewe and Myatt were charged, and in 1998 a trial was held. The arrogant Drewe defended himself. In a nod to the fact that Drewe was the mastermind of the scam, in 1999, after a five month trial that mesmerized England, John Drewe was found guilty of forgery, conspiracy to defraud, theft, and using a false instrument. He was sentenced to six years in prison. When John Drewe was released from prison he disappeared. John Myatt, who pled guilty and was the chief witness against Drewe, was sentenced to only one year. Based on his good behavior, Myatt was released after four months.

Here's the best part of the saga. In spite of being convicted of forging over 200 paintings in a seven-year period, John Myatt is held in high esteem by almost everyone who knows him or has come in contact with him. Myatt retains his well-known sense of humor even after serving his time in jail. He is a pillar of his community, serving as head organist and choir director at his church, and, has retained the respect of everyone who was involved in bringing him to justice, including the judge, prosecutor and jurors who sent him to jail. Why did Myatt keep on painting fakes when he knew Drewe was going to sell them as authentic? "It was unforgivable, I know. It was a dreadful combination of greed and vanity, spiced with the thrill of danger. It was like being in a dream."

Like many other forgers, John Myatt has had an exhibition of real Myatt fakes (as opposed to fake Myatt fakes, which, yes, also exist), and has become successful selling "genuine fakes." (At this time, approximately 140 of the 200 Myatt forgeries are unaccounted for.) The Tate and Victoria and Albert museums reluctantly admit that they might never discover the total extent to which their archives have been tainted by John Drewe.

CHAPTER THREE
UNSCRUPULOUS ARTISTS

The forger must become a skilled art historian,
a restorer, a chemist, a graphologist and a
documentalist if he is to exploit his talents
as a charlatan. It is not a vocation
for the indolent.

— Frank Wynne

Put yourself in the position of an artist who,
after years spent in a vain struggle for success,
finally achieves it at a single stroke by putting a
famous signature to his own work . . . What a
delectable moment, when he puts to shame the
connoisseurs who described his work as dilettante
when it bore his own name, only to praise it to the
skies when he presented it above the signature of a
master.

— Frank Arnau

The art forger is always driven by one or more basic motives. In alphabetical order they are ambition, greed, poverty, revenge, and vanity. A few truisms.

Classical drawings are easier to forge than classical paintings because it is harder to paint than draw. In addition, it's more difficult for science to detect fake drawings than fake paintings. It's also easier to get caught forging old master paintings than more modern artists. After all, there is much more detail that needs to be copied in the old works. There is not much forgery of watercolors, although there are exceptions. Not only are watercolors difficult to paint, prices are historically lower for them than oils. Bottom line: Most experts insist that over 40% of works by significant artists for sale are fakes. In Korea up to 75% of works attributed to Lee Jung-seop (1916–1956) are fakes.

There is a reluctance on all sides to finger forgers. Sometimes it's because the party who gets taken is emotionally or professionally involved with the artwork. More often than not, however, museums and their curators are embarrassed to admit mistakes; dealers don't want to burn bridges; collectors don't want to admit they were duped, and most important, conflicts of interest and catty rivalries abound in every aspect of the world of art.

In an additional break for forgers, in every country in the world enforcement is highly splintered, making it less likely the artist will be caught and convicted. In Slovakia for example, no one has ever received a prison sentence for forgery; cases of forgery are not even investigated. In America, enforcement is indeed splintered (to say the least), so enforcement is sporadic. There is no federal statute against intentionally selling fakes. Most of the cases are handled by either the postal service (mail fraud) or the FBI (wire fraud.) In addition, US Customs, the Department of Justice, the US Attorney's Office, the Drug Enforcement Administration, and the National Park Service get involved when appropriate. States have a rich variety of laws that make art fraud a crime.

Who are the most forged artists? (Remember, a flurry of fakes almost always follows the death of an artist, so this list is subject to constant revision.) There is disagreement about which artist is the most copied, although Jean-Baptiste Camille Corot (1796–1875) the French landscape master, whose fame peaked in the 1860s, leads everyone's list. There is an old joke that uses a different set of numbers whenever it is told. It goes like this: Out of the 3,000 paintings Corot produced in his lifetime, 8,000 are in the United States.

A French collector who died in the 1920s left a collection of almost 2,500 works by Corot, all of which turned out to be fakes. Corot signed innumerable works of imitators, apparently feeling honored to be copied. In addition, the happy, even-tempered Corot would never prosecute forgers because he felt sorry for their families.

Albrecht Dürer (1471–1528) has been copied for over 500 years; in the 1600s Archduke Wilhelm of Austria had almost 100 fake Dürers in his collection. Picasso, Matisse, Marc Chagall (1887–1985), Salvador Dali (1904–1989), Joan Miro (1893–1983), Amedeo Modigliani (1884–1920), Maurice Utrillo (1883–1955), and Vincent van Gogh (1853–1890) are also high on every forger's hit parade.

In 2004, police in Helsinki, Finland seized over 400 fake Dali paintings, prints, etchings, woodcuts and sculptures from one exhibition. Every piece in the show was a fake.

Marc Restellini, an Italian art scholar, abandoned his six-year undertaking to write a catalogue raisonné on Modigliani due to pressure (and death threats) from collectors who feared that his work would expose the fakes in their collections: Word had leaked out that Restellini had concluded that one in nine Modigliani paintings were fakes, and that one in four drawings by the Italian master were fakes.

More Modigliani. When his friends criticized his sculptures, in a fit of tragic anger, the emotional Italian artistic genius tossed all of them in the waters of Livorno. Not too long ago youthful forgers claimed that they had raised the treasures from the deep and offered the sculptures for sale. The pieces they trumpeted as Modiglianis were fakes. Regarding Utrillo, Paris dealer Paul Petrides, who wrote the artist's catalogue raisonné, has recorded over 1,000 forgeries of his works, and that only includes the Utrillo fakes that have been brought to his attention.

Johannes van der Wolk, curator of the Kroller-Muller Museum in Otterlo, Netherlands, home to one of the world's most extensive van Gogh collections (278 paintings and drawings) has estimated that there are between 100 and 200 van Gogh forgeries hanging on walls worldwide. The Kroller-Muller Museum itself admits to numerous van Gogh fakes in its permanent collection. Not even the Van Gogh Museum in Amsterdam (with a collection of over 200 van Goghs) is immune; it has almost 20 paintings considered to be fake van Goghs.

While the raw number of van Gogh fakes is small by comparison, their impact is great. The authenticity of Van Gogh's three most famous works that stunned the art world when they soared to auction records in the go-go 1980s (including the so-called "Yasuda Sunflowers") is being hotly contested. As they say, the dead Vincent keeps painting and painting.

American artists are not immune to forgeries. There are more fake works of Albert Pinkham Ryder (1847–1917) than any American artist except Ralph Blakelock (1847–1919). How about this: Zhou Tiehai (born in 1966 in China), an artist who lives and works in Shanghai, doesn't paint but calls works his own that other artists create from his ideas. "Ten years ago," he once said, "I wanted to show people how easy it is to make art.

And I did that." Uli Sigg, a major art collector, said, believe it or not, "The fact that he [Zhou Tiehai] doesn't paint doesn't bother me . . . It's accepted today. It doesn't have to have traces of your own hand." I can see Caravaggio (1571–1610) and the other Old Masters turning in their graves. Even after an artist dies there is no guarantee he will rest in peace: The Alberto Giacometti (1901–1966), Victor Vasarely (1906–1997) and Jean Arp (1886–1966) estates and foundations are embroiled in battles for control, accused of mismanagement, and worse.

Here are a number of prime rules about fakes supposedly spoken years ago by a "Frank X. Kelly" to Thomas Hoving, 77, the arrogant director of the Metropolitan Museum of Art in New York (called the Met) from 1967 to 1977:

First, the fake must look juicier, more appealing, more energetic, and slightly older than an original;

Second, surface image is all that matters because scientific analysis almost always produces conflicting evidence;

Third, the less contrived a fake's provenance, the longer it will go undetected;

Fourth, if a forger produces enough fakes, and if enough time elapses before they are exposed, they will become models for other fakes, and once that happens, few can ever be detected;

Finally, to avoid detection, paint over old canvases but never copy the original exactly, rather, combine elements from the artist's other works so experts don't have a concrete original with which to make comparisons. And paint fast, because the appearance of spontaneity is critical.

I believe that while these points are compelling, they themselves are fake. That is, I think Hoving made up Frank X. Kelly (or even if Kelly exists, Hoving made up the quotes) to spice up his book on fake busting, "False Impressions: The Hunt For Big Time Art Fakes."

Why do I think that? Because Frank X. Kelly is too pat, too convenient, too shrewd. In addition, Kelly's observations sound exactly like observations Hoving would make, words and music. To paraphrase Thomas Hoving himself, I took one look at the list of rules and my gut cried out "Frank X. Kelly is a fake." Speaking of Thomas Hoving, he once said (then denied) that the trustees, not the public, own the works of art in the Met, and therefore it has no accountability to the public. Long time Met curator Gary Tinterow sings the same song.

Artists who forge amaze us because they must have serious, creative artistic talent to be successful. Additionally, they generally wear the white hats in any discussion of art fraud because they are almost always exploited by unscrupulous dealers, and everyone loves an underdog. Who doesn't secretly admire those talented artists who puncture the pompous, prim, and pretentious art establishment.

Obviously, there could be no fakes if artist/forgers didn't create them. Nevertheless, except for a few exceptions, it's clear that there would be few unscrupulous artists if there were no unscrupulous art dealers, collectors, museums, and auction houses.

THREE CHARACTERS YOU'D LOVE TO HAVE DINNER (OR AT LEAST A DRINK) WITH

Zhang Daqian

In a field awash with colorful characters, Zhang Daqian (1899–1983) also known as Chang Dai-Chien and several other names, was one of the most colorful artists of all time. Outgoing and happy, the generous Zhang had a long, flowing beard and carried a walking stick to augment the floor length robe he always wore. In addition to being a con man, Zhang Daqian was a connoisseur, a collector and a dealer.

Zhang was born on the Chinese mainland into an artistic family which encouraged the precocious youth. As a young man in China, Zhang concentrated on learning the techniques and subjects of classical Chinese painting. After completing what Americans call high school, at his family's request Zhang went to Japan with his brother to learn commercial weaving and textile dying. Zhang learned his lessons well, but he wanted to be a painter. In 1949, Zhang, along with many other artistic people, fled the communists and began a life of traveling that included stops in Hong Kong, Argentina, Brazil and the United States. He moved to Taiwan in 1977 where he died at 84, surrounded by a coterie of admirers, all on the make (and take).

Chinese and Western art are different in most ways, but Zhang's seven-year stay in California left an indelible mark on the artist. In fact, the basic reason Zhang is considered China's greatest modern painter is that he made the transition from the ancient to the new with his invention of the splashed ink and color painting technique, a technique that breathed new life into a centuries-old moribund Chinese painting scene.

In 1956, Zhang met Picasso in Paris, which the press trumpeted as a historic meeting of the masters of Eastern and Western modernist art and started calling Zhang the Picasso of Chinese art. Basking in the resultant publicity, Zhang had exhibitions all over the world for the next decade.

Zhang Daqian became one of the most accomplished con men in history. He has usually been labeled the most gifted master forger of the twentieth century. (Speaking of fakes, Zhang, noted for his inexhaustible work and play ethic, is reputed to have produced over 30,000 paintings, of which about 1/6th have survived. Of these 5,000 surviving works, some 4,000 are fakes.)

During his aforementioned stay in Japan, Zhang learned how to age and darken silk and paper. These skills were central to his 60-year career as a forger. In addition, Zhang collected the tools of the forgers trade, including a large collection of old silks and old seals, both important in Chinese painting. Zhang wanted to test the experts of the art world, for whom he had little respect. An impressive number of the 4,000 paintings he forged are hanging in the most important museums in the world: Nobody knows, or can even guess, the actual number. Throughout his life Zhang openly bragged that his fakes were hanging in every major collection of Chinese art, and in every major museum in the world. Also, Zhang was able to emulate painters who lived over a number of centuries.

In 1997, to celebrate the opening of its Chinese galleries, the Met displayed a huge (over seven feet tall) scroll entitled "Riverbank," which the museum touted as being painted by the legendary tenth century painter Dong Yuan, a painter who helped shape the Chinese landscape tradition over 1,000 years ago. Several of the world's experts on Chinese painting, including Sherman Lee, retired director of the Cleveland Museum of Art and author of several scholarly books on Chinese art, and James Cahill, retired professor of Chinese art at Berkeley and also a venerated author on the subject, publicly denounced the monumental work as a fake.

Cahill, who has made a career out of exposing Zhang Daqian fakes, had expressed doubts about the painting when he first saw it almost two decades earlier (in 1980), asserting that the painting dates from the 1950s. Who do these (and other) experts believe painted "Riverbank?" Zhang Daqian, that's who. These experts advance a litany of reasons that have to do with technique and related matters. In addition, there is other evidence "Riverbank" is a fake.

C.C. Wang is a collector who sold "Riverbank" to Met trustee Oscar Tang. Tang subsequently loaned it to the museum. Wang originally obtained "Riverbank" from none other than Zhang Daqian. The Met, in an attempt to appear responsive to the alarming (to them) and growing furor over the provenance of "Riverbank," held a symposium in 1999 that merely replayed the controversy, as the museum knew it would.

Zhang Daqian was such a beloved character, as well as an internationally renowned painter, no one held his scamming against him. After all, they would say, in the world of Chinese art, copying of classic paintings has been an accepted practice for centuries. Let's not spoil their fun by pointing out that it's not the copying that is criminal, it's the passing the copy off as an original that crosses the line.

Icilio Federico Joni

Icilio Federico Joni (or Ioni) (1866–1946) may be the most spirited and interesting Italian forger of all. Joni is Siena's most famous and beloved forger. In fact, Joni, who is known as the "Prince of Sienese Fakers," is considered one of the town's most distinguished citizens.

This accolade is probably due to Joni's personality (a candid man of principles); his talent (he was so good that other artists copied his fakes, thereby creating a sub-culture of fake fakes); his leadership of a large school of artist/fakers; and his powerful impact on the local economy. Joni also made a number of dealers filthy rich due to his constant supply of fake masterpieces. Joni was one of the colorful characters of his time. He was an expert gymnast, raised falcons in his studio, and gave new meaning to the term party animal. He was also very talented and very shrewd.

Lord Kenneth Clark called him "an impudent rascal . . . [motivated] less by greed than by natural naughtiness. He enjoyed the fun of fooling the experts and museum directors, and would go to any lengths to achieve it." His specialty, which was forging Old Masters (Middle Age and Renaissance works), was particularly difficult, but all the more reason for the irascible Joni to work in those periods.

Joni also enjoyed great success forging Biccherna wooden book covers of the thirteenth through the seventeenth centuries, which were used as covers for tax records. To give you an idea of how talented Joni was, he had never seen a Biccherna but his forgeries were not only right on the mark, they were more sought after by collectors than the originals.

Joni's fake paintings hang (or hung, since they are usually taken down when museums discover they've been duped) in every important museum in the world, including the Cleveland Museum of Art and the National Gallery in London.

Bernard Berenson plays a large role in the Joni story. As a young man, B.B. (as he demanded to be called) purchased numerous Jonis believing they were the real thing. When he discovered the truth, using friends as fronts, Berenson sold many of these fakes through auction houses as genuine. (B.B.'s wife's brother had an antiques shop in London, which she and B.B. also flooded with fakes painted by Joni. To each other they laughingly referred to the shop as their very own Iniquity Shop.)

Berenson kept two Joni fakes in his villa, I Tatti, believing they were authentic. Many years later, while visiting Berenson, Joni pointed out a painting on his host's wall as one that he had painted. B.B., who by this time had convinced himself that he was infallible, would not believe the artist. Any artist would be annoyed by this degree of arrogance, but Joni was not only annoyed, he was also insulted that Berenson would not admit that he (Joni) had the talent to create a masterpiece that he (Berenson) would hang on his wall.

Joni was an Italian patriot, particularly devoted to his home town of Siena. He resented all of the foreigners (like Berenson) who came to Italy to reap the financial rewards off the backs of past and present Italian artists. Outspoken throughout his life, in his sixties Joni decided to write his autobiography. Art dealers panicked, fearing his revelations would jeopardize their business, so they offered Joni a substantial bribe not to publish it. Always his own man, Joni went ahead and published the book in 1932. Surprisingly, very little was said in the book about his forgeries, the dealers who forged the authentications, or the art critics who were easily bribed.

Alceo Dossena was one of Joni's colleagues, as were Igino Gottardi, Fulvio Corsini, and Bruno Marzi. The talented ring turned out fakes of Duccio di Buoninsegna (c. 1255–c. 1319), Donatello (c. 1386–c. 1466) and Simone Martini (c. 1283–c. 1344) in quantity, but could never keep up with the demands of the greedy dealers. To fool the experts, the members of the ring scoured local farmhouses for old wooden panels to be used for backing the fake paintings (the use of wood predates the use of canvas). To age the wood and give it the right patina, it was left out in the sun, covered with earth and urine.

A retired wood carver in Siena said, "We were extremely poor in those days. It was considered a kind of social revenge to fool the rich foreigners, as well as a lot of fun." A perfectionist, Joni devised ingenious methods to give his fakes the cracks of aging, and like all great forgers, became an expert in producing just the right paints and performing tricks to age his works. Joni's fakes were so good, as he said in his autobiography, "Collectors coming to Siena were warned to be careful, for everything found in Siena must be the work of Ioni."

Showing a flash of his intellect and humor, Joni goes on to say, "I could not decide which were the bigger fools, the Florentine dealers who talked like this, or the foreign visitors who lapped up their story without so much as wondering whether it would not be equally easy to take Ioni's stuff to Florence."

While Joni was a unique individual in makeup and temperament, he was a typical forger in his excuses: "They are not forgeries. You can say that a man who makes false banknotes is a forger, because he uses a printing press, or a man who makes false coins, because he uses a die. But an artist who creates a work of art on his own, in imitation of the style of an old master, is not a forger; he is at worse an imitator, and he is creating something of his own."

Like almost all forgers, Joni skips the part about passing the work off as the masters. Joni relates that a friend, while admiring his latest productions, said to him, "Be careful you don't imitate any particular master too closely, otherwise your work will always be too easy to recognize, simply by confronting it with an original." Joni followed his friend's advice all of his life, and, in fact, was never arrested for forgery.

Today, the fakes of Joni et al are extremely valuable in their own right. In 2004, almost 60 years after Joni's death, in Siena's Santa Maria dell Scala, a major exhibition of some 70 works of Joni and his collaborators and colleagues was held to rave reviews. The show, with works gathered from all over the world, was entitled "Fakes by Master Artists." Gianni Mazzoni, professor of the history of modern art at the University of Siena, who curated the show, famously said of Joni, "He only made original works that seemed old, and as they went from dealer to dealer, they became old."

Eric Hebborn

Eric Hebborn (1934–1996) was perhaps the most literate and intelligent forger of them all. Hebborn was born in a Cockney family in England and demonstrated his artistic talents at an early age, winning awards and scholarships.

Hebborn learned the tricks of the forger's trade as a picture restorer. He realized that when his restored pictures were elegantly framed and contained elements he'd added without detection (say a dog or cat in an otherwise dull landscape), they sold for more money than they would otherwise have.

This observation led Hebborn into faking. The artist meticulously prepared himself for his life of crime. He studied day and night to determine the correct tools to use, such as paper, paint, and ink. He also examined in minute detail the styles of the artists to be faked. His preparation paid off.

Eric Hebborn went on to produce thousands of fake ancient masterpieces that fooled the greatest experts in the art world, including experts at the British Museum, the National Gallery in Washington, and such luminaries as Sir John Pope-Hennessy. In fact, Hebborn faked almost every European master from the fourteenth to the twentieth century, and wrote an autobiography in 1991 entitled "Drawn to Trouble" to brag about it.

Like many other forgers, Hebborn claimed that he didn't copy difficult masterpieces by Van Dyke, Peter Paul Rubens (1577–1640), Nicolas Poussin (1594–1665) and others. What he did, he says, was think himself into the master's style. It also helped that he made a career of using the appropriate ancient paper, paints and tricks to age his works.

Hebborn moved to Rome in 1963 and opened a gallery. The amiable artist, parlaying his sharp mind and engaging features (bushy hair and beard), moved in the top international art circles, including the group that surrounded the surveyor of the Queen of England's pictures, Sir Anthony Blunt. Blunt was also the director of the Courtauld Institute in London, which he ran as a fiefdom. With Blunt as one of Hebborn's best salesmen (albeit a secret one), how could Hebborn fail? He couldn't and didn't.

Hebborn sold most of his forgeries through the high powered Colnaghi Gallery, the London dealer. In the late 1970s, a curator of the National Gallery bought two paintings which he thought were from different eras. After checking, however, the pieces were determined to be produced from the same stock. The curator, Conrad Oberhuber, alerted the art world, and a third similar fake surfaced at the Morgan Library in New York. All three of the fakes were traced back to Colnaghi's who realized they had all been acquired from Hebborn. What did Colnaghi do?

Believe it or not, the gallery waited a full year-and-a-half before revealing the deception to the media, but then didn't even mention Hebborn's name as the forger. Did Eric Hebborn go into hiding, which would have been logical? Hebborn never considered it. He was an adventurer. A player.

In the years after the Colnaghi debacle, Hebborn proceeded to create another 500 fakes, all of which he sold. Throughout his storied career, Hebborn never forgot his humble background and never, ever, backed down from his position as savior for the masses who resented (as he did) the stuck-up phonies of the art elite who sold and/or authenticated his works. Hebborn enjoyed the fruits of his labor to the fullest, particularly while leading la dolce vita in Rome.

Hebborn was never prosecuted for his life of forgery. The reason may be that he had a trick: When peddling a drawing or painting he acknowledged the expertise of the museum, dealer, or collector and let the purchaser tell him what he was showing and set the price. Hebborn also had a strict rule about whom he conned. He never sold to amateurs, for example, only to recognized experts or buyers acting on expert advice.

Hebborn specialized in selling to dealers because, he felt, they were making all of the money. More important, he knew that the dealers make their living by being able to tell the fake from the real. So if I pass my fake successfully, his reasoning went, I will have won the battle of wits and the hot-shot dealer will pay for his mistake in judgment.

The greater the experts, the more Hebborn enjoyed deceiving them. Always reflecting his background, he called his marks "those vulgar, avaricious creatures with good backgrounds, smart accents, fine education and infinite pretensions, who control the art trade from the top and to whom a work of art is as good or bad as the amount it fetches."

In 1996, Hebborn published his "Art Forger's Handbook" (in Italian, later translated into English), which told the reader everything he wanted to know about forging, and then some. Probably because of the book (although we'll never know), the life of one of the most fascinating forgers in history came to a crashing close. A few weeks after publication of the sensational book, while walking in Rome, 62-year-old Eric Hebborn was hit on the head from behind by a heavy, blunt instrument, probably a hammer. The tragic murder remains unsolved.

Sorry Pal, You're Messing with the Wrong Artist

Alceo Dossena

Alceo Dossena (1878–1936) was a brilliant forger, working in marble, bronze and terracotta. Originally a restorer, many label Dossena the best forger in history. His case is a classic example of putting principles ahead of money.

Dossena was versatile and worked openly on a grand scale out of a large studio on storied Via Margutta in Rome, surrounded by other artists and dealers. What his neighbors didn't know was that the clever forger had a secret studio behind his public one. In addition to his training and raw artistic talent, Dossena invented a concoction of corrosive chemicals which he dipped his works into, giving them a deep, believable patina. Each sculpture was dipped into his concoction (which was located in his secret studio) some 40 times. Dossena, unlike most forgers, did not limit himself to any one period in history; he produced masterpieces spanning a period of over fifteen hundred years.

His dealers, Alfredo Fasoli and Romano Palesi, sold his beautiful sculptures to major collectors and museums around the world. The most august museums scooped up his pieces, including the Museum of Fine Arts in Boston (which thought it was purchasing a tomb by Mino da Fiesole (c. 1429–c. 1484), the Cleveland Museum of Art, the Saint Louis Art Museum, the Frick Collection, the J. Paul Getty Museum, and the Metropolitan Museum of Art, among others. (In 1952, Saint Louis purchased a four foot "Etruscan" terracotta statute (in pieces) of Diana, but it wasn't until 16 years later, in 1968, after in-depth research and numerous tests, the museum reluctantly admitted that it had been duped.) Like art dealers throughout the ages, Fasoli and Palesi got rich, while Dossena the creator, died in poverty. It is estimated that Dossena's works sold in America alone brought (in today's dollars) several billion dollars.

One day, out of the blue, Dossena announced to the world that he had been faking classic sculptors, including Donatello, Andrea del Verrocchio (c. 1435–c. 1488) and other masters. The bombshell admission stunned the art world. What triggered Dossena's confession?

In 1927 one of his Italian agents, Alfredo Fasoli, made a small but fatal mistake. Fassoli brushed off Dossena's request for a personal loan to pay for his mistress's funeral. Not only did Fasoli hurt Dossena's feelings, his timing was atrocious; after selling a Dossena fake Donatello for millions of lira, Fasoli gave the forger only a few pennies (so to speak.) Dossena found out about the deal.

Represented by a well-connected attorney (Mussolini's right-hand man Farinacci), the court ruled that Dossena was unaware that his works were being sold as original antiquities and granted him a substantial monetary settlement from his dealers. They say that there is nothing like a woman scorned, except maybe an artist who is not only cheated but is also insulted.

Lothar Malskat

The German Lothar Malskat (c. 1912–c. 1987) is a classic case of the triumph of bruised ego. In 1937, Malskat restored frescoes in the cathedral of Scheswig, Germany. In the course of restoring the medieval frescoes, the playful artist added turkeys to the mix (turkeys were not introduced into Germany until the sixteenth century, much later than the age of the original frescoes). After World War II, Malskat, still an unknown artist, hooked up with a fellow unknown artist named Dietrich Fey. Both were disgusted that dealers and collectors only wanted works of name artists. "So we decided to give them what they wanted," Malskat said with his patented devilish grin.

Malskat started painting masters from Rembrandt to Degas to Utrillo and most everyone in between. Fey signed and sold the works to German dealers and collectors. (How good was Maskalt? In the course of the scam, Maskalt produced some 2,000 fakes of over 70 modern and ancient masters. He was so proficient he could create a French Impressionist masterpiece in less than an hour.)

In 1948, Dietrich Fey was accused of selling forged paintings but was able to talk his way out of the charge. Also in 1948, the well-connected Fey received a legitimate commission. He was hired to restore the 700-year-old frescoes in the oldest church in Lubeck, Germany, the Lutheran Church of Saint Mary, which was built from 1250 to 1350. The cathedral had been damaged by allied bombing in March, 1942.

Fey hired Malskat to help him with the commission. In typical fashion, artist-turned-dealer Fey assigned all of the work to artist Maskalt, who was happy to oblige. After all, he was getting paid an hourly wage, and he enjoyed the prestige of restoring the famous frescoes. When Maskalt went up on the 90 foot scaffolds, he found the original frescoes had been burned off by the Allied incendiary bombs. After consultation with partner Fey, the pair decided that it would be foolish to give up the lucrative commission.

No problem. Maskalt covered the scaffolding with cloth to conceal his work from prying eyes. He then whitewashed the walls and filled them with pictures of family, friends, historical figures and even movie stars. He only removed the cloth from the sections that were complete, so that when local political and art officials came to inspect his work (which, remember, was a full 90 feet from the ground) they were duly impressed.

In 1951, the 700th anniversary of the church, the restoration was complete. A celebration of the restoration, the likes of which Lubeck had never seen, was held. Even Chancellor Konrad Adenauer attended the glorious event, for which millions of commemorative stamps were issued by the government. The stamps showed a detail of Maskalt's handiwork. The tipping point came when Fey received an award at the ceremonies for excellence in restoration and Maskalt's name wasn't even mentioned. Piqued, Maskalt went to the police and confessed creating fake paintings and fake frescoes.

Art historians and experts did not believe Maskalt until the police raided Fey's apartment and uncovered almost 30 fake paintings and drawings. This led to the church where close examination of the frescoes revealed an old Gothic king was really Rasputin, and the Virgin Mary was modeled after Maskalt's sister and a movie star. After a lengthy trial, which ran over from 1954 into 1955, the pair was found guilty. The well-connected mastermind Dietrich Fey received a sentence of 20 months, while the (relatively) innocent Lothar Malskat got 18.

Other ramifications? The church head retired (read was forced out), the city's art director left town, and his assistant was fired. The red-faced officials scrubbed the embarrassing evidence (the very frescoes that had been previously praised) from the church walls.

Giovanni Bastianini

Giovanni Bastianini triggered an international war of words. Bastianini, born in Italy in 1830 and died in 1868 at only 38 years of age, mostly faked the works of Renaissance sculptors. This is unusual because most artists forge drawings and paintings.

An art dealer, Florentine Giovanni Freppa, discovered the impoverished 17-year-old youth who had a talent for sketching masters of the Renaissance. Freppa commissioned young Bastianini to sculpt fakes, which he sold to the Louvre in Paris and the V & A in London, among others. In 1857, 1861, and 1863, the South Kensington Museum of London (now the Victoria and Albert Museum) purchased Bastianini fakes believing they were Florentine Renaissance pieces. Not only that, in the mid-1800s, the V & A purchased an English forger's ivory fake of a fake Bastianini they owned, thinking it was a piece by Luca della Robbia (c.

1400-c. 1482). Thus, the V & A owned a fake of one of its fakes. But hold on, there is good news. In 1896, the V & A purchased a Bastianini bust of Savonarola and exhibited it as an example of neo-Renaissance nine-teenth-century sculpture. In other words, the museum now acknowledged that Bastianini was a star in his own right.

In 1866, the Louvre in Paris purchased what it believed was a Renais-sance sculpture at auction. The piece (which became known as the "Beni-vieni Bust") was lauded by the museum and public alike as a Renaissance masterpiece more than 300 years old and was displayed in a place of honor. When a French art dealer named di Nolvos reneged on a pay-ment, with the permission of an irateBastianini, his dealer Freppa wrote an article in a Paris art publication exposing the scam that he and Bastianini had been perpetrating. In a move that set the pattern for museums, the Louvre, despite its stature as one of the world's top muse-ums, first ignored, then stonewalled the startling announcement, refus-ing to admit it had been duped.

A heated debate ensued between French historians on the one side and Freppa/Bastianini on the other. What became an international dual between individuals proud of their homelands amused the general pub-lic. Bastianini's arguments were so strong they finally convinced the Louvre he had created the bust; without fanfare the museum removed the bust from display. In 1891, after the "Benivieni Bust" scandal revealed Bastianini as the true sculptor of the controversial piece, the English joined the fray. The V & A acquired a wax model of a bust, knowing that it was a preliminary study by Bastianini for the Louvre's fake Bastianini. After Giovanni Bastianini died, his talent was so widely recognized that authentic piece after authentic piece was attributed to him. It boggles the mind to think of what this genius might have accomplished had he lived beyond the age of 38.

Henricus Anthonius van Meegeren

The small, dapper, and high-strung Han van Meegeren (1889–1947) was surely the least talented but most famous forger of the twentieth century. How to explain this dichotomy? The Dutch forger fits the clas-sic model of an aspiring artist who had modest talents but an inflated ego. In the early 1930s, when art critics labeled his paintings lacking in originality, van Meegeren took it personally and swore revenge on the art establishment. The pompous and arrogant van Meegeren devised a plan. He'd paint a fake, allow the critics and experts to drool over it, and then confess that he had painted it. That'll show them.

During a four-year period van Meegeren perfected an aging process that worked perfectly, giving his fakes a patina almost indistinguishable from the originals. He would obtain genuine seventeenth-century canvases (and frames), scrap off the original art, and then paint his fakes on them. In 1936, van Meegeren moved to the south of France and, in six months of seclusion, was ready to make his big move. He had decided to paint a Vermeer from the master's early life about which little was known. He called the forgery "Christ and the Disciples at Emmaus." Van Meegeren paid his attorney to take the fake painting to 83-year-old Abraham Bredius, far and away the most influential Vermeer expert alive. The old man took the bait.

Bredius declared to the world that a previously unknown Vermeer had been discovered. Moreover he raved about the beauty and quality of the painting. In the art world, Bredius's reputation was so strong no other opinions were even solicited, much less forthcoming. Within months, van Meegeren's Vermeer was the top attraction at the Boymans Museum in Rotterdam. The artist was so obsessed with his mission that he stood next to the painting everyday and proclaimed it a fake. Much to his annoyance (but deep down joy) the scholars, critics, art historians and other experts would try to convince van Meegeren he was wrong, that the painting was an authentic Vermeer.

Not only did van Meegeren feel vindicated regarding the ignorance of the art establishment, he became rich (to the tune of what would equal $7,000,000 today) with the sale of the fake Vermeer to the museum. Since it was clear to him that his plan was not going to work, van Meegeren did the next logical thing. He started painting more forgeries.

Numerous successful fakes were produced by van Meegeren into the 1940s, which he sold to the most celebrated collectors and museums in the world. Having no use for modern art, van Meegeren faked paintings in the style of seventeenth-century masters, including (besides Vermeer) Franz Hals (1580–1666) and Pieter de Hooch (1629–1684). He would not exactly copy the masters, but rather would paint in their style.

The most amazing thing about van Meegeren's fake Vermeers is that they bore little resemblance to the master's work, but since his first block-buster Vermeer fake set the standard, his subsequent fakes were compared to it and accepted. The world was authenticating fakes based on prior fakes. Van Meegeren was able to sell his fakes for large sums (over $60,000,000 in today's dollars) which he profitably invested in real estate.

In 1943, during the German's occupation of the Netherlands, van Meegeren sold a fake Vermeer to the notorious Nazi who also loved art, Hermann Goering. In payment, van Meegeren accepted some 200 Dutch paintings the Nazis had plundered from Holland earlier in the war. In 1945, after the war ended, van Meegeren's Vermeer was found in Goering's extensive personal art collection by a knowledgeable American officer and traced to van Meegeren. The artist was arrested and charged with collaborating with the enemy, an offense punishable by death.

Van Meegeren confessed after a little over a month in prison. He told the authorities that he was a saint not a collaborator. He wanted credit from the authorities for retrieving several hundred Dutch paintings from the Nazis' and sticking them with a fake Vermeer that he painted. The world press went wild, and the ego centric van Meegeren basked in the media circus, loving the attention. Although he went from vilified traitor to folk hero, much to his frustration, down deep nobody believed the artist.

A police officer taunted van Meegeren, saying if you painted Goering's Vermeer, why don't you do it again, copying it from memory. The arrogant artist snapped back, "I have never painted a copy. But I shall paint you a new Vermeer. I shall paint you a masterpiece." Under the court's supervision, and to the astonishment of a fascinated court, press, and public, van Meegeren painted his last fake Vermeer. Even more satisfying to van Meegeren, his eventual trial was marked with a parade of experts trying to explain, or even deny, their previous rapture over the fakes. The collaboration charges were dismissed.

Hold on. Not satisfied with his victory in court, the egotistical artist demanded that he be charged with forgery. The bewildered authorities had little choice so they obliged him. Even though he had fooled the art establishment, major museums, and even the Dutch State, Han van

Meegeren felt that by being officially charged with forgery, his artistic talent would finally be unequivocally recognized. In November 1947, an ecstatic van Meegeren was convicted of forgery and sentenced to one-year in prison. Han van Meegeren's joy was short lived. He died one month later, in December 1947.

SVENGALI

Elmyr De Hory Meets Fernand Legros & Real Lessard

Always on the run from the authorities, the mysterious man gener-ally known as Elmyr de Hory (1905–1976) used (more or less) hundreds of aliases in the course of his extensive career as one of the most prolif-ic and successful forgers of all time. For our purposes, we'll stick with Elmyr de Hory.

Born in Hungary, Elmyr spent his early years trying to achieve his dream of becoming a famous artist. He was able to sell very few of his paintings, and those he was able to sell brought in very little. Elmyr left for Paris, figuring (correctly) that that was where the artistic action was and that maybe, just maybe, he could take his flagging career to a high-er level. In Paris, Elmyr studied art under Leger. Always the hustler, while in Paris Elmyr sought out, and made a point to meet, the artistic names of the day including Picasso, Matisse, Derain, Renoir, Dufy and van Dongen. Elmyr analyzed their works to learn the secrets of making money as a painter. When the always practical Elmyr realized that de Hory paintings were not saleable, he ratcheted up his analysis of his con-temporaries. "I can draw and paint as well as any of them, so why are they selling and I'm not?"

According to Elmyr's biographer, the notorious Clifford Irving (famous for his Howard Hughes scam), Elmyr's life as a forger began acci-dentally. I don't believe that. First of all, nothing Irving said has credibil-ity. (When I think of Clifford Irving, I'm reminded of what Mary McCarthy famously said of Lillian Hellman, "Every word she says is a lie, including 'and' and 'the.'") Second, Elymr de Hory was a clever, calculat-ing man who never left anything to chance. I think Elymr had a "Eureka" moment. It's not the drawings and paintings, it's the artist. The signature. With a vengeance, Elmyr purchased some old paper and frames and produced a few drawings. He then signed Picasso's name, and prepared to sell them.

The shrewd Hungarian realized he needed a story to explain why he, a lowly painter, had drawings by the great Picasso. He concocted the story that he was able to save a small collection from his royal family's estate back in Hungary and these works were a part of that collection. Elmyr also realized that in order for his story to be believable he had to look the part of an ex-European aristocrat. A quick study, the well-read, intelligent artist knew that his clothes needed to be perfectly cut, his manners needed to be beyond reproach, his accent needed to be just to the right of Middle European, and he had to appear to love the ladies, even though he was gay.

And, hey, why not a monocle to round things off. After his first nervous attempt to sell his Picasso drawings to an art dealer was successful, Elmyr de Hory never looked back. He moved on from drawings to paintings because they were more of a challenge, and because there is much more money to be made forging paintings than drawings. In the 1950s, the tipping point occurred when Fernand Legros (1931-1983) met Elmyr de Hory in Miami. Legros realized that he'd found his meal ticket and Elmyr would never be the same.

Legros (who most people believe was an Egyptian born ex-ballet dancer) was ambitious and greedy. Legros bedded de Hory, and while between the sheets convinced the artist he should be his dealer. And to show what a good guy he was, Legros agreed to perform the dealer duties for a mere 40% of the sales price. The oral agreement (as Sam Goldwyn supposedly said) wasn't worth the paper it was written on because Legros sold de Hory fakes to galleries across the United States and kept both the sales prices and bulk of the money from the unsuspecting artist.

Later in the 1950s, Legros met a beautiful young man named Real Lessard. Lessard was a bushy-haired, freckled, French Canadian with a quick smile and cheerful disposition. Born in 1939, he was ten years younger than Legros. Suddenly, all of the dynamics changed: Lessard was not as innocent as he looked. Real Lessard went from Fernand Legros's lover, to prodigy, to business partner in record time. The Latin-looking, fast-talking, sharp-eyed Legros had a violent nature. When the volatile couple weren't clawing and fighting with each other over real and imaginary infidelities, they sold fake de Horys as fast as the artist could create them.

To give you an idea of how aggressive Legro and Lessard were, they once held an exhibition in Paris entitled "Homage to Raoul Dufy," in which 26 of the 33 "Dufys" were by Elmyr de Hory. Another example: In a page out of John Drewe's playbook, Legros and Lessard would acquire old art books and replace the photographs of works by famous artists with pictures of de Hory fakes. In still another classic scam, Legros &/or Lessard would cross the border into Canada transporting fake de Hory paintings. You know the routine. A customs agent would question the works and Legros (or Lessard) would respond that the paintings were copies. Invariably the agent would call in an expert, who, to help the customs agent collect duty, would declare the pieces originals. The dealers would pretend to be upset and grudgingly paid the fine. Legros and Lessard would then use the custom documents as proof of authenticity.

Elmyr stuck to Post-Impressionists (the artistic world he knew best) and traveled with Legros and Lessard in the European, South American and American circles of excess and snobbery. In Elmyr's long, remarkable career Legros and Lessard sold over 1,000 Elmyr fake drawings and paintings to museums, dealers and collectors.

Elmyr was a brilliant man who studied hard and was clever and thoughtful in his life of crime. For example, he once discovered in an art book that Matisse had produced a series of some 200 drawings in 1941 and 1942 and had them published in 1943. De Hory continued the series, dating them 1944. Elmyr never made direct copies; major league forgers never do. What he did was produce versions of the real thing.

Elmyr was so good, in the 1950s his drawings and paintings started to appear in art books and catalogues as authentic masterpieces. Kees van Dongen even once authenticated a de Hory fake as his own. And Pierre Matisse, the artist's brother, did the same regarding one of his brother's drawings. Elmyr claimed that he never offered a painting to a museum that they didn't buy.

Elmyr wanted to quit painting fakes number of times. Since he loved the high life, however, he was always broke and needed to keep forging in order to feed his extravagant lifestyle. The fact that his dealers were shortchanging him didn't help his cash flow.

Elmyr De Hory was suspected of being a forger many times in his career, but since he was always, constantly, fleeing to a different country, and always, constantly, changing his name, he was almost never caught. When he was caught he managed to slip out of the fingers of the law.

An unusual combination of circumstances triggered the beginning of the end for Legros and Lessard; both involve Texas collector and philanthropist Algur Hurtle Meadows (1899–1978). Meadows invited a local Dallas art dealer to view the art collection in his Dallas mansion to discuss the possibility of selling some of the pieces. The dealer was appalled by the number of obvious fakes, and, delicately as possible under the circumstances, pointed out the problem to Meadows.

Meadows reacted aggressively, calling in an independent body, the Art Dealers Association, to assess the situation. The committee, which included the well-known dealer Klaus Perls, discovered that almost all of the paintings Meadows owned were fakes. In early 1967, the group issued their report to Meadows: Forty-four of the 58 paintings he had purchased in the last four years were fakes. (These fake paintings were by all created by Elmyr de Hory and sold to Meadows by Legros and Lessard, who had also forged the certificates of authenticity.) Meadows begged the experts he had hired not to issue their report. They refused.

At the same time this was going on, Legros sent a French auction house a photo of a fake Derain he wanted to sell. Derain's widow was called in and cried fake, which led to the auction house checking its files. It discovered that Legros had also offered them two Dufys and a Vlaminck. The authorities were called in and raided Lessard's apartment. The police found four paintings, forged custom stamps, and other faker's paraphernalia. Yes, Legros and Lessard were poised to sell Meadows his 45th, 46th, 47th, and 48th de Hory fake. Meadows was easily convinced to press charges. Fernand Legros and Real Lessard were charged with forgery and fraud and served short prison sentences for defrauding Algur Meadows.

Elmyr's life on the run basically ended when he moved to the island of Ibiza. He enjoyed the sun and parties, but mostly reveled in being the center of attention. But he was still painting fakes and being ripped off by

Legros and Lessard. The two dealers had absolutely no shame: They were giving Elmyr a monthly allowance of $400 and keeping the huge sums the fakes were commanding (as originals) for themselves. In 1976, a day before the Spanish police were to turn him over to the French authorities, Elmyr de Hory killed himself with an overdose of barbiturates.

In 1999, the Terrain Gallery in San Francisco held a Elmyr de Hory show, selling real de Hory fakes, as opposed to fake de Hory fakes, which also exist. An interesting sidelight illustrates how notorious Fernand Legros became. He was Herge's inspiration to create the character of Endaddine Akass in one of the beloved comic strip character Tintin's adventures.

Geert Jan Jansen Meets Adrien Venema

Geert Jan Jansen (also spelled Janssen) was born in the Netherlands in 1944. Jansen began painting when he was three years old. As cute as it was, his precociousness led nowhere. The self-taught artist became a mediocre artist who couldn't sell his works. But he tried. In the 1980s, he opened a gallery in Amsterdam to exhibit his paintings. They still didn't sell.

Like most forgers, Jansen eventually concluded that it wasn't the quality of the painting that sold for the fabulous sums,, rather it was the name and fame of the artist that motivated people to lavish big bucks on works of art. Desperate for money to keep his gallery afloat, Jansen tried out his theory by forging the name of famous Dutch artist Karel Appel (1921-2006) to posters and selling them as original lithographs. From there it was a short jump to forging an Appel painting, which sold for a mighty sum at auction. Jansen was hooked. While living in the Netherlands, the Dutch police spend more than a decade unsuccessfully trying to pin the crime of forging on Jansen but nobody would come forward and say they bought a Jansen fake. To escape the heat of the police in the Netherlands, Jansen and his lover, Ellen van Baren, moved to France. In France, the minor league forger Jansen met Adrien (or Adriaan) Venema, a major league crooked French art dealer, who smelled fresh meat.

Venema was so impressed with the few forgeries Jansen showed him, he offered the artist, who was deep in debt, a full partnership and proceeded to play the part of Svengali. Venema supplied Jansen with all the tools of the forger's trade, including vintage typewriters and old paper. Venema even had a collection of stamps which bore the names of the experts regularly called upon to authenticate various masters, such as Dali and Picasso. Based on a lifetime of fraudulent experience, Venema taught Jansen the art of producing fake signatures for the fake paintings, as well as the art of producing fake certificates of authenticity to back up the fake paintings.

So far there is nothing unusual about the Venema/Jansen partnership but there is an inspired twist. Venema had Jansen move to a remote castle in central France where, uninterrupted, and safe from prying eyes, Jansen ground out some 2000 fakes over a three decade period. (Jansen wasn't only good, he was prolific; he could produce a fake Picasso in 15 minutes.) Geert Jansen said that he tried to get into an artist's soul. "It is essential that I like who I fake or I am incapable of imitating them."

He was so good at faking that the experts at the auction houses where Venema peddled Jansen's fakes consistently proclaimed their authenticity. Karel Appel, after seeing over a dozen Jansen fakes authenticated the fake paintings as his own. On a regular basis Venema would collect paintings from the workshop and make the rounds of European galleries, selling the fake paintings with the fake provenance and getting rich in the process. Venema was clever enough not to flood the market. He parceled out the Jansen fakes of Picasso, Modigliani, Gustave Klimt (1862–1918), Rene Magritte (1898–1967), Fernando Botero (born 1932), Raoul Dufy (1877–1953), and Karel Appel (and other prominent Dutch artists), in small batches over the years. This tactic helped conceal the source of the fakes.

In 1993, the scam began to unravel, although Jansen didn't know it at the time. Jansen and his lover began to sell the works themselves. While his lady friend successfully sold a few of his fakes, unfortunately for Jansen, painting and selling are two different talents. At an auction house in Munich, Germany, a nervous Jansen (using a fake name and business card) submitted for auction three works he had painted. A combination of the seller's demeanor, and the fact there was a misspelling in the Appel certificate of authenticity, caused the official to conduct a thorough investigation. The trail led from Germany to France to the isolated chateau. (Born in 1941, Venema committed suicide in 1993, at the age of 52. Yes, Adrien Venema died before getting caught in the scam.) In 1994, the year after Venema's death, the French police raided Jansen's hideout and seized a staggering 1,600 canvases. The French police department bragged to the press about solving the case they labeled "the largest art swindle since World War II," arresting "the master forger of the century," as they called Jansen.

Not so fast. For six long years, from 1994 to 2000, the French tried to obtain sufficient evidence to prosecute Jansen, but in spite of a vigorous public campaign, not one fake Geert Jan Jansen was reported. The frustrated French authorities finally took matters into their own hands. They threatened to prosecute the country's auction houses (which they regulate) with complicity if they didn't cooperate. The tactic worked. The auction houses caved-in and the authorities obtained sufficient evidence to bring charges against Jansen and his lover, van Baren.

The trial was as farcical as the infamous Otto Wacker trial years earlier in Germany, where the experts lost all credibility. Nevertheless, in 2000 Jansen was convicted of fraud by the court in Orleans, France, and was sentenced to prison. He served a mere six months. Jansen was banned from France for three years. The judge also ordered all of the 1,600 works found in Jansen's chateau destroyed. However, with the help of Rudi Fuchs, director of the municipal museum in Amsterdam, Jansen fought the onerous order because a number of the paintings in Jansen's possession were authentic. Sanity eventually prevailed. A large number of his paintings (and other works that he owned) were returned to him after being in held in France in locked storage for over a decade. Shortly thereafter, Jansen began realizing his youthful dream.

In 2005, he had a show in Zwolle under his own name. In following years, exhibitions followed in Zeist and other towns in the Netherlands. Famous now in his own right, the pieces flew off the walls for good prices.

Back home in the Netherlands, celebrity Geert Jan Jansen (now almost 70, grey, paunchy, and bespectacled), holds, you guessed it, workshops for art students, teaching them how to paint Picassos and Appels, or which ever artist's soul they wish to inhabit. To his students (and whoever else will listen), Jansen rationalizes his career of faking.

"When a musician reproduces a sonata of Bach, one applauds him. Me, I reproduce a sonata of Picasso and I am placed under arrest." A clever argument that misses its mark: The musician does not pretend that he is Bach.

William Blundell Meets Germaine Curvers

The lean, suntanned Australian artist began copying artists as a hobby in the 1960s. He sold a few of his works, but generally gave them to friends. In those days, he would also put a clue in the works to signal that they were copies and didn't sign them with the artist's name. However, in 1998, while testifying in a disputed will case, Will Blundell confessed to what he had been up to for the last 20 or so years.

His life changed in the early 1980s, he said, when the flamboyant (picture her carrying a glass of champagne in one hand and a cigarette in a holder in the other), manipulative, larger-than-life Belgian-born dealer Germaine Curvers saw a Blundell copy and asked if he could paint a few for her. Could he! In the next 20 years, using the tools of the forger's trade supplied by dealer Curvers, Blundell painted some 4,000 fakes. Now, however, the pieces had phony signatures and no clue that they were fakes.

Although he painted fakes from Picasso to Pollack in the 1980s and '90s Blundell specialized in a number of well-known Australian artists including Arthur Streeton (1867–1943) and Brett Whiteley (1939–1992). Blundell admits to painting hundreds of Whiteleys, and could knock off twenty or thirty fake sketches in a couple of hours. Whiteley was easy, Blundell says, without a hint of maliciousness.

Curvers sold Blundell's fakes to collectors and through auction houses throughout Australia. If genuine, Blundell's 4,000 fakes would be worth more than $100,000,000 today. Curvers placed orders with Blundell for forgeries of certain artists she knew she could sell or had an order for.

Blundell is a colorful artist in his early 60s (born 1947 in Australia), whose lean physical appearance and close-cropped hair tends to disguise his roguishness. He worked out of an attic that had a drop-dead view of Sidney harbor. Blundell denies his works are forgeries, nor is he a copyist: He just has an overwhelming urge to feel like a particular painter on a particular day. "If it's a gray day I'll say I'll do a Streeton," he says, "cause he used to specialize in doing gray days on Sydney Harbour. [If it's a sunny day] I like the Roberts [paintings] of Sydney Harbour, his nice blues, Prussian blue water colors and light blue skies."

Blundell calls his works innuendoes and considers the word fake to be rude. Not surprisingly, he conveniently overlooks the fact that he forged the names of the artists he was copying to his innuendoes. It's interesting to watch this artist's mind at work.

He claims that he sold his innuendoes for next to nothing to the dealer Curvers for her to use as decorative pieces Yet when questioned on television how he felt about Curvers selling his fakes as originals, Blundell replied, "I was not at all upset, I was happy for her." Another time, however, Blundell exclaimed he had no idea that Germaine Curvers was selling his paintings as the real thing. When quizzed about how much money Curvers made selling his decorative pieces, he quoted the figure $400,000. (Dealer Curvers paid artist Blundell some $40,000 over ten years, that is about $150 per fake.)

The real relationship between Will Blundell and Germaine Curvers will probably never be known because Curvers is dead. Although he loves the spotlight (he wears gold jewelry to match his gold teeth capping), Blundell isn't talking, at least about that aspect of his life. On her deathbed, the 71-year-old Curvers said that her only regret was she didn't sell the Blundell fakes for more money.

THE ART OF A PEOPLE IS MORE IMPORTANT THAN THE LAWS OF A PEOPLE

In order to qualify as Aboriginal art, Dreaming designs are not considered authentic unless they are painted by an Aborigine. Why? Their cave and rock paintings have religious origins, and their creation (Genesis) stories are known as dreamings, or dream time. Most Aborigines still live on a tribal basis, and only family members are allowed to paint their dream stories.

Unlike almost all Western art, where the so-called schools casually cross national, ethnic, religious and color lines, to be considered Aboriginal art the work must be produced by an Aborigine. Otherwise, the art is considered cultural appropriation.

Who are the Aboriginals? Aboriginals are the original inhabitants of Australia, having settled the country some 60,000 years ago. There are roughly 400,000 people in Australia (about 2% of a population of 21,000,000) who claim Aboriginal ethnicity. They are black, have no written language, speak in a patois that is almost undecipherable to others, and pass their art down from generation to generation. Not unlike the American Indians, the Aboriginals have been discriminated against since the white settlers arrived. The indigenous people have the poorest health and lowest wealth and life expectancy in Australia (their lives are 17 years shorter than that of other Australians.) They are the most likely to be illiterate and unemployed.

In one of the most disgraceful chapters in history, between 1910 and 1970 the arrogant white settlers rounded up and took away from their parents about 100,000 children of the Aborigines. They claimed that the Aborigines were incapable of raising their own children and that their race was doomed. In early 2008, newly elected prime minister, Kevin Rudd, heroically made a formal apology for past injustices to the almost half-a-million Aborigines. Hopefully, compensation will soon be paid to the "stolen generation." Aboriginal art has become the face of Australian art to the world since 1970, and is considered the only true Australian artistic heritage.

Ray Beamish

Ray Beamish, a white Welshman living in Australia, lived with the highly regarded Aboriginal artist, Kathleen Petyarre for ten years. In the Aboriginal culture they were considered husband and wife. In 1996, Petyarre won the award for best Aboriginal art, the $18,000 Telstra National Aboriginal and Torres Strait Islander Award. Beamish and Petyarre had a falling out and Beamish moved to Melbourne. In 1997, a fuming Beamish announced to the world that he had painted Petyarre's award-winning Aboriginal work.

Not only did this stunning revelation disqualify Petyarre's painting from the most renowned and longest running award for Aboriginal art, further probing revealed that Ray Beamish had produced some of Australia's most important Aboriginal paintings which had been previously attributed to Kathleen Petyarre. Petyarre at first denied Beamish had worked on the dream painting, but in Melbourne Beamish painted other works to prove he had painted the winner. Petyarre grudgingly admitted that Beamish was co-author of the award winning painting. Beamish claimed that he painted well over 90% of it.

Pamela & Ivan Liberto

Rover Thomas (c. 1926–c. 1998), who started painting his dream paintings late in life, became one of Australian's most successful Aboriginal artists. Shortly after Rover's death the Libertos began forging his paintings. Then, in 2002, they began selling the fake Rover Thomas paintings. The couple sold their fakes through auction houses in Australia, including Christie's and Sotheby's. From 2002 to 2006, the Libertos, both in their sixties from Toorak, Australia, made over $300,000 selling fake Rover Thomas paintings, which financed a lavish lifestyle.

Pamela was the salesperson. She would always go to a different auction house and claim that she had inherited the paintings from her father, who had worked with Rover Thomas at a diamond mine in Kimberly. Incredibly, the auction houses believed her and conducted no further checks. (The judge, who heard the subsequent case, called it "absurd" that the auction houses relied solely on her story as authentication.) As in most cons, a mistake took Pamela and her husband down.

Pamela made a return visit to Sotheby's in 2005, where (this time) the Aboriginal art expert became suspicious. When experts confirmed the painting being offered was a fake, the authorities moved in. At the couple's residence the police seized paints, books, catalogues, images of Rover Thomas' work on a digital camera, and two Rover Thomas fakes in progress. Arrested in early 2006, a jury found both Libertos guilty on six counts. In late 2007 the judge sentenced the couple to three years. He required them to serve nine months in prison and suspended the remainder of the sentence.

LONELY? CREATE A FICTIONAL CHARACTER

Elizabeth Durack

In 1997, a bombshell dropped on the Australian art market. Elizabeth Durack (1915–2000), an acclaimed artist who had almost 100 solo exhibitions and was awarded several awards because of her artistic accomplishments, admitted that she had invented an Aboriginal artist named Eddie Birrup and then started painting under his name. Durack wrote an entire manuscript about the imaginary man that discussed his life in detailed biographical notes and even conducted a purported interview with Eddie in his native (Aboriginal) tongue. Perhaps even stranger, Durack always spoke of Eddie Birrup in the third person. Her daughter, owner of an Australian art gallery and in on the scam, even had an Eddie Birrup website. Durack entered her Eddie Birrup paintings in Aboriginal art exhibits to critical acclaim. In 1997 when Durack confessed to the fraud, the international art world was stunned: Why would a successful, white, establishment artist create a fictional Aboriginal artist and then produce, display, and sell paintings under the fictional artist's name when she was in her seventies?

Elizabeth Durack was born, raised and lived most of her life in remote Western Australia. She was of Irish extraction and spent much time during her life with Aborigines, whom she admired and loved. Affected and inspired by these relationships, Durack was one of the first white artists to adopt what are called indigenous painting techniques. Durack's creation of the fictional Eddie Burrup produced a storm of outrage in Australia because the case compromised the burgeoning worldwide Aboriginal art market. But there was a reason more basic than economics.

Reflecting centuries-old prejudices, the white establishment dismissed white Durack's trickery out of hand. But, in a classic case of what goes around comes around, the Aboriginal community protested vehemently. It claimed that Durack had appropriated Aboriginal culture for commercial purposes and that since all Aboriginal paintings allow access to the unique vision of an Aboriginal elder, she had wantonly (and illegally) entered their sacred tribal civilization. When pressed to explain her elaborate hoax, Durack advanced numerous reasons for conducting it. Her excuses, however, sounded mystical instead of compelling. On analysis, maybe the word mystical explains everything.

Peter Thompson

In the 1840s, Englishman Peter Thompson pulled the same scam as

Elizabeth Durack. Thompson, a forger of seventeenth-century master drawings, also created an imaginary artist and named him Captain John Eyre. Eyre was purported to be born in 1604. Thompson killed Eyre off in 1644, but had about 300 of his creation's drawings and paintings mysteriously appear in his make-believe house shortly after the imaginary Eyre's death. In 1852, Thompson made his move and brought out a limited edition of Captain John Eyre's etchings, which the unsuspecting public bought.

Frederick Schultz & Tokeley-Parry

New York art dealer Frederick Schultz, 54, was acclaimed as one of America's most reputable antiquities dealers. (Schultz was a former president of the National Association of Dealers in Ancient, Oriental and Primitive Art.) What the public didn't know was that Schultz was surreptitiously banking and selling looted artifacts provided by his partner, a 56-year-old antique restorer named Jonathan Tokeley-Parry (real name Jonathan Foreman). Tokeley-Parry was smuggling Egyptian antiquities into America.

The scam began in the early 1990s when Tokeley-Parry began stealing artifacts from archaeological sites in Egypt. To hide the prize objects from the authorities Tokeley-Parry found a unique use for his talents as a restorer; he covered the artifacts in a clear, liquid plastic, and when the plastic dried he painted it in colors that made the pieces look like cheap reproductions or cheap authorized government replicas. In a nice touch, to get them through customs, he even wrapped them in gift shop paper. Since Egypt passed a law in 1983 that gave title to the state of all antiquities found in Egypt after that date, both the smuggler and smugglee (is that a word?) realized they needed to create an old, believable provenance for the pieces. No problem for the two fertile criminal minds.

Tokeley-Parry had a deceased distant relative named Thomas Alcock. What they did was fabricate false provenances by creating an entire Thomas Alcock collection. Then, in order to make it appear to buyers that the works predated 1983, fake labels (using tea and baking to age them) were created. This professional handiwork fooled the government officials and buyers thousands of times in a four-year period: Tokeley-Parry admitted to smuggling over 2,000 artifacts out of Egypt alone. A remarkable coincidence brought the lucrative scheme to a crashing halt.

Tokeley-Parry sent his assistant to the British Museum to have 24 papyrus texts authenticated for a suspicious buyer. The curator at the museum recognized one of the pieces being offered; it was part of a collection discovered in 1966 by one of his colleagues. The curator notified the authorities.

Tokeley-Parry and Schultz were charged with conspiring to receive and smuggle stolen Egyptian antiquities. In 1997 Jonathan Tokeley-Parry was sentenced to six years in a UK prison. In absentia, Egypt sentenced him to 15 years of hard labor. In New York in 2002, Frederick Schultz was sentenced to 33 months in prison and fined a paltry $50,000. In 2003, a Federal Court of Appeals upheld the conviction.

Here's the most searing indictment of Schultz. During the time he was engaged in the crime of antiquity smuggling, in his role as advisor to president Bill Clinton, Schultz was officially urging lawmakers not to target the very crime he was committing.

A Fictional Character Doesn't Do It for You?
Then Create an Entire Civilization

Brigido Lara

Brigido Lara, a Mexican peasant with a grammar school education, was so prolific as a forger of pre-Columbian ceramics he created an entire civilization; which became known as the ancient Totonac style. A self-taught artist, Lara (born c. 1940 in Mexico) began copying antiquities dug up on his family's farm when he was a child of ten. In 1974, Mexican police arrested Lara and a group of his friends for possession and sale of pre-Columbian ceramics. The artworks were extensively tested by experts appointed by the Mexican government. The scholars and historians declared that the pieces were authentic so Lara and his friends were imprisoned.

Invoking the van Meergeren defense (how can I be guilty of possessing and selling off our national heritage when all I did was create fakes), Lara requested clay from his captors. The authorities were confused, but complied. Lara proceed to create exact reproductions of the identical pieces which had convicted him. These fake antiquities were then turned over to the same experts who had authenticated the original group. The pompous experts returned the same verdict: These are authentic antiquities. Lara and his band were released.

Brigido Lara was subsequently hired by the State Anthropology Museum in Xalapa where he was put in charge of restoring ancient pieces and advising on fakes. Lara is now licensed by the Mexican government to produce original replicas, which are all signed by him. When Lara was most active he created some 4,000 fakes, many of which remain in the collections of the top museums in the world. Lara, like many other forgers, has his own interpretation and explanation of his fakes: He calls them original interpretations, and his own originals.

Brigido Lara also denies that he sold his pieces as original pre Columbian art. Rather, he says he sold them to tourists, collectors and dealers as his own work and that he only learned later that the dealers and collectors would doctor his works, age them, and sell them as authentic pre-Columbian art. The museums purchased the fakes in the late 1950s and early '60s when pre-Columbian works flooded the market. At that time, no one questioned where the hoard came from.

In 1987, the Saint Louis Art Museum and the Dallas Museum of Art admitted publicly that several of their prized pre-Columbian sculptures were fakes; Saint Louis admitted to possessing three. The Met was stuck with a three-foot-high sculpture of an ancient Mexican wind god.

Did the museums reveal the forgeries on their own? Of course not. Brigido Lara, who created the fakes, tipped off the reporters.

Salim Al-Kari and Wilhelm Moses Shapira

In 1861, Wilhelm Moses Shapira (1830–1884) opened an antiquities shop in Jerusalem's Old City. Salim Al-Kari was a tourist guide. Al-Kari led the suckers to the shop and Shapira sold them fake artifacts. A nice little money-making scam. When the Moabite Stone was discovered in 1872, Al-Kari and Shapira saw a golden opportunity to get rich beyond their dreams. The pair literally created an entire (fraudulent) Moabite civilization.

Al-Kari was the forger. He created thousands of figurines, dishes, pottery, crude scripts, biblical figurines, crypts, stone heads, manuscripts and the like. Shapira was the salesman. And could he sell.

Shapira peddled almost 2,000 fake Moabite inscriptions to the Berlin Museum alone. In 1883, the pair decided to go big time: Shapira took strips of parchment, creating the so-called Torah Scrolls, to the British Museum. The following year, 1884, the Torah Scrolls were exposed as fakes. A few months later, the disgraced Wilhelm Moses Shapira committed suicide in a Rotterdam hotel.

THINKING BIGGER THAN A FICTIONAL CHARACTER OR CIVILIZATION? REWRITE YOUR COUNTRY'S HISTORY

Shinichi Fujimura

The damage that forgers cause society is normally tied to the monetary disaster that purchasers of the fakes invariably incur. In the big picture, however, what is more significant is the damage to the reputation of the authentic artists. After all, if the public is studying forgeries believing they are the real thing, its evaluation of the artist becomes warped, negatively. The case of Shinichi Fujimura (born in Japan in 1950) transcends both of these results. His scam changed the course of Japanese history, at least for a time.

Fujimura, an amateur archaeologist, began claiming discoveries of stone artifacts in the 1970s. In 1981, while in his early 30s, he stunned the nation when he announced that he had discovered stone tools dating back over 4,000 years, the oldest artifacts then known in Japan. An overnight hero, in the next 20 years, digging in almost 200 historic sites in Japan, Fujimura discovered older and older antiquities, pushing back the history of Japan hundreds of years with each discovery.

Fujimura became the darling of the press and public alike. He always seemed to be in the right place at the right time and was nicknamed The Devine Digger and God's Hand for his luck in finding significant artifacts. He explained his almost extrasensory perception by claiming he could see 500,000-year-old landscapes. Basking in his celebrity, Fujimura even conducted television interviews where he would lead the camera crew to a site and then miraculously discover historically significant stone implements. What Fujimura had been doing over the previous two decades was planting tools from his mundane collection and claiming they were real ancient artifacts proving earlier and earlier human settlement of Japan.

For the entire time, there was little or no public debate over Fujimura's extraordinary discoveries; the Japanese wanted to believe. Not only that, in Japan's academic community it is considered bad form to question elder scholars. Also, once removed from the soil, few anthropologists bother to examine the artifacts uncovered in a dig. Not unlike other great cons, Fujimura went too far. In 2000 he exhibited stone tools he claimed to have discovered in stratum dating back to the Paleolithic Age (600,000 years ago) which, not coincidently, made Japan home to the most advanced people in the world. Later in 2000, a suspicious newspaper, *Mainichi Daily,* videotaped Fujimura at dawn burying stone tools in the soil of his latest dig and then tapping the dirt down with his boots. After confronting the con artist with the evidence and obtaining a confession, the paper ran front page photographs exposing the hoax. One of Fujimura's junior associates admitted that he did not scientifically date the strata of the discoveries, which it was his duty to do, relying on his elder's assurances.

Stunned by the scam's newspaper exposure, the reaction was brutal. The previously quiet (and admiring) academicians issued statements denouncing Shinichi Fujimura. Textbooks were rewritten expunging Fujimura and his discoveries. Museums removed Fujimura discoveries from their galleries. Funding was cut off from institutions Fujimura was associated with. And everyone began to question an academic community which allowed such a harmful scam to flourish for over two decades. For the moment, the chastened Japanese realize that the claim of humans on their island some 600,000 years earlier is merely a chimera.

HOORAY FOR HOLLYWOOD

John Decker

John Decker (1895–1947), real name Leopold von der Decken, was born in Germany. He settled in Los Angeles, and was known as a bon vivant, hard-drinking, hard-loving, hard- living artist. A Hollywood version of Francis Bacon (1909–1992). Decker even looked the part. He was muscular and had impressive facial features which set off his dark red hair and thin reddish mustache. Even in Hollywood's golden age when anything goes was more than a phrase, Decker stood out. His secluded home (really a cabin) on Bundy Drive in the Brentwood section of Los Angeles served as headquarters for his celebrated circle of best pals, including John Barrymore, Errol Flynn, and W. C. Fields, aided and abetted in their high jinks by Vincent Price, Anthony Quinn, and Thomas Mitchell.

During his lifetime, Decker achieved a certain notoriety and commercial success from the portraits he painted in the style of the old masters. His sense of humor was legendary; portraying W. C. Fields as Queen Victoria is one of Decker's most famous spoofs. Interspersed with the fun and games almost demanded by the high life (or maybe as a part of it), Decker would discuss his forging when he was sufficiently oiled. His beloved coterie was never certain if Decker was kidding or not.

In 1947, however, only two months after his death, a remarkable postscript to Decker's life emerged that convinced his friends that their leader was indeed a talented forger. A memorial exhibition was held in Decker's honor. Included in the show were paintings supposedly painted by Gustave Courbet (1819–1877), Gauguin, Matisse, Modigliani (three), Picasso (two), Rembrandt, and van Gogh. All were owned and painted by John Decker.

Later investigation into Decker's life revealed a cunning side to the hell-raiser. It turns out, Decker was a careful forger who studied his subjects, used the proper paints and canvases, and even purchased letters of authentication. His favorite co-conspirator was the notorious Wilhelm Valentiner (1880–1958), who sold Decker his signature (on authentications) when he (Valentiner) was director of the nearby Los Angeles County Museum of Art.

Anthony Tetro

Tony Tetro was a flamboyant, likeable, Hollywood-type forger who was actively faking from the early 1970s (when he was in his early twenties) to the late 1980s. Cutting through all of his self promoting, listen to Tetro as he delivers all of the classic forger's liturgies:

He never sold anything as real;

He never knew that his fakes would be sold as originals;
He didn't paint fakes, he painted reproductions;
He absorbed the techniques and emotions of the masters and emulated them;
He blames the art dealers.

Tetro had no formal art training but made up for it by reading art books and visiting museums. He was meticulous in his forging. He went to great pains to produce fakes as close to the originals as possible, including buying old canvases and frames and traveling to France for art supplies not available in America (such as stretcher bars.) Tetro also used a computer process that eliminated the dot pattern in photographs. While a magazine photograph has 120 dots per line, Tetro's system had 700 dots per line. This meant that his photo copies looked like lithographs. In addition, Tetro was careful not to leave a paper trail. He relied on handshakes, and as his con expanded, he established offshore corporations to accommodate dealers who wanted to pay by check.

Tetro's high-flying, partying life in LA started to unravel when the Feds picked up Mark Henry Sawicki, owner of a Sherman Oaks, California gallery. In 1989, Sawicki was charged with ten counts of art forgery and grand theft. Sawicki copped a plea and agreed to finger Tetro as the forger furnishing his fakes in return for probation, community service and a small fine. Tetro was charged with conspiracy to commit grand theft and some 40 counts of forging lithographs. In addition, he was charged with forging Hiro Yamagata (born 1948) watercolors.

In 1993 Tetro pled no contest in a Los Angeles courtroom to one count of conspiracy and six counts of forging Dalis, Miros, Chagalls, and others. Today Tony Tetro, in his late 50s, advertises on the Internet and continues to paint fakes. Now he marks them as his own work.

HE WHO HOB-NOBS WITH CELEBRITIES ALWAYS GETS THE WORST OF IT

Tod Volpe

Tod Volpe was born in 1948 into a modest Italian family in New York. Volpe honed his skills in an unlikely venue; the funeral business. These skills included the art dealer staple; a soothing manner.

In 1968, with his cousin, Volpe made his move by buying an old-warehouse in downtown Manhattan. He was inspired to specialize in the arts and crafts side of the art world when he found a Gustav Stickley recliner and was fascinated by its design. Possessing the instincts of his legendary hero, Joseph Duveen, Volpe named the period of the pieces he amassed "Mission," trumpeting their importance as masterpieces of American design, and placing grotesque price tags on them.

Business boomed, not only because of Volpe's tactics, but also in large part because Volpe had learned the fine art of presentation and lighting perfected by Duveen: He made ordinary furniture look like priceless antiques. The biggest names in collecting (and America) became customers of the hard-working Volpe, who was available to his clients 24 hours a day, and, like Duveen, considered no request unreasonable.

Volpe had collected such an large number of the Hollywood A-List (led by Jack Nicholson and Barbra Streisand), he moved west to better infiltrate the anointed. In Los Angeles, Volpe took life up a notch and added paintings to his arsenal. Like Duveen, Volpe did nothing in halves. To impress his clients, he joined them in leading the high life, with the usual big house, bigger parties, fast cars and, what else, drugs. Unfortunately for Volpe, this lifestyle can only continue if the money keeps rolling in, and the bursting of the art bubble in the 1990s began to take its toll. To compensate for the lack of legitimate income, Volpe began using the usual tricks of desperate art dealers.

He sold fakes, he borrowed money against pieces that he didn't own, he inflated appraisals, and even conned money out of numerous best friends, including fleecing Jack Nicholson out of over $500,000. In 1998, Volpe was convicted of fraud and embezzlement, sentenced to 28 months in a federal pen, and ordered to return almost $2,000,000 as restitution. After serving two years, Tod Volpe is back in business. Even his autobiography, "Framed," sold well.

NEVER PLAY POKER WITH A GUY NAMED SLIM

Alfredo Martinez

Marinez's scam sounds like a variation of the three card monte. Alfred Martinez (born c. 1967 in Brooklyn) lived in New York and forged paintings by Jean-Michel Basquiat (1960–1988), the street graffiti artist turned celebrity, for an unusual reason.

No complaining about the art establishment for him. Martinez wanted to buy a partnership with an art dealer, so to raise the money he painted the fakes and then also faked the provenances. Here's how his scam worked.

In late 2001, Martinez had two Basquiat drawings (which belonged to his friend Tom Warren) in his possession. Martinez copied the drawings and the certificate of authentication that accompanied them. Martinez then returned the real drawings to Warren along with the fake certificate of authentication. He then sold the forged drawings, accompanied by the genuine certificate of authentication. Still dreaming about being an art dealer, Martinez tried to personally sell the fakes. Big mistake.

Unfortunately for Martinez, the so-called buyer of his cache of over a dozen fakes was an FBI agent. He was arrested for selling several hundred thousand dollars worth of Basquiats. During the trial in 2002, after originally pleading not guilty, Martinez changed his plea to guilty after Tom Warren, the photographer acquaintance of Martinez, revealed to the court that Martinez had earlier told him about his forging Basquiat.

The court imposed a three-year sentence on Martinez, who was still in his thirties, but the art world had not heard the last of the six-foot-two-inch, 300+ pound artist, even though he was in prison. Martinez had always been fascinated by guns and loved to paint them. While he was in prison from 2002 to 2004, the warden felt paintings of guns would incite riots so he forbade all painting by the artist. In retaliation, Martinez conducted several successful (and publicized) hunger strikes. One lasted almost two months. Also, while incarcerated, using improvised materials, such as jam, floor wax, Kool Aid, and coffee grounds, Martinez painted quite a few works on homemade paper. He smuggled the works out of his jail cell, labeling them legal documents. The flamboyant Martinez's efforts have resulted in several solo exhibitions. In addition, he has enjoyed sales to high-profile collectors, something that eluded him before going to jail. No question about it. Notoriety, no matter how gained, sells.

The Unscrupulous

Wolfgang Kuffner

German Wolfgang Kuffner (1760–1817) famously copied a Dürer self-portrait, which had been hanging in the Nuremberg City Hall, returned the copy, and kept the original.

Albert Sorlin-Dorigny

Sorlin-Dorigny is a French art collector who was also a restorer. At the end of the nineteenth century, Sorlin-Dorigny removed precious Ottoman ceramic tiles from the graves of two sultans who lived in the 1500s, ostensibly to restore them. The tiles, known as Cini (pieces of earthenware decorated with opaque colored glazes) are masterpieces of Turkish tile artwork. Sorlin-Dorigny kept the originals and gave copies back to Turkey. In 1895, Sorlin-Dorigny sold the priceless artifacts to the Louvre Museum in Paris. Turkey has had a patrimony law since 1906 but has been lax (to say the least) in enforcing the law. Now, however, following the lead of Italy, Turkey is showing concern for its heritage and is planning to recover the looted Cini from the French.

James Austin

James Austin, a restorer in Washington, accepted a painting by Thomas Moran (1837–1926) from an unsophisticated client who inherited the painting from a neighbor. The painting was grimy and the nice lady wanted it cleaned.

Austin, knowing Moran is considered one of America's premier landscape artists (even though he was born in England), immediately sold the valuable painting, without telling the client, of course. For over one year, whenever the lady inquired about the progress of the cleaning, Austin would bob and weave, putting her off. Finally, Austin could hold the client off any longer, so he returned the painting. No problem, right? Wrong. Austin returned a photograph of the painting which he had touched up with a bit of paint.

The story has a happy ending. The client eventually noticed the switch and went to the police. After investigating the scam, James Austin was charged in 2000. He pled guilty and was sentenced to jail and fined.

MY KID COULD DO THAT, BUT I'M NOT SURE HE'D WANT TO

Jupp Jenniches

Jupp Jenniches was a simple-minded museum attendant and all-around handy man who worked at the Cologne (Germany) Art Club, for almost 30 years. In 1945, returning to work after WW II, Jenniches found damaged paintings floating in the basement of the bombed-out gallery. He took seven of the works home and cleaned them. Jenniches sold the creatively cleaned paintings to a dealer/artist named Robert Shuppner. (Jenniches may or may not have known that Shuppner had been sentenced in 1942 to 3 1/2 years for selling fakes and was also forbidden to deal in art in the future.) In any case, Jenniches decided to up the ante and started selling Shuppner works that he himself painted. He added forged signatures to his fakes.

In 1947, while guarding an exhibition entitled "From Nolde to Klee" which was on display at the gallery, Jupp Jenniches had a classic my-kid-could-do-that moment. Jenniches brought some tracing paper from home and traced several Emil Nolde (1867–1956) and Paul Klee works on display. At home, Jenniches transferred the images to drawing paper, filled in the colors, and forged the artist's signatures. He then forged certificates of authenticity. When caught and Jenniches's story came out, the German public was amused rather than outraged. The judge agreed and Jupp Jenniches served no prison time.

WASN'T THERE A CLOSET IN THIS HOUSE TO HIDE IN?

Shaun Greenhalgh

Another poor Englishman, Shaun Greenhalgh, made headlines in the UK, not only because of his forgeries but also because he put together the most unusual English mob since "The Lavender Hill Mob" or "The Ladykillers." Shaun was a gifted artist who possessed unusual talent in that he could paint (pastels and oils) and sculpt (marble, stone and silver) with equal skill.

Shaun found little success in the marketplace. He was convinced that he was unable to sell his pieces because he was self-taught and hadn't attended the right schools. His feelings of inferiority were fueled by the fact that he lived with his parents in council housing (called public housing in America), a non descript terrace house in Bromley Cross, Bolton, Greater Manchester.

In 1989, when he was 29 years old, chunky, anemic Shaun had it. Frustrated by rejection and encouraged by his parents, he realized his talent was in copying, not creating. He decided on a plan to show up the art world. First, Shaun enlisted his 66-year-old, wheelchair-bound father, George, and his 65-year-old mother, Olive, to join him in his scam. The trio did its homework. They scoured books, periodicals, catalogues, sales receipts, and historical documents of all kinds to find items that Shaun could copy.

After acquiring the proper materials (say Roman gold to create a Roman artifact), Shaun would copy the selected piece depicted in the document they were studying. Shaun had the unusual talent of being able to create fakes from antiquity right up to today. Shaun's father, George, would then create a written provenance (paper trail) for the fake. Because Shaun was shy, his mother, Olive, would work the phones, making phone calls setting up appointments for her husband. A shy artistic genius, a wheelchair-bound elderly father, and a socially-adept elderly mother: It was a dream team.

Picture the con. See George Greenhalgh (in action from the age of 66 to 83), being pushed into a meeting in a wheelchair by his equally aged wife. Listen to the old man in his broad Lancashire accent explaining to the mark that the painting or artifact he was showing them had been in his family for hundreds of years. "Can you identify it for me," he would ask.

A natural salesman, in his pitch George always claimed that he never knew if the so-called family heirloom was worth anything. "Oh, is it really? Well then maybe I can be convinced to part with it. Why don't I see if I have any documentation about it at home." It was the realistic provenances the old man had forged that cinched the deals.

The con lasted 17 years and it netted the family gobs of money. Scotland Yard estimates the team sold some 120 fakes, and raked in an estimated $20,000,000 in the period from 1989 to 2006. Examples:

In 1993 and 1994, George sold the Bolton Museum in Manchester, England, a fake Thomas Moran sketch and watercolor. (When arrested,

Shaun bragged to the police that he could produce a Moran landscape worth more than $20,000 in half an hour.) In 2002, George went back to the Bolton Museum and pitched a fake 20 inch statue of an Egyptian princess (a relative of King Tut) to the Bolton Council for their Museum. The museum sent the piece (which Shaun had created in three weeks in his garden shed from a block of alabaster using an ordinary mallet and chisel) to the British Museum and Christies for authentication. Experts at the museum and auction house both concluded that the Princess Amarna (as it was known because of its artistic style and Egyptian period) was a genuine 3,300-year-old antiquity.

The key to the scam was the meticulous research the family had conducted and then how they wove a story around it. George produced a genuine 1892 catalogue which detailed the sale of contents of the home of the Fourth Earl of Egremont. George said his grandfather was at the sale and bought the Princess. As a clincher, he said that the statute passed through generations of his family and he had the (fake) letters to prove it.

In 2003, the statue was purchased for about $1,000,000 by the Greater Manchester Council with public money. The museum bragged about the acquisition (which made headlines all over the world), and put the forged Princess Amarna on display. Alerted in 2006 of a possible scam, the Bolton Museum withdrew the Princess from display and re-examined the piece. This time they determined it was a Greenhalgh fake.

As in most cons, a small mistake brought the scammers down. In 2005, George presented three fake Assyrian stone reliefs to the British Museum ostensibly for authentication (but really for sale.) George, however, had previously sold the museum a Roman plate he claimed to have discovered. This coincidence made museum staff suspicious so they conducted a more detailed inspection. When they discovered a spelling error and an anomaly in the reliefs, they called the Metropolitan Police Art and Antiques Unit. The scam fell apart later that year, in 2006, when the police raided the Greenhalgh's family's modest home and discovered what can best be described as a forgery factory. They found, according to Scotland Yard, "blocks of stone, a furnace for melting silver, half-finished sculptures, piles of art books, and a bust of Thomas Jefferson." In 1997, the Art Institute of Chicago had purchased what they thought was a sculpture by Gauguin (called "The Faun") from a London dealer who had purchased the piece from Sotheby's in 1994 for $50,000. It was a Greenhalgh fake.

After the Greenhalghs were arrested, the Gauguin was exposed as a fake in 2007. The habitually candid, but now clearly embarrassed director James Cuno, would not reveal how much the Chicago Institute had paid for the fake. It must have been a bundle. (Reports say $125,000.)

Following guilty pleas in 2007, the son, now 47, was sentenced to nearly five years in prison. His 83-year-old mother was given a one-year jail sentence (which was suspended), and the 84-year-old father was given a two-year sentence, which was suspended due to his medical condition. The public was fascinated by the story of a poor family running a con that was, in essence, a two decade long, highly successful major cottage industry.

Other angles to this story also intrigued people. For example, although the money flowed like wine for almost 20 years, Shaun Greenhalgh and his parents continued to live in relative poverty in their council house, even though, when arrested, they had about $1,000,000 in the bank. And that's only what the authorities could find.

Here's another. After their acquisition of the Princess Amarna, the town and museum spokespeople crowed, publicly, that while they had paid close to $1,000,000 for the antiquity, it was worth twice as much, the town and museum had taken advantage of the Greenhalgh family and were bragging about it. Outraged by the trial, a large segment of the public vowed to try to overturn Shaun Greenhalgh's prison sentence.

DREAM NO LITTLE DREAMS, THEY STIR THE IMAGINATION OF NO MAN

Tom Keating

Tom Keating (1918–1984) is one of several artists born in modest circumstances in England who bedeviled the art establishment. Keating was a colorful Englishman from a poor Cockney family who started his art career as a restorer and ended it as a television celebrity and author. In between, the man who looked like an impish pixie with a bushy white beard, which was as much a signature as his jolly laugh and infectious sense of humor, painted and exhibited his own works along with his restoration efforts. While neither endeavor paid the bills and barely put food on his table, Keating decided it was the system that was rotten, not his paintings or restoring. He felt the system was rife with unscrupulous critics, dealers, and auction houses, all of whom got rich at artist's expense.

Like Don Quixote, Keating had a dream. Like the hero in Cervantes's classic novel, Keating's planned adventure was idealistic and impractical. He decided to paint so many fakes his works would destabilize the corrupt system of the art establishment. Actually, the plan to paint thousands of fakes of hundreds of different masters was not as crazy as it sounds.

As an art restorer and artist, Keating had a head start on his plan. He knew how to use paints, glycerin, turpentine, ammonia, and other tools of the trade. These talents allowed him to fake such diverse masters as Rembrandt (his favorite), Modigliani, Jean-Honore Fragonard (1732–1806), Thomas Gainsborough (1727–1788), and Pierre-Auguste Renoir (1841–1919). Destabilizing the art establishment with his fakes was the idealistic dream aspect of the planned adventure. But in the process, he also invented creative forging techniques, and, studying the lives of the artists he painted, Keating also became adept at faking provenances.

Keating would visit the National Gallery and other museums in London and, when no one was looking, touch the surface of the canvas to feel the vibrations from the artist who painted the piece. How's that for a Quixote touch? In any case, for some 25 years, Keating pursued his dream, turning out over 2,000 forgeries of 120 different artists.

Kating called his fakes Sexton Blakes, either after a fictional detective or using down-home slang. He enjoyed toying with the establishment, almost always leaving clues in the works that they were fakes. Like Don Quixote, Keating may have been a little off center but he was honest: He never made a secret of his ability to make fakes. Besides putting clues in the forgeries, he boasted about his fakery in pubs and at dinner parties. Even to casual acquaintances.

In the early 1970s however, the impossible dream began to unravel. Thirteen Tom Keating fake Samuel Palmer watercolors were offered for sale at auction. The auction house officials noticed certain similarities and began an investigation. Geraldine Norman, a writer for the *London Times* who was following the story, found the wayward Keating. She convinced the larger-than-life artist to tell the story of his life in a book "The Fakes Progress," which Keating dictated to Norman and her husband. The book, published in 1977, was a big hit in England. Unfortunately for Keating, the authorities also read it and one month after the book's publication he was arrested on nine charges of conspiracy to defraud and deception. The irrepressible Keating confessed, saying, "The only thing that amazes me is that I wasn't exposed in the press a lot sooner."

In 1979, during the trial, the charges were dropped and the criminal case was dismissed when it was determined that Keating was too sick to be tried. In 1982, Keating's life took a most unusual turn; he was hired to host a television show about art.

Keating's natural approach made him a star. The following year he hosted a second series on art that reinforced his celebrity. Everyone in England, except the art establishment, loved the colorful rascal who had duped the experts. After all, who doesn't love a dreamer? In 1983, cashing in on his new-found fame, Christie's held the first of six successful auctions of Keating paintings. Yes, original and fake paintings by Tom Keating now bring high prices and have become important works to collectors, particularly in England.

SNAPSHOTS

Ernest Durig

Swiss born Ernest Durig (1894–1962) was a stocky, serious looking forger who immigrated to America in 1928. As one commentator phrased it, Durig led a childhood, and indeed a life, marked by misadventures, impostures, and hints of mental illness. Durig had a mediocre artistic talent but he was relentless. He called himself professor and fulfilled a life-long obsession to be close to the rich and famous by ingratiating himself by drawing or sculpting their portraits gratis. We're talking major league celebrities here like popes (Benedict XV), presidents (James Monroe), and premiers (Benito Mussolini).

Durig's deep-seated passion, however, was the great French sculptor Auguste Rodin. Throughout his life, Durig claimed to have been Rodin's last pupil and a dear, close, personal friend of the master. How did Durig manifest this preoccupation with Rodin?

Over more than four decades Durig produced over 1,000 fake Rodin drawings, most of which were female nudes. Although the forgeries were mediocre at best, his fake Rodin's made their way into the world's top museum and were eagerly sought after by collectors.

There is one bright spot in the life of this tortured artist. In the 1930s, on a trip to Greenwood, Wisconsin to visit his wife's relatives, a planned one week visit stretched into a three month love-in with the locals. During that time Durig agreed to sculpt plaster busts of many of the leading citizens of the small Wisconsin community for free.

Durig also created a huge (15 foot) peace memorial cast from white cement and white sand, charging only for the cost of materials. And this was in the height of the depression when Durig desperately needed money. (The memorial was dedicated in 1937 in front of a large audience, and to this day it sits on the square, next to the city hall.) The enigmatic artist/forger Ernest Durig died in poverty.

Emile Delobre

Parisian born Emile Delobre (1893-1956) was winning artistic awards in his teens, and studied at Beaux Arts with some of the biggest names in French Impressionism, including Matisse. A gentle and warm man, committed to his extended family, Delobre was hired by art dealer Nathan Wildenstein (1851-1934) who observed him in the Louvre copying a painting and hired him on the spot. To the world, Delobre's job for Wildenstein was consultant/restorer, and the artist did some of that.

It appears Delobre's real role was to paint fakes for Wildenstein. For example, most experts attribute de la Tour's "The Fortune Teller" to him. The painting was purchased by the Met in 1960 from Wildenstein (who else) for the then hearty sum of $675,000. Emile Delobre, the French Impressionist artist with the masterly talent, retired in 1972, having forged innumerable artists, including Rembrandt, in the course of his lengthy, cozy relationship with Nathan Wildenstein.

Georges Wildenstein

Georges Wildenstein (1892–1963), son of gallery founder Nathan Wildenstein, was accused by writer Hector Feliciano of collaborating with the Nazis in WW II. In his 1997 book *The Lost Museum*, Feliciano maintained that even though Georges had fled Paris in 1940, the Wildenstein Gallery remained opened during the war, and was run by employee Roger Dequoy. Maintaining regular contact with Georges in America, Dequoy dealt regularly with the Number One Nazi art dealer, Berlin based Karl Haberstock. In 2000, a Court of Appeals in France ruled against the Wildenstein heirs who had filed a lawsuit against Feliciano. In 1955, Wildenstein had his New York vice-president, Emmanuel Rouseck hire an attorney named John Broady to tap the phone of art dealer Rudolph Heinemann.

Why? Heinemann was known to have worked on big sales with archrival M. Knoedler & Co. The bug was active for about six months but yielded nothing but a lawsuit.

Philips Wouwermans

There are two interesting versions of the death of Pieter Van Laer (1592–1642), the Dutch artist who lived most of his life in baroque Rome. Called *Il Bamboccio* (which means, depending on who is translating, puppet, little clumsy one, large baby, or rag doll) because of his physically deformed body, Van Laer specialized in street scenes that offended the nobility but were popular with the peasants.

Van Laer followers were mostly Dutch, except for Italian Michelangelo Cerquozzi (c. 1602–1660). They were called Bamboccianti. There are the two versions of Van Laer's death: Both relate to the forger Philips Wouwermans.

1. After Van Laer died of natural causes in 1642, Philips Wouwermans (1619-1668), one of the stars of the Dutch golden age, stole everything Van Laer used in his work, including his brushes, paints, and even his designs. From that moment on, Wouwermans forged Van Laer paintings.

2. Van Laer killed himself because Wouwemans was imitating/forging his works. Take your pick.

Jan van Beers

Jan van Beers (1852–1927) was a Belgian artist who put a unique twist on the art of forging. What the creative van Beers did was pay inferior artists to make copies of his paintings.

When the paintings were good enough, van Beers signed his own name to the fake. When, on the other hand, van Beers felt the work was not up to his standards, he had the copyist sign his (van Beers) name. That way, if a fake Jan van Beers aroused suspicion, Jan van Beers himself could disown it, pointing to the fake signature. Van Beers was creating genuine fakes and fake fakes.

Jef van der Veken

Belgian Jef van der Veken (1872–1964) was Belgium's top restorer in the 1930s, 40s and 50s. He was so talented he worked for several museums in Brussels. We all know that restoring and forging are first cousins. The question is, when does the relationship cross the line and become incestuous? In van der Veken's case, he went from traditional restoring to creative restoring, where he would add his own ideas to old paintings. From that point, he moved into painting decorative pastiches in the Gothic and Renaissance styles.

Along the way, when he realized that unscrupulous dealers like Emile Renders were reselling his pastiches as originals, van der Veken decided to join the con. He began forging Jan van Eyck (c. 1395–c. 1441), Hans Memling (c. 1430–c.1494) and other Flemish primates.

Here's a rare twist. Jef van der Veken's most famous fake was commissioned by the authorities. In 1934 a panel of the van Eyck masterpiece altarpiece "Adoration of the Mystic Lamb" was stolen from the cathedral of Saint Bevo in Ghent. Van der Veken was called upon to paint a copy. The fake is so perfect, today no viewer can distinguish between it and the companion authentic van Eyck panels.

Van der Veken has begun to receive recognition of sorts. In 2004/2005, the Groeninge Museum in Bruges, Belgium, hosted an exhibition entitled "Fake or Not Fake." Jef van der Veken's work was at the heart of the show. And in 2007, the Bruce Museum in Greenwich, Connecticut, in a show about fakes, displayed a painting in the style of Jan van Eyck by Jef van der Veken.

Luca Giordano

Luca Giordano, born in Naples in 1632 (died in 1705), appears to be the most prolific forger of the Old Masters. By the time Luca was thirteen he was copying Raphael and Michelangelo. After winning a lawsuit brought by a client who had purchased a forgery of a Dürer, young Luca, pushed by his domineering father, shifted into high gear. Giordano, like all great forgers, was able to insert himself into the psyche of the artists he copied. His known oeuvre includes at least a dozen of a Raphael painting (which was hanging in the Vatican), some twenty Giulio Romano drawings, and innumerable Caravaggios. There are countless Luca Giordano fakes hanging today in the world's museums and in the homes of collectors. Remember, regardless of who painted them, the best forgeries are still hanging on walls.

Robert Lawrence Trotter

Robert Lawrence Trotter of Kenneth Square, Pennsylvania took his antique and furniture restoring talents in the wrong direction. Between 1985 and 1990, Trotter altered over 50 nineteenth-century folk art paintings, which he then sold to dealers and auction houses throughout New England and the East. He claimed they were Early American works by deceased or fictitious artists. In executing his scam, Trotter used numerous pseudonyms. When the authorities sought cooperation from the 16 collectors they were able to identify as having been duped by Trotter, only five wanted their money back and agreed to cooperate with the investigation.

In 1990, Robert Trotter pled guilty and was sentenced to ten months in federal prison for faking, forging, and selling American primitive paintings. As part of his plea bargain, Trotter agreed to forfeit the seized works to the US Justice Department, which donated four to Yale University and one to Buffalo State. For study purposes.

Marcantonio Raimondi

Over the ages, some of the biggest names in Italian art have been forgers at least once in their lifetime, including Andrea del Sarto (c.1486–c. 1531), Raphael (1483–1520), and even Michelangelo (1475–1564). An Italian scholar assembled a catalogue of Guercino (1591–1666) fakes that filled two volumes. Marcantonio Raimondi (c. 1480–c. 1534) was a remarkable Italian printmaker and engraver. Raimondi was inspired by Dürer and was his most prolific forger. Dürer, who was obsessed about people copying his works, sued Raimondi in Venice. The Venetian Senate found Raimondi guilty and rebuked him.

In the early 1500s, Raimondi established a workshop of engravers who could beautifully and accurately duplicate works of art. The great Raphael became Raimondi's main client, with the master using Raimondi's prints as a way to get his art known to the general public.

Raimondi was so good, Raphael needed merely to make a sketch. He would then turn it over to Raimondi who would fill in the details and engrave a complete work of art. Raphael's assistants would supervise the dirty work of printing. Altogether, Raimondi engraved some six hundred plates and his methods were copied all over Europe, particularly by the Germans, who flocked to Rome to learn from him. After Raphael's tragic early death, Raimondi continued to work with his circle, particularly Giulio Romano (c. 1499–c. 1546.)

Romano was a rake who designed erotic scenes and convinced Raimondi to engrave them, landing the master engraver in jail. (Remember, Rome was part of the papal states in Raimondi's time and the Popes took no prisoners when it came to moral issues.) While the evidence is spotty, a good guess is that Raimondi was captured during the tragic Sack of Rome in 1527, losing his fortune and career. Like so many other greats in that violent time, he reportedly died a beggar.

Robert Thwaites

Thwaites is another who, unlike most forgers, didn't produce fakes to support a lavish life style or to expose what he considered the idiocy of the art establishment, but rather, like Myatt, he needed the money to avoid financial disaster. The graphic designer, whose eyesight was failing, needed money to pay his son's tuition at a private school where the fees ran, hold on to your hat, over $100,000 per year.

To raise the money in the early 1900s, Thwaites began to forge the work of Victorian artist John Anster Fitzgerald (1823–1906). Thwaites, who had no formal training as a painter, became so proficient he sold a fake Fitzgerald to the BBC's Antiques Roadshow television star, Rupert

Maas. (Maas, the show's resident art expert who also own his own gallery, resold the work at triple his cost.)

Another Thwaites Fitzgerald forgery sold to a second gallery owner for over $200,000 at auction. Thwaites claimed the paintings were bequeathed to him by his grandfather. His five-year career of forgery (1999–2004) came to an end when a prospective buyer raised questions about the authenticity of another Fitzgerald painting. When the police raided Thwaites' house in Herefordshire they found substantial evidence of his faking career. Subsequent technical examination revealed that Twaites had used nickel titanium in his his fakes, which wasn't patented until 1936 (Fitzgerald died 30 years earlier.) In 2006, Twaites, relieved the ordeal was over, pled guilty and was jailed for two years. He became the prison's unofficial portrait artist, but wouldn't take any payment for his work. Twaites must have seen plenty of prison movies, because he wisely stated, "What you need more [than money in jail] is friends or people to look after you." Released under strict supervision in 2007, the 55-year-old Robert Twaites continues to paint in the style of Fitzgerald, but is now careful to label his paintings as fakes.

John-Pierre Schecroun

John-Pierre Schecroun was born in Madagascar in 1929. He arrived in Paris and enrolled in the famous Ecole des Beaux Arts. The artist also worked in Leger's workshop. At the two key positions, Schecroun learned two things, one good and one bad. It was fortunate that he learned that he would never be a great painter in his own right, thereby saving himself a lifetime of frustration. The bad news is Schecroun learned the moves of the rich and famous painters which de discovered he could easily ape.

The young forger was smart and clever. He limited himself to copying the artists he had studied (and studied under), including Leger, Picasso, Braque, and Miro. Schecroun became a major forger of Leger. Instead of painting in oils, Schecroun only worked with watercolors and pastels, which were easier and faster for him. Schecroun worked with various art dealers and was successful until he was arrested in 1962 and charged with forgery. The artist confessed that he had created innumerable works, including approximately 80 Picassos, which he sold for substantial sums. (Schecroun bragged that he could create a Picasso painting in three minutes.) He later claimed that he really didn't sell the fakes himself but pled guilty to the crime to protect his friends. Throughout the trial, the forger maintained that his intention was to expose the idiocy of art dealers who refused to buy his works but paid huge dollars for the forgeries he could draw or paint in a few minutes. The artist was given a two-year prison sentence in France for painting over 100 fakes. After being released from jail, Jean-Pierre Schecroun fakes sold well when he held shows of his works.

CHAPTER FOUR
KING OF UNSCRUPULOUS ARTISTS

Salvador Dali

Salvador Dali (1904–1989) is the most well-known (and avaricious) twentieth-century artist in history. His fame is a reflection of his shameless self promotion rather than his artistic talent, although his melting watch painting is one of art's most vivid images. Dali was born and died in Figueres, Spain. Other than that, nothing was ordinary about his life, although there is general agreement that Dali's surrealist works prior to World War II are worthy of scholarly analysis and comment.

The Surrealist Movement was formed in Paris in the early 1920s; its goal was a revolutionary transformation of society. Dali was admitted to the group in 1929 and was soon considered the leader of the Surrealists with his paintings of grotesque distortions, genitalia, insects and what have you. In 1929 Dali met his future wife, the Russian who designated herself Gala. She divorced her husband in 1932, married Dali in 1934, and choreographed Dali's life from the moment they met. As if he needed any help.

In 1939, Dali was expelled from the Surrealist Movement for being too greedy, and for publicly expressing his support of the Spanish dictator Franco. Dali also thought Hitler was interesting, and said so. Publicly. After moving to the United States in 1940 (to sit out the war), Dali perfected the tricks of self-promotion which he started as a youth. Self-promotion had been rampant in America, but Dali took it to new levels. He became the larger than life DALI. He dressed the part with colorful, ridiculous clothes, always bulged his eyes in public, and carefully groomed his mountainous moustache. Hello hustler, good-bye artist.

American society loved Dali, which meant that America loved Dali. Dali would do anything for a buck. Wherever one looked, Dali's imprint was there. There was no escaping his glowering face, upturned moustache, and distinctive signature, whether (for example) on perfume bottles or the cover of magazines (*Time* 14 Dec. 1936). Back in Spain, Dali and Gala put together the mother of all entourages (eat your heart out Andy Warhol) with whom they played out their sexual fantasies and other lurid dreams. Entourages, whether in America or Europe, cost money. So, to live the high life, the greedy couple now perfected the scams they had begun some years earlier.

Dali figured out that the painting was inconsequential, his signature was what was important. Consequently, Dali had his collaborators do the work (that is, paint the pictures) and then he would sign the painting and have his picture taken standing next to it, brush in hand. The painting would thus be miraculously transformed into an authentic Dali. (The Italian artist Giorgio De Chirico would also sign copies of his friend's paintings in return for money.) Dali would also claim prints of his work were limited editions, but kept the plates and secretly struck an illegal number of additional prints, signing them all (thereby making them originals.) Dali even made fake copies of real prints and copies of original paintings. Dali signed blank pages and sold them to a network of accomplices. It has been estimated that he signed (believe it or not) hundreds of thousands of blank sheets of paper.

Bottom line: Dali was almost never involved in the supervising or execution of the stones or plates of his lithographs. In fact, most Dali prints for sale today are mere photomechanical or offset reproductions. Because of these maneuvers, it is almost impossible to buy a legitimate Dali: Sotheby's and Christie's stopped selling his prints almost 30 years ago. Dali got rich by hardly lifting a finger. The finger he lifted to the world is best not described here.

In 1982, a Dali Museum was opened in, of all places, Saint Petersburg, Florida. The museum is on the campus of the University of South Florida and is modest but quite nice. What isn't modest is the enormous gift shop, which engulfs you when you enter the museum. Could a Dali museum be designed any other way? A new building is planned for 2010. Museum gift shop junkies can hardly wait.

CHAPTER FIVE
UNSCRUPULOUS DEALERS

There is something in art that corrupts
even honorable men.

— Sophy Burnham

Before World War II, art dealers were kings. Actually, emperors would be a more accurate description. During the time dealers ruled the roost, some 90% of the selling of art was conducted through them. Since most transactions were conducted in private, prices were not generally known. This secrecy (a trait that has always dominated the art business) was an asset to the dealers, because this made it easier for them to buy low and sell high, without their collector clients knowing what hit them. All this has changed. While dealers are still a factor in the art world today, they are less and less prominent. Sort of like telephone operators.

Why has the role of art dealers diminished since World War II? Auction houses. Auction houses have taken over the function of selling weighty art. This has serious consequences, especially to the collector, because the world now knows whether a painting sold, and if it sold, what price was paid. While the lifting of some of the veil of secrecy that has historically engulfed the art world has numerous advantages, the fact that auction houses are now the dominant force in the art business is not necessarily good news. Auction houses can be as unscrupulous as art dealers.

What does it take to be a successful art dealer? Remember, art dealing is a unique business because the end product has no intrinsic value. Value is determined primarily by reputation of the artist and how that reputation is transmitted and interpreted in the marketplace by dealers, curators, collectors, auction houses, and especially the press.

Having said that, just what does it take to be a successful art dealer? On the surface, not much. On the buying side, you have to know where the art is, which pieces to buy and how much to pay for them. On the selling side (but before buying) a dealer needs to know to whom the works can be sold, and how much they can be charged.

The reality is much more complex. Art dealers must have the basic traits and abilities of all con men. That is, they have to be (in alphabetical order) believable, charismatic, charming, intelligent, likeable, street-wise, tough, and utterly ruthless, while at the same time generating trust, with the ability to make everybody their best friend. And, all con men must have no shame.

It's hard to imagine, but art dealers have an even higher mountain to climb. Dealers must also appear to be connoisseurs, suave, sophisticated socialites who are worldly, well-connected, and know more about art than anyone else on the entire planet. Finally, art dealers must give the impression they are rich, whether they are or not.

THEIR ANCESTORS MUST BE TURNING IN THEIR GRAVES

Frederick Hill and James Berry Hill

The 70-year-old Berry-Hill Galleries in Manhattan is one of America's best known dealers. It specializes in Early American paintings, and is the successor of Berry of London, which was established in the seventeenth century. Third-generation owners, Frederick Hill, and his cousin, James Berry Hill, pled guilty in 2003 to a felony count of failure to collect sales tax and falsifying records for a number of paintings and paid a $750,000 fine in a plea agreement. But that was a mere warm up. Also in 2003, the Hills encumbered their inventory of paintings to one creditor (ACG Credit) for over $20,000,000. At the end of 2004, Sotheby's listed for sale a George Bellows painting named "The Kids." The Hills wanted the painting but needed cash, having blown through the $20,000,000 they had previously borrowed.

No problem for the Hills. They set up a shell corporation (Coram Capital), transferred title of their inventory of paintings to it, and then pledged the previously encumbered paintings as collateral for a second loan of $8,000,000 from a loan company (ARCK). To make the fraud work, the Hills hooked up with a man named Andrew Rose.

Andrew Rose made the first loan to the Hills on behalf of ACG Credit. He then left the firm under a cloud, set up his own loan firm (ARCK), and made the second (illegal) loan to the Hills. In late 2004, the Hills were the successful bidders on the Bellows painting, using a little over $6,000,000 of the $8,000,000+ they had borrowed illegally from Rose. In May 2005, still hungry for cash, the Hills and Rose rigged a Christie's auction by consigning but then hiding their ownership in 43 paintings and bidding them up.

Bidding on your own works is illegal except in rare exceptions, such as divorce situations. No problem. The Hills sent Andrew Rose to the auction house, claiming that the paintings were owned by a divorcing couple. The Hills had to buy back 21 paintings at the auction, but by inflating the value of the 22 others, they raised some fast cash. As it turns out, not enough. Also in May of 2005, to raise additional money, the Hills sold a wealthy Texas collector named James McGlothlin half of that Bellows painting. The agreement contained a typical buy/sell agreement. At this point, Christie's reacted to the gossip on the street. In an unusual move, the auction house withheld the 22 paintings (hyped by Hill/Rose) and conducted an investigation.

The auction house determined that the Hills had perpetrated a price-fixing scheme, so it cancelled all of the Hill/Rose purchases and offered to refund the money of the other purchasers of the Berry-Hill/Rose paintings. This auction was the trigger. Lawsuits started to fly (including one from McGlothlin) and the Hills declared bankruptcy in late 2005, showing a debt of some $50,000,000 and 100 creditors. Christie's was the largest unsecured creditor. In mid-2006, American Capital, an art financing company, loaned the Hills $21,000,000 to keep them in business. The most unfortunate victims of the scam are the collectors and artists who consigned works to Berry-Hill that the Hills sold prior to the bankruptcy but kept the money. These individuals are unsecured creditors and the large secured loans have preference over them.

Jean Charles Millet

In the early 1900s, French art dealer Jean Charles Millet, born in 1898, grandson of great Barbizon School (realistic landscapes) painter Jean Francois Millet (1814–1875), took an authentic Millet painting to a little known artist by the name of Paul Cazot (or Cazeau) to be restored. When the grandson saw the impressive results, he had a classic "Eureka" moment. "Forget legitimate dealing, the money is in fakes." The pair teamed up: Cazot forged elder Millet's paintings and grandson Millet supplied the signatures and authentications.

Not satisfied with besmirching his grandfather's legacy, the grandson branched out (with Cazot) and over the years sold some 4,000 fake Degas, Monets, Pissarros, Corots, and many others. (Millet sold the museum in Barbizon its entire collection of his grandfather's works. The works were all fakes.) In 1930 a disgruntled French collector blew the whistle when he realized he had purchased a fake Millet from the grandson. The grandson confessed, but that's not the best part of the story. The best part is the defense offered in the 1935 trial where the pair insisted they had only cheated certain buyers, whom they considered fair game. Here's Millet: "You can sell anything to Americans and the English. They know nothing about art . . . All you have to do is ask a fabulous price."

Jean Charles Millet, besides acting like a stereotypical obnoxious Frenchman, also had a bizarre sense of humor. He boasted to the authorities, "I had a good time [selling fakes.]" This from the grandson who was peddling fakes of his famous grandfather's works. Some grandson.

NOT EVEN FATHERS ARE IMMUNE

Anna Casella & Giorgio Corbelli

Giorgio Corbelli owned an Italian auction house named Semenzato which operated on the Italy's shopping channel. In 1999, the Italian police began a fraud investigation into the possibility that the jovial, mustachioed Corbelli was selling fake lithographs. In 2001, some 6,000 fakes were confiscated and Corbelli was arrested.

The fraud concentrated on artist Michele Casella (1892–1989), although forgeries of other contemporary Italian artists were peddled. The authorities also arrested a couple of Corbelli's partners, including, believe it or not, Anna Cascella, daughter of the artist most forged. In 2002 the well-connected Corbelli (he was the controlling shareholder of the Naples football club, two television stations, and a company named Finearte) was incarcerated in a Roman prison.

PRINTS A CINCH TO SCAM? COUNT UP AFTER THE HARVEST IS OVER

Leon Amiel

Leon Amiel began his career in art importing and publishing art books. He had operations in New Jersey and France, and his works were well-regarded and legal. But late in the 1970's, Leon Amiel got greedy. He became an art dealer. Amiel began producing, and then selling, fake limited edition prints of Dali, Chagall, Miro and Picasso. By the time Amiel died in 1988, he was a major force in the art business because he was the biggest source of prints in the world. The problem was, all of the prints (and blank pieces of paper signed by Dali) he sold were fakes.

Amiel had printing presses that enabled him to produce thousands of fake lithographs an hour as opposed to 30 or 40 an hour using prior methods. Amiel brought his entire family into the scam; his wife Hilda, daughters Kathryn and Joanne, and even his granddaughter, Sarina, who would return from college to the plant in New Jersey where she would sign the prints with the appropriate artist's name. Amiel was the wholesaler; the center of an international network of dealers that the Government estimated cost unsuspecting collectors and tourists over $1,000,000,000. When Amiel's factory was raided by the Federal authorities in 1991, investigators found (and confiscated) more than 75,000 counterfeit prints: Over 50,000 were fake Dalis and over 20,000 were fake Miros.

In early 1992, the government filed a 30 count criminal indictment against Kathryn, Joanne, and Sarina. In 1995, after a lengthy trial, Amiel's daughters and granddaughter were sentenced to various prison terms and fines for federal conspiracy and mail fraud (Leon's wife, Hilda, died in 1993 so she escaped punishment.) In 1996, the Court of Appeals upheld the verdict. Over an eight-year period, since 1987, the Federal Trade Commission brought criminal charges against 14 dealers to crack this worldwide ring. Three dealers and distributors (Philip Coffaro, Thomas Wallace and Lawrence Groeger) pled guilty to mail fraud and testified for the government in various cases.

Cornell Gabos

Hungarian born Cornell Gabos, 70, moved to Cleveland, Ohio, where he formed Renaissance Fine Arts and became a well-known dealer and art auctioneer. Nobody was safe from his gregarious personality and story telling ability, including diplomats, politicos, celebrities and sophisticated collectors. Over a 20-year period he sold over 3,000 counterfeit etchings and lithographs (mostly fake Dalis) as museum quality pieces. Gabos accompanied the fakes with false appraisals and bogus certificates of authenticity, which he produced. Gabos was charged in 1994, and ordered to repay over $2,000,000 to injured parties. In response, Gabos abandoned his gallery and fled to Europe, where he remains at large.

Pierre Marcand

Frenchman Pierre Marcand established Magui Publishing in the early 1980s to produce Dali fakes and began selling them, through his Beverly Hills art gallery and in other ways. In 1983, Marcand closed his French operation and moved everything to California.

Marcand's sales pitch claimed that Dali had approved and supervised the preparation of the prints, that Dali himself had signed each one, that the prints were scarce, that the etchings were hand produced from an eighteenth-century press, and finally, that the prints were valuable and would increase in value. None of this was true. After selling over 20,000 Dali fakes in less than ten years, Marcand was stopped in 1989 when the Federal Trade Commission filed for an injunction to halt the scam. In a raid on a Marcand warehouse, the authorities hauled away almost four truckloads of incriminating evidence, including more than 1,000 blank pieces of paper bearing Dali's signature, and printing presses used to produce fake prints by Dali, Chagall, and others. The FTC prevailed and in 1991 the court imposed a fine of almost $2,000,000, which the court figured was the amount Marcand had illegally made through his fraud.

Leon Amiel, Jr.

In 2008, after a two-year investigation, the Feds charged Leon Amiel's son, 36-year-old Leon Amiel, Jr., with following in his father's footsteps; that is wholesaling fake prints. Amiel, Jr. was charged with nine counts of fraud, including distributing 2,500 fake Dali and Alexander Calder (1898–1976) prints, claiming they were limited editions. Amiel used various tactics to move the fake prints, including eBay. Young Amiel used the name Leon Glass to conceal his family's background of art fraud.

In a second simultaneous indictment, seven individuals were charged in 2008 with raking in more than $5,000,000 selling fake paintings and prints of Picasso, Miro, Chagall, Dali, Andy Warhol (1928–1987), and Roy Lichtenstein (1923–1997), which were imported from Spain and Italy. The European arm of the worldwide forgery ring, which was headquartered in Spain and Italy, cautioned their American customers not to flood the market with the fakes (and fake authentications) they produced. Unfortunately for the Europeans, the Americans were much too anxious and numerous marks in America began to complain to the authorities. An investigation was launched in 2006. In raids in Spain, the authorities found thousands of fakes in and around Barcelona, which ultimately led to the 2008 indictments. (Also in early 2008, as part of this on-going investigation, federal authorities seized dozens of artworks in a raid on the Kass/Meridian Gallery in the upscale River North area of Chicago. The 22-year-old gallery is owned by Alan and Grace Kass who have been suspected for many years of selling fake Picasso, Dali, Chagall, and Miro prints.) The seven fraudsters from Europe and America included James Kennedy and Northbrook, Illinois dealer Michael Zabrin.

Donald Austin

Donald Austin, based in Chicago, owned 30 Austin Galleries at the height of his scamming. In 1994, Michael Zabrin, 56, who worked for Donald Austin at the time, testified for the prosecution. He helped establish that Austin sold reproductions worth pennies for up to $13,000 each, and that Austin's take from the scam was some $4,000,000. In 1994, in less than two hours, a jury convicted Donald Austin of selling counterfeit works of art (mail fraud). He was sentenced to 8 1/2 years and ordered to pay back $500,000 to defrauded customers.

TWO-TIME LOSERS

Michael Zabrin

In 1994, when Donald Austin's employee Michael Zabrin cooperated with the government, he received a light sentence for distributing fake art. In 2007, Zabrin was again convicted of art fraud and sentenced to five months in jail. In early 2008, the Feds again charged Michael Zabrin with selling counterfeit art.

James Kennedy

Between 2005 and 2007, James Kennedy, 56, made over $1,300,000 selling fake prints at art shows across the US and on eBay. In 2008, Kennedy was charged with selling the fakes. In an ugly footnote, James Kennedy threatened physical harm to Michael Zabrin for cooperating with the authorities. He was arrested in early 2008 and charged with that additional crime.

Speaking of James Kennedy, this is the same guy who drove up to Milwaukee in 2004 to see an acquaintance who owned an art gallery. Kennedy told the dealer, William DeLind, that he sold antique French posters out of his home for three decades but the poster business had slowed down so he was shifting gears. The pitch was that he had purchased a number of works by Picasso, Chagall, Matisse, Miro and Monet for very good prices. Perhaps, Kennedy told the dealer, you would like to take these masterpieces on consignment and sell them for me. And the best news is, since I really need the money, I'm willing to let them go for only, let's say, um, $10,000 or $20,000 each. DeLind knew that the paintings were worth much more than Kennedy was asking if they were real. Plus, they looked like crude fakes. So he never hung the works in his gallery but called the authorities instead. One month later when Kennedy returned to the gallery to pick up his sales proceeds and unsold paintings, the police were waiting.

The authorities couldn't believe their good luck. Kennedy had arrived in Milwaukee with a van crammed with more than 500 false paintings, sketches, and posters. The police arrested Kennedy and called in Dmitri Rybchenkov, an art expert with the firm of American Conservators, Inc. When Rybchenkov examined the works at the police station he burst out laughing. He called the items a joke, and gave us one of the year's best quotes. Looking at the mass of artworks in Kennedy's van, Rybchenkov said, "It's an insult to the professional counterfeit community."

In this case James Kennedy was charged with attempted theft by fraud and possession of forged artwork.

William Mett

William Mett (born c. 1943 in Milwaukee) who owned Center Art Galleries in Hawaii was an integral part of the Dali scam. Mett and Marvin Wiseman (born in Boston c. 1944), sold fake Dali lithographs and etchings, raking in some $2,000,000 from the scam.

In 1987, authorities raided Center Art galleries and seized five truck-loads of incriminating evidence, including over 12,000,000 fake lithographs. In 1989, a federal grand jury indicted Mett and Wiseman on 93 counts of mail fraud, wire fraud, and securities fraud relating to selling fake Dalis.

In 1990, after an acrimonious trial and 12 days of deliberations, the jury found Mett guilty on 73 counts, Wiseman guilty on 63 counts, and the gallery guilty on 72 counts. For selling more than $35,000,000 fake Dali lithographs, Mett served three years in federal prison, Wiseman served 2 1/2 years, and the judge levied fines of almost $2,000,000. The pair served their time in the minimum security prison in Lompoc, California.

Did the two con artists learn any lessons in jail? Of course not, they're art dealers. So what did the pair do after scamming the public of more than $35,000,000? They stole over $1,600,000 from two employee pension benefit funds. In 2000, Mett and Wiseman were found guilty of 12 counts of conspiracy and embezzlement and were sent back to prison. The food must have been really good at Lompoc.

Farah Damji

Farah Damji, a Manhattan art dealer, had it all. Not yet 30 years old in the 1990s, the stunning, well-dressed, coiffed (and corrupt) native of Uganda parlayed her good looks, upper class British accent, and knowledge about art into ownership of five galleries. The high-flying Damji, however, was not what she appeared to be to her legion of admirers. In her attempt to convince the world that she was rich, Damji ran through money like water flows through a dam when the locks are opened. Desperately trying to stay one step ahead of her creditors, Damji moved fast, changing her name and addresses in rapid succession. She also altered checks: In one of her more brazen moves, Damji altered a certified $38.00 check to read $38,000. Equally hard to believe, Damji even altered a judge's order in an eviction case that had been filed against her. In 1994, the authorities moved in. Farah Damji pled guilty to five felony counts of grand larceny, possession of forged instruments, and, yes, tampering with official records. In 1995, the glamorous Farah Damji began serving six months in jail, followed by four years probation, plus minor restitution.

After her release from Riker's Island prison, Damji moved to England (where she was raised) and started her scamming anew. To maintain her luxurious lifestyle, Damji stole credit cards and ran up humongous charges; stole anything not nailed down; and when charged, called witnesses and prosecuting officials on the phone (masquerading as a government official) in an attempt to get the charges dropped. The duplicity didn't work. In 2005, Farah Damji, 39, was again jailed, this time for 3 1/2 years for credit card fraud. The London judge who sentenced Damji called the former art dealer "a thoroughly dishonest and manipulative woman."

Guy Hain

Frenchman Guy Hain is considered one of history's greatest forgers of nineteenth- and twentieth-century bronzes. His defense, which always fell on dead ears, has consistently been that his sculptures were not artistic forgeries but rather technical ones. (There is a French law that states that after twelve bronzes are cast, all of which must be numbered, any others must be labeled reproductions.) Hain never marked any of his fakes as reproductions; but he considered that a detail. He forged almost 100 artists, but Auguste Rodin (1840-1917) was his favorite subject when it came to faking.

The Rudier family foundry was the official caster of Rodin, and Hain cuddled up to scion Georges Rudier. Once he had access to Rodin's original casts, Hain would change the Rudier family's mark from Bernard or Georges Rodier to Alexis Rodier, the legendary original caster of Rodin. He did this to make it appear the pieces were cast during Rodin's lifetime and with the artist's supervision and approval. When necessary for his con, Hain even imitated the Rudier foundry seal.

Hain sold over $25,000,000 in Rodin forgeries (some at record prices) before the French police caught up with him. Hain copied other sculptor's work, including such geniuses as Giacometti, Jean-Antoine Houdon (1741–1828) and Constantin Brancusi (1876–1957) by using plaster molds, or by making after-casts from finished bronzes, using silicon molds.

In raids, over 20,000 kilos of bronze and other materials were seized by police from various foundries in remote areas of France; Hain used these to produce his fakes in secrecy. Even though the authorities confiscated almost 3,000 bronzes in various stages of completion, there are still an incredible 4,000 to 6,000 Hain forgeries currently in circulation worldwide. Like all brilliant forgers, Guy Hain sold his fakes through third parties, who consigned them to auction houses, who, in turn, sold them to the world's museums and collectors.

In 1997, Hain served a prison term in France but did he learn? Nope. He went right back to forging bronzes. In 2001, Hain began serving a four-year term in a French prison after being convicted (again) of the scam which the authorities now believe exceeds $60,000,000.

Shirely Sack
In 1978, elegant, blond art dealer Shirley Sack served five years for fencing stolen art. In 2001, Sack, along with New York gallery owner Arnold Katzen, was caught in Boston on tape by the FBI trying to sell an undercover agent a Degas and a Modigliani painting for over $4,000,000. The artworks were stolen and the duo was back in (or never left) the business of laundering drug money. In 2004, Shirley Sack, 74, and Arnold Katzen, 65, copped a plea for potential tax evasion and received sentences of three years probation and forfeiture of their interest in the paintings.

In Every Brilliant Mind There Is a Dull Spot

Steven Cheung

From 1969 to 1982 Steven Cheung (born in Hong Kong in 1935) taught economics at the University of Washington. A Nobel Prize candidate, the renowned economist also previously taught economics at Hong Kong University. In 1998, Steven Cheung and his wife, Linda, opened an Asian antiques store in Seattle which they named Thesaurus Fine Arts. In addition to selling Asian antiquities over the counter, the Cheung's sold hundreds of items a year on eBay. Cheung and his wife were pillars of local society when they opened their shop. But instead of selling legitimate Asian antiquities, the Cheungs peddled fakes.

Experts allege two interesting things. One, unlike most scams where the bad is mixed in with the good, every antiquity for sale in the store and listed on eBay was a fake. Two, the experts say that they know of no other art dealer who made such sweeping claims for inferior fakes. A critical element that made the selling of the fakes so successful was that each item was accompanied by a scientific certificate of authenticity from a Hong Kong testing laboratory. (The lab uses a scientific procedure called thermoluminesence [or TL], which is a procedure pioneered in the 1960s at Oxford for use in archeology. The procedure tests the age of ceramics by measuring the radiation absorbed since the last high temperature firing.)

As you have probably guessed by now, Steven Cheung established and owns the Chinese lab (named Ad signo) that issued the certificates of authenticity for the fakes. In 2003, the authorities closed Thesaurus Fine Arts, eBay banned the Cheung's from their site, and the Internal Revenue Service (IRS) indicted the Cheung's for tax evasion. In 2004, the Washington State Attorney General filed consumer fraud charges against the couple. Steven and Linda Cheung are fugitives living somewhere in China.

Vilas Likhite

Doctor Vilas Likhite was named an associate professor at Harvard in 1972. The brilliant doctor preferred medical research to teaching and became well-known through his numerous writings about his experiments. Likhite convinced himself that his (non-approved) drugs could solve most any problem, so he began injecting patients with the drugs. By 1979, a concerned and disillusioned Harvard allowed Likhite to resign his position instead of being fired. He began seeing private patients.

In 1981, in a classic coincidence, two of Likhite's patients went to the same doctor for a second opinion. The doctor, Robert Schwartz, realized that Likhite had injected both patients with an unapproved treatment. Having been forced out of Harvard, and being investigated by the state, Likhite's private practice was reduced to a trickle. To top things off, the Massachusetts Board of Registration in Medicine investigated Likhite and cancelled his medical license in 1989. Likhite turned to selling forgeries to solve his problems. Dodging charges throughout the 1980s, in 1989 Lkhite was convicted of selling fake art in Massachusetts.

Anxious to escape his past, Doctor Vilas Likhite moved his act to Orange County, California, which is south of Los Angeles and has a reputation for harboring con artists and scammers. Luckily for Likhite, his Massachusetts problems had not been news in California. A likeable rogue, frail with a comforting grandfatherly-type grin, Likhite had a very clever con. He would slowly and shrewdly develop acquaintances into close friends and then dupe them into buying his fakes.

Like all good cons, Likhite made his story big and beautiful. He claimed to own over 700 pieces of art worth over $1,000,000,000 maintaining that he inherited the works from his father who had been given the art by a maharaja in India. He also claimed that his father's will prohibited him from selling the works at auction. Therefore, he would say, I can offer the precious paintings to you. The truth was that Likhite bought almost all of his paintings at flea markets and garage sales.

In California, Likhite added a nice element to his false story. He said he was friends with the rich and famous Johnson family of Boston and was employed by their company, Fidelity Investments, as an art consultant. Vilas Likhite's years of selling fake paintings came to an abrupt end in December, 2004 when he was in his mid-60s. The Los Angeles police arrested him for selling a fake Cassatt to an undercover agent posing as a rich South Korean collector. The defrocked doctor was convicted and sentenced to one-year in jail.

Likhite had hundreds of suckers who bought into his story, but the most heart-wrenching victim was the Harvard graduate student who bought what she believed was a real Modigliani back in 1985. She paid Doctor Likhite one hundred dollars a month for years and years before Likhite was exposed and she learned the painting was a fake.

Steven Cooperman

Sixty-five-year-old Steven Cooperman, a Beverly Hills eye surgeon, was convicted of faking an art theft (with attorney James Tierney) to collect over $12,000,000 in insurance. His medical license was taken away. In 2007, Cooperman surfaced again in the news. This time he pled guilty to accepting over $6,000,000 in secret payments for serving as lead plaintiff in class-action lawsuits filed by New York law firm Milberg Weiss.

YOU WANT MONEY? HELP YOURSELF

Michel Cohen

To understand the premium the insular art world, the largest unregulated money market in the world, places on secrecy, informality, and trust, one need only examine the Michel Cohen case.

Michel Cohen was born in France and immigrated to the United States in 1981 at the age of 29. Cohen lived in California and New York. An astute observer and indefatigable worker, the handsome Cohen began his career in art by selling large edition prints. He was successful and soon began dealing in more expensive prints. Finally, he moved into paintings, where he saw the big money being made. In the 1990s Cohen made serious money and significant contacts in the art word. After closing his New York gallery, he basically became a wholesaler (also pejoratively called a runner), taking color transparencies, and ultimately paintings, from seller to buyer.

When he could afford it, Cohen also bought and sold paintings on his own account; his life was one of nonstop buying, selling, and hustling paintings. He was happy with small markups, but, what he lacked in percentage of profit, he made up in volume. Most important, during this period, dealmaker Cohen made money for the galleries and auction houses, which, everyone knows is the way to gain their respect and confidence.

So here we have nice story: A French-born art dealer with a nice house and a nice family who has made a nice fortune in America through intelligence and hard work. The American dream incarnate. Nice. But Michel Cohen wanted to double-down on his dream. Naturally, this meant he needed more and more money.

Feeling infallible, and spotting what appeared to be a shortcut to serious riches in the go-go 1990s, Cohen began playing the stock market and then plunged into the volatile, commodities and futures markets. No go. Cohen saw only one way to cover his mounting losses.

The con was on. Here are a few specifics of what many are calling the biggest art fraud ever. (No one is certain at this point, but it is generally believed that Cohen's scam made him in the neighborhood of $100,000,000 from some of the savviest people in the art world.) Once he decided to cross over the line, Cohen worked fast.

In April of 2000, Cohen, still in his 40s, convinced Sotheby's to loan him $1,300,000 to buy a Picasso. The following month he struck again for a $2,500,000 loan to buy a painting by Chagall. Two months later, the auction house loaned Cohen $1,000,000 more to buy another Chagall. Just four days later, they loaned him $1,500,000 more to purchase another Picasso (this loan was later raised to $3,600,000.) The firm also made Cohen a secured $1,500,000 loan. In all of the cases, Cohen assured Sotheby's he had buyers lined up. The auction house never bothered to check. "We had a longstanding relationship . . . there had never been any problems." The usual terms were put in place for transactions of this type: Repay the loans, plus interest and a share of the profits. Sotheby's and Michel Cohen became partners in the paintings.

In late 2000, the Richard Gray Gallery gave Cohen $2,200,000, in advance, for the purchase of a Picasso most everyone knew was stolen. Instead of delivering the painting to Gray, Cohen sold it to a buyer in Iowa for about $5,000,000. Gray sued, and is still looking for his money or the painting.

One more. During this period, Cohen sold half of a Monet to the Beadleston Gallery in New York, and 100% of the same Monet to Francois Gobi, a Paris dealer. He raked in $7,500,000 in the process. Cohen never owned the painting which everyone knew was hanging in the Met. No problem. Cohen claimed it was about to be returned to its rightful owners after being plundered by the Nazis. When Sotheby's loans became due in December, 2000, Cohen passed several bad checks as a delaying tactic. Now on guard, Sotheby's sued for their $9,500,000, plus costs, ending the scam. In a matter of days, 49-year-old Michel Cohen disappeared. Over two years later, he was found and arrested in Rio de Janeiro, Brazil. The United States began proceedings to extradite Cohen for the crimes of wire fraud and transporting stolen goods across state lines.

During the period he was awaiting extradition, Cohen feigned sickness, and while being transported from one hospital to another, escaped from the ambulance. A bribe is suspected but not proven: Perhaps he just conned his jailers with the charm all great con artists have. Michel Cohen, a man with no enemies, a rarity in the art business, remains at large. Incredibly, most of his victims say they would work with him again, giving him a chance to pay back the money he scammed. It's only business they say. The art business, that is.

THE DOG ATE MY HOMEWORK

Monsignor Michele Basso
Art fraud, as we know, can be as much about fake documentation as it is about fake art. For instance, in 2001 Monsignors Michele Basso and Mario Giordano, two former senior officials in the Vatican, were charged with selling works they falsely attributed to Old Masters, including Michelangelo and Guercino. The clerics were faking certificates of authenticity on Holy See stationary, stamps and all. What could be more reassuring to a purchaser than that?

After obtaining extraordinary permission to raid Basso's apartment in the Vatican (which has been an independent country since 1929), the Italian police confiscated a hoard of works of art which were stashed there. In one of the most creative defenses of all time, when confronted, Msgr. Basso claimed he was selling the artworks to raise money for a hospital in Albania.

John Douglas O'Loughlin

Born in Adelaide in 1941, O'Loughlin was a dealer who turned forger when he realized the aboriginal art market was taking off. He painted and sold paintings (to collectors, dealers, and museums) he claimed were Dreamtime art by famous Aboriginal artist Clifford Possum Tjapaltjarri (1932–2002). Possum (as he is known) is one of Australia's top Aboriginal artists. O'Loughlin also created fake documentation for his fake paintings

In 1999, various experts went to the authorities questioning the authenticity of the Possum paintings hanging on O'Loughlin's Sidney gallery walls. After first claiming the works were by Possum, O'Loughlin eventually admitted he had painted the fakes. In the process, he came up with one of the most original defenses any court has ever heard. O'Loughlin claimed he was entitled to create Possum Dreamtime paintings because he became a cousin of Possum after drinking kangaroo blood with the artist.

In 2001, O'Loughlin pled guilty to five counts of making a misleading statement with intent to obtain financial advantage (read Indigenous Art Fraud.) The court granted him three-year bail. O'Loughlin is the first Australian art dealer to be convicted of Aboriginal art fraud.

Rudolph Sagl

In 1989, Rudi Sagl pled guilty in Canada to tax evasion. Shortly thereafter, in 1991, the 80-year-old German native moved from Canada to Atlanta. (In Canada Sagl was the world's leading maker of police radar detectors.)

Moving aggressively, Sagl borrowed tens of millions from the South Trust Bank in Atlanta, pledging his art collection of over 70 pieces as collateral. Sagl told the bank the paintings were worth over $40,000,000. By 1997, Sagl and his company, Bel-Tronics, were in receivership. The bank repossessed the paintings but only found 42 of the 72 pledged paintings. Ouch. Then another bombshell hit the bank.

When the bank had the paintings appraised it was informed that the 42 paintings they recovered were fakes and were worthless. Shell shocked, Sun Trust listened for the next bombshell. Incoming. Sagl told the bank not to worry, the remaining 30 pledged paintings were at his house outside of Toronto but there was a small problem. His second wife, Bridgette, claimed half ownership in the paintings. Can there be more? Duck.

That doesn't really matter, Sagl told the bank, because the house was robbed and the 30 pledged paintings were stolen. Numb, the bank listened for the killer. It hit. Not only were the pledged paintings stolen, Sagl said, their authentication documents were also stolen. In 2001, Sagl declared bankruptcy, claiming that he had over $6,000,000 in debts and less than $4,000 in assets. The high-life does not come cheap; nor does alimony when you sleep with your wife's sister.

IS NOTHING SACRED?

Oded Golan

Israeli Oded Golan, born c. 1951, is charged with running a con of biblical proportions, literally and figuratively: It had worldwide ramifications among billions of devout Christians and Jews. Golan is one of Israel's major collectors of antiquities. Nothing wrong with that.

The trouble is it appears Golan took his collecting a monumental step further. What Golan apparently did was acquire real antiquities and then give the common artifacts a biblical association by adding killer inscriptions. This act made the pieces worth millions.

Golan performed this con (with his partners) numbers of times over two decades without getting caught. In late 2002, however, overconfidence and greed finally won out. Golan orchestrated an announcement of the discovery of a first-century, two-foot-long limestone Ossuary (a box for dead people's bones) that had on its side an ancient inscription, which identified it as the last resting place of James, son of Joseph, brother of Jesus. The news stunned the art and religious worlds. If genuine, the so-called James Ossuary would be the world's most significant biblical artifact ever unearthed. Anxious to believe, in one day the Geological Survey of Israel authenticated the box.

In record time Golan made a deal with the Royal Ontario Museum in Toronto to display the Ossuary. Why that particular museum? Probably because Golan knew it had previously hosted an exhibition of Rodin sculptures without giving the works a thorough examination. The pieces were Guy Hain fakes. In any case, record crowds jammed the museum to stare at what was touted as the only physical evidence that existed of the family of Jesus. A few months after the wildly successful exhibition, a second blockbuster find surfaced: a 3,000-year-old stone tablet.

This black stone tablet also contained an ancient inscription which recorded the renovation of Solomon's Temple in the ninth century BC, which was the first physical evidence that the legendary Temple existed. Again, desperate to believe, the experts authenticated the artifact in one day.

Suspicious Israeli officials began to thoroughly investigate the history-altering artifacts and their provenance. They discovered that Oded Golan owned both spectacular finds and had secretly offered to sell what has been called the Joash (or Jehoash) Stone to the Israel Museum. A team of scientific experts was assembled by the Antiquity Authority. This time, the experts determined that the Ossuary dated back some 2,000 years but that the critical words, brother of Jesus were gouged through the original patina. In addition, the patina of the artifact was determined to have been recently added. Regarding the 3,000-year-old stone tablet, the experts found that the patina was also recently manufactured and applied. Language added to make the antiquities much more valuable was the key to the scam.

When Golan was arrested, police raided his various apartments and found tools and materials of the forgers trade, including drills and soil samples from every archeological dig in Israel. In 2005, various friends and Golan were charged under a 28-page indictment, including fraud, receiving money through deception, damaging antiquities, and violating Israeli antiquities laws. Only Oded Golan and dealer and writer Robert Deutsch remain at the bench. The highly-charged trial is dragging out over several years.

Although Golan's fakes are in the collections of many of the world's top museums, the favorite mark for the forgers was one man, Shlomo Moussaieff, an Israeli diamond merchant. The con men sold Moussieff, now in his eighties, so many fakes they made him the world's leading collector of biblical antiquities.

Shlomo Moussaieff

Shlomo Moussaieff, an 84-year-old Israeli, epitomizes the collector who lives in complete denial. The diamond merchant, who sells items in the seven-figure range (and above), insists that everything in his collection is authentic. Moussaieff makes this claim in spite of the fact that he has acquired most of the pieces from Oded Golan and his accomplices. Moussaieff, who has spent tens of millions of dollars on his collection of antiquities in order to prove the truth of the bible has been swindled out of most of his fortune in his quest.

The Israel Museum

This is going to sound like a bad movie. In 1988, the Israel Museum in Jerusalem placed $550,000 in a Swiss safe deposit box as an anonymous seller (who turned out to be Oded Golan) placed an ivory pomegranate the size of a thumb in another. In other words, a museum gave over a half million dollars to someone it never met.

The biblical artifact said (in ancient Hebrew) "Belonging to the temple of the Lord, holy to the priests." Because the pomegranate has a hole it its bottom, scholars believed that it was used as a scepter carried by a temple priest. The prized possession was displayed as the centerpiece of the 23-year-old museum and labeled as the only relic of King Solomon's Temple. In 2004, after biblical scholars began questioning the museum's other spectacular acquisitions from dealer Oded Golan, a scientific examination of the inscription and patina proved the pomegranate was a fake. Golan had used the same scam on the James Ossuary and the Joash Tablet, taking legitimate historic pieces and add a stunning biblical inscription, thereby increasing their value a thousand fold. The Israel Museum removed the fake pomegranate from display.

THANKS FOR THE CONSIGNMENT, SUCKER

Kurt Lidtke

Kurt Lidtke, 44, owned the Pioneer Square Gallery in Seattle, which he opened in 1992. Things went swimmingly for Lidtke for several years. He married a celebrity television reporter, opened a second gallery, and was admired by the Seattle community where he was a prominent member of society. Before long, however, complaints and law suits from all over the country began to surface. It turned out that what Lidtke was doing was taking paintings on consignment, selling them, but neglecting to tell the owners that their paintings had been sold. Lidtke was pocketing their money. When the unsuspecting owners would inquire about their paintings Lidtke would smooth-talk his way out of trouble.

In 1999, Lidke's dream life started to unravel. A collector named James Clark consigned 23 paintings by Mark Tobey to Lidke. Tired of the runaround concerning his works, Clark sued, which opened the floodgates. In 2004, after a scathing article in the *Seattle Times*, Lidtke closed his 12-year-old gallery and went into hiding. Since then, the lawsuits and judgments have been piling up. In 2007, Kurt Lidtke pled guilty to nine counts of first degree theft; selling paintings and not remitting the proceeds to the owners of the pieces, and failing to return art he had been given on consignment. "In a few months, no one will remember it [my scam]," Lidtke says. He's probably right.

Michael Lord

Art dealer Michael Lord, 54, owned the most prominent gallery in Milwaukee. The local media tagged him "the long-time leading light in the Milwaukee art scene." They didn't know what Michael was doing when they weren't looking.

Lord was constantly in trouble with the law. For instance, between 1996 and 1999, the State of Wisconsin filed 14 warrants to collect almost $200,000 in back taxes Lord owed. Between 1999 and 2004, Lord was selling paintings for say $200,000 and telling the owner he received only $100,000, pocketing the difference; he was taking paintings from clients to sell for them, but the paintings disappeared, with elaborate excuses and explanations; he was taking paintings on consignment from New York Galleries without sending them their money or returning the paintings. (Ironically, Lord was Milwaukee's only direct line to the New York art world.) How was Michael Lord able to get away with these flagrant tricks for so many years?

Lord was gentlemanly, affable, well-groomed, and put up a great front, spending money lavishly. Everyone liked and trusted Michael Lord. As is true with many cons, Michael Lord's house of cards collapsed on a fluke. He was arrested in 2003 for stealing $175,000 from his great-aunt's estate. Lord pled guilty to the theft and in 2004 was sentenced to 20 days and five years probation. In quick succession over $1,400,000 in civil claims were filed against Lord and the Feds brought criminal charges. In early 2006, Lord pled guilty to two counts of felony theft and was sentenced to 14 months in jail. He was also ordered to serve 40 months of extended supervision and pay restitution of $634,750. That odd number is the amount the Court could confirm Lord scammed from 15 customers. Lord says he intends to repay everybody. Sure.

Fred Banks

Fred Banks worked an identical scam in San Francisco, that is, selling consigned works but not remitting the money to their owners. Doing business all over the world with his brother and wife out of his Harcourts Gallery, which he opened in 1967, Banks was a integral part of the San Francisco cultural scene for some 30 years. After the inevitable lawsuits started flying, Banks filed for bankruptcy in the mid-1990s. Court documents revealed that Banks had scammed millions of dollars from hundreds of artists, collectors, galleries, and museums, including the Utah Museum of Fine Arts. Gallery owner, Rachel Adler, who Banks owes $137,000, said, "I have always suspected something. This is one of those cases in which, if someone dies, you'll want to open that coffin, just to make sure." It looks like the scammers will have the last laugh. Fred Banks, the art dealer, and his wife, the bookkeeper, have disappeared.

Richard Sebastian Esterhazy

In 1986, Richard S. Esterhazy opened an art auction house in Hollywood, California. Born in Hungary in 1954, the blond hair, blue eyed con man sweet-talked (with his smooth British accent) hundreds of artworks out of unsuspecting individuals. In 1989, Esterhazy closed his auction house and disappeared. He escaped with hundreds of works of art that had been turned over to him on consignment. The crack Los Angeles police art theft department, which is led by Don Hrycyk and is probably the best in the country, is searching for Esterhazy.

Jay Halperyn

Jay Halperyn's life, 61, had been filled with judgments and liens. To start over, in 2001, Halperyn, who uses numerous variations of his name, followed the well-traveled route to Palm Beach, Florida, where he opened a gallery named Style di Vie in the tony Worth Avenue section of town.

Struggling to make ends meet, Halperyn met and conned a local named H.E. (Gene) Rayfield, Jr. Rayfield made loans totaling hundreds of thousands of dollars to his friend Halperyn. Halperyn ran through Rayfield's money and was indicted on bank fraud charges in 2004 and declared bankruptcy in 2005.

Following an FBI investigation, in 2006, Halperyn was indicted for making false statements on loan applicatiions. He was sentenced to 37 months in federal prison.

The ugliest aspect of the story is that a judge allowed Rayfield to confiscate the artworks of the fifty or so artists (and others) who had *consigned* paintings and other works to Halperyn's gallery, which was shut down.

HE PRETENDED TO BE WHAT?

Tom Doyle

In a rare twist, Tom Doyle, born c. 1958, is a man who scammed by imitating an art dealer. Norman Alexander, a retired executive and collector, was in his early 70s when a mutual friend introduced him to Tom Doyle in 2004. Mr. Alexander, who lives alone (except with servants) on New York's tony upper east side, had suffered a debilitating stroke and Doyle seemed like the answer to the prayers of the childless millionaire. Doyle offered to handle Mr. Alexander's affairs, including selling Alexander's residence which was too large for him, and, oh yes, his art collection. To give his assertion of art expertise legitimacy, Doyle (who had served time for swindling $200,000 in jewelry from a Tennessee woman) claimed to be descended from Joe Duveen, the greatest art dealer of all time.

Mister Alexander believed the con man and gave him a Degas

bronze sculpture worth at least $600,000, which Doyle said he wanted to buy. In 2005 Doyle gave Alexander a $100,000 down payment on the Degas sculpture and bobbed and weaved when pressed for the remaining $500,000. Unknown to Mr. Alexander, as soon as Doyle received the artwork, he sold it to a dealer for $225,000, pocketing a quick $125,000. Eventually Norman Alexander became suspicious and contacted the authorities. In 2004, Mr. Alexander won a default judgment in a civil suit against Doyle for breach of contract. In 2006, Tom Doyle was charged with the felony of grand larceny. In 2007, he pled guilty in a plea deal.

THE TWO GREEDIEST DEALERS? CLOSE ENOUGH

Edward and Samuel Merrin

Edward Merrin and his son Samuel, owners of the Merrin Gallery in Manhattan, were key players in the artifact smuggling racket. Not only was the pair trafficking in looted antiquities, they also conducted one of the more unique scams seen in the world of unique scams.

In the early 1990s, the Merrins entered into a cost-plus oral agreement with two wealthy collectors, William Ziff and his wife. The agreement called for the Merrins to sell the collectors antiquities at their cost, charging a sliding commission, which was dependant on certain conditions. In the next decade, the Ziffs paid the Merrins a whopping $65,000,000 for their plundered antiquities.

Were the Merrins satisfied with the grand and glorious commissions called for in the agreement with their client? Never. They got greedy and double dipped, scamming the Ziffs twice. The Merrins were taking their actual acquisition costs and inflating them. They tacked on millions of dollars when they presented their costs to the unsuspecting Ziffs. In their sophisticated scam, the Merrins utilized false invoices and related tactics. Obviously, the Merrins earned substantially higher commissions because of the inflated costs they presented to the Ziffs. The big money, however, was in the other part of the scam.

The amount between what the Merrins paid for an artwork and the amount they claimed they paid was the major payoff. The amount they added on was only limited by their imagination. And the Merrins had extremely potent imaginations. In 2005, Edward Merrin, 77, and Samuel Merrin, 42, were charged in a 12-page indictment with conspiracy and wire fraud. In 2007, in what can only be considered a mockery, the father, Edward, was given a one-year probation, a $3,000 fine, and ordered to pay restitution of less than $45,000. Samuel's attorney claims the son's case was dismissed.

SOME DAYS WHEN YOU SCRATCH YOUR HEAD YOU BREAK YOUR FINGER

David Stein

David Stein (nee Henri Haddad) was born in France in 1935. A short, heavy set man, his considerable artistic talent and conversational skills offset his less than movie star looks. Starting early in life, Stein changed his name regularly and bounced worthless checks all over Europe. Beginning in the 1960s, Stein forged all of the usual artists, including Matisse, Kees Van Dongen (1877–1968) and Andre Derain (1880–1954), but his specialty was forging Chagall and Picasso. Stein preferred working in watercolors, pen and ink, and pastels. He typically produced sketches because they are seldom catalogued and therefore harder to check. Also, he could produce fake sketches fast, and Stein liked to work fast.

Greedy, but talented, Stein acted as his own dealer. Because he knew that it would be a mistake to flood any one market with too many of his fakes, Stein constantly moved across Europe selling his fakes. Stein never copied a master, but rather painted in their style. He would seek out, wherever possible, less famous works to imitate, to avoid detection. Then he would add the signature of the original artist.

Drawn to America by the higher prices art was commanding, Stein opened galleries in New York and Palm Beach, Florida. Stein loved the high life in America, and continued to paint fakes and produce phony certificates of authentication to feed his extravagances. As we've seen, the smallest mistake can take down a major scam.

In 1966, a dealer customer of Stein purchased a fake (unknowingly) and asked for a certificate of authenticity. No problem, this is a typical request. Stein readily agreed to deliver the certificate. He told the customer he would have to write to Paris for it. Using special paper, a

French typewriter, and fake rubber stamps similar to the ones used by French galleries, Stein created a certificate of authenticity. Without thinking, Stein delivered it to the customer in three days, reiterating that he had written to Paris for it.

POW! The dealer connected the dots. Three days was much too short a time to write to France from America, and to receive a reply from France. The dealer contacted the authorities. Approximately one month later, after a fruitful investigation, the police raided Stein's Park Avenue apartment. But Stein escaped. Stein was eventually captured in Los Angeles while on the run to Mexico. He was brought back to New York where he was incarcerated in the infamous tombs.

In 1967, Stein was indicted on 97 counts of grand larceny. In early 1969, Stein copped a plea, pleading guilty to six counts and cooperated with the authorities in return for a three-year sentence. After serving a few months in jail, he was deported to France where he was found guilty of selling counterfeit paintings and served two short prison terms.

While in prison in New York, Stein began painting in the style of the same artists he had forged, however now he signed his own name to the works. For some reason known only to them, the authorities in America made the ridiculous legal attempt to stop Stein from painting whatever he chose and signing his own name. Common sense prevailed and Stein won the right in court to continue the practice. France readily agreed to the arrangement. Copies by David Stein now sell for decent prices. His French wife, Anne-Marie, wrote about her husband's life of faking in the cleverly-titled book, "Three Picassos Before Breakfast: Memoirs of an Art Forger's Wife."

THE "GUARANTEE" CON

Alistair Miller

Alistair Miller ran a very clever scam against residents of Great Britain. Miller, who had been banned in England from serving as a director until 2011 due to fraud he committed in the spirits business, got around that restriction by setting up a company in 2000 called Ashley Jenkins, Ltd., and fronting it with his wife, Mercedes Carbo. In this con Miller used the name David Newman. The company, which was a boiler room operation, advertised that it had an office at 72 New Bond Street, which is in the heart of London's vibrant art world. Actually, it was just a mail drop. The advertisement also listed a telephone number in London that rang in Seville, Spain where the con was headquartered. Miller had glorious, glossy brochures printed that laid out the scheme.

On your behalf the pitch went, Ashley Jenkins would buy paintings and prints of Spanish artists who were not yet, but soon would be, discovered. These works would then be loaned or sold on your behalf to owners of major companies to decorate their offices. You could expect a 10 1/2% profit, but the return would certainly be much, much, much higher. Much higher.

Once the mark made a purchase (always over the phone), the scammers went in for the kill. A few months after the initial purchase the buyer would get a call saying his or her painting had increased in value from the $2,000 they had paid for it to, say, $4,000, and the company would like to buy it back at the inflated price. The investors were so excited by this turn of events that they invariably agreed to purchase, say, a $6,000 soon-to-be released issue which they were assured would increase in value the same way.

The 750 British investors who fell for the scam never saw one of the phantom paintings or prints nor received any money back. Collectively they were conned out of over $10,000,000. In 2003, the British government closed down the scam and Alistair Miller and Mercedes Carbo disappeared.

Mirek Klabal

Miroslav (Mirek) Klabal, 63, had a similar angle to his scam, which he worked over a 30-year period, in venues as diverse as Naples, Florida; Toronto, Canada; Greenwich, Connecticut; and New York City. The quintessential con man, Klabal was handsome, social, and lavished gifts on his marks. Women loved his attention, especially how he kissed their hand when meeting.

Klabal claimed to have paintings by modern masters that he had obtained cheap from distressed individuals at distressed prices. Because of this, he maintained, he could offer the works to his friends for a fraction of their real value. To round off the con, Klabal would then guarantee that he could help them sell the (fake) paintings at a huge profit, or he would buy them back at a premium.

In the course of conning his friends out of tens of millions of dollars, lawsuits followed the Czeck born dealer like kids chasing the Good Humor man's truck. The cases, which have had mixed results, were usually settled. Mirek Klabal continues dealing in New York as a small time, chastised art dealer, but he floods the Internet with propaganda worthy of a political candidate.

BELIEVE IN COINCIDENCES? FANTASY? YOU'LL DINE OUT ON THESE CASES

Gerald Peters & "the Canyon Suite"

Here's the back story. In 1975, Emilio Caballero, a water colorist of some renown, and an art teacher at West Texas State Normal College (now West Texas A & M University), under heavy pressure from the college administration agreed to resign as chairman of the art department and return to full time teaching. A few months later, Emilio Caballero changed his mind and a bitter lawsuit followed A happy, easy-going gentleman turned into a bitter, cynical man. (Georgia O'Keeffe taught art at the college some 60 years earlier.)

Fast forward to 1984. Emilio Caballero's son, Charles, married Terry Lee, who is a granddaughter of Ted Reid, an ex-student and lover of O'Keeffe. In 1986, Georgia O'Keeffe (born in 1887) died at the age of 99. In the spring of 1988, Ted Reid died.

Got it? Good. Now here's the most coincidental story in the history of mankind. In the fall of 1988, Emilio Caballero claimed that Ted Reid gave him a package back in his painful year of 1975. Further, Caballero maintained that he put the package Ted Reid gave him in 1975 into his garage without opening it. (Let's begin counting the questionable, improbable, dubious, inconceivable, unbelievable, ultimately unconvincing statements made by the various players.) That's one.

Also in 1988, Caballero claimed that back in 1975 when Reid gave him the package he not only didn't open it, he never asked Reid what was in the package. That's two.

Also in 1988, Emilio Caballero claimed that in 1987 he stumbled upon the package that Ted Reid had given him 12 years earlier. That's three.

Also in 1988, Emilio Caballero claimed that in 1987 when he stumbled upon the package that Ted Reid had given him 12 years earlier he still didn't open the package but instead gave it to his daughter-in-law, Terry Lee Caballero, wife of his son Charles. That's four.

Terry Caballero claimed that when she opened the package for the first time in 1987, she found 29 watercolors on paper. She contacted an art dealer to sell them for her. After year-long negotiations, nefarious art dealer Gerald Peters paid Terry Caballero $1,000,000 for the 29 paintings. Peters claimed that he believed the works were by Georgia O'Keeffe because Juan Hamilton (O'Keeffe's live in companion who managed her affairs) orally authenticated the paintings as genuine O'Keeffes. That's five.

In 1989, Keiko Keyes, a paper conservator (expert), conducted an examination of the 29 paintings and discovered that one of the works was painted on Fabriano paper, which was manufactured decades after it and the other 28 were purported to have been painted. In 1989, Peters claimed that he secretly withdrew that particular painting from the group but didn't bother to check into the authenticity of the other 28 paintings. That's six.

Meanwhile, Peters hired Charles Eldridge Hall, Distinguished Professor of American Art at the University of Kansas, and an expert on Georgia O'Keeffe, to write an essay on the "Canyon Suite" (as Peters had cleverly labeled the works) to affirm the authenticity of the paintings.

The tactic worked. In 1989, the scholar not only affirmed the authenticity of the 28 paintings, he placed them in Peters' claimed time period of 1916–1918. Later, Hall claimed that he based his essay on the fact that Peters told him that Juan Hamilton had authenticated the group. That's seven.

In 1990, Peters pitched J. Carter Brown, director of the National Gallery in Washington, D.C., that he had 28 genuine works of Georgia O'Keeffe, which she painted when she was young and living in Canyon, Texas. The National Gallery agreed to display and try to sell the "Canyon Suite" in the hope that a buyer would surface and then donate the paintings to the museum. Peters put a price of $9,000,000 on the group of 28 watercolors. Peters neglected to tell anyone at the museum about the fake painting he had pulled from the group of 29 he bought from Terry Caballero. That's eight

The National Gallery officials, up to and including the museum's director Brown, all raved, publicly and privately, about their O'Keeffe coup. The museum officials and curators later insisted that they didn't bother to check the provenance of the 28 watercolors because they relied on art dealer Gerald Peters' claim that Juan Hamilton had orally authenticated them. That's nine.

The National Gallery displayed and tried to sell (on Peters' behalf) the "Canyon Suite" for two full years. The fact that the paintings were accepted, displayed, and hawked for two years by the National Gallery gave them an aura of respectability and authenticity. That's ten.

In 1991, while the works were still hanging in the National Gallery, Peters hired his friend Eugene Thaw, a prominent collector then based in Peters' home town of Santa Fe, New Mexico, to appraise the "Canyon Suite." Thaw appraised the 28 paintings at $7,600,000. He later claimed he believed in their authenticity because the paintings were hanging in the National Gallery and because Peters told him that Juan Hamilton had orally authenticated them. That's eleven.

Also in 1991, the National Gallery and the Georgia O'Keeffe Foundation announced that they would jointly publish a catalogue raisonné of O'Keeffe's paintings. (Juan Hamilton, now a director of the Georgia O'Keeffe Foundation, joined the scholars working on the catalogue raisonné.) Barbara Buhler Lynes, the catalogue's author, joined her fellow scholars in praising the "Canyon Suite." That's a dozen.

Armed with this heavy ammunition, art dealer Gerald Peters made his big move. Peters pitched the 28 watercolors to billionaire Kansas City banker and art collector, R. Crosby Kemper, Jr. Peters sent Kemper professor Hall's 20 page confirming essay and the Thaw appraisal of $7,600,000. Peters stressed to Kemper that Juan Hamilton had authenticated the group.

Most important, Peters convinced the director (and six curators) of the National Gallery to assure Kemper that they agreed with the attribution of the paintings to Georgia O'Keeffe. Peters also convinced the National Gallery brass to assure Kemper that all 28 paintings would be included in the forthcoming O'Keeffe catalogue. That's a baker's dozen.

In 1993, Kemper paid Peters $5,000,000 for the 28 watercolors. "I thought I was getting the bargain of the century," Kemper later said.

After the Kemper purchase, Earl Powell, newly appointed director of the National Gallery, wrote Kemper lauding the paintings and confirming their value, while trying to convince him to donate the group to the museum. Powell gave Kemper every reason to believe that the paintings would be included in the catalogue raisonné of O'Keeffe's works, which would establish them as authentic O'Keeffes and send their value to the moon. That's fourteen.

The director's enthusiasm convinced Kemper to keep the "Canyon Suite" in Kansas City and to make the paintings the centerpiece of his newly established Kemper Museum of Contemporary Art. In 1994, the group of watercolors was unveiled to a glittering crowd of museum notables, dealers, collectors, celebrities, and hangers-on, imported from far and wide.

For the next several years the "Canyon Suite" was the darling of the art world, traveling all over America to universal acclaim by art critics and museum officials alike. Several books were even written about the phenomenon.

In late 1999, inevitable reality hit the fairy tale. Kemper received a letter informing him that the soon-to-be-published catalogue raisonné of Georgia O'Keefe's works would not include his 28 paintings. The letter said that the scholars had changed their minds, and, without explanation, stated they no longer believed the paintings to be the work of Georgia O'Keefe. To his horror, Kemper realized that the 28 watercolors for which he paid $5,000,000 were fakes and, therefore, worthless.

R. Crosby Kemper was stunned. He was also mad as hell that the National Gallery didn't extend him the courtesy of delivering their bombshell in person. In early 2000, not wanting to further alienate a wealthy collector, the museum sent a delegation to Kansas City. The group explained to the distraught Kemper that O'Keeffe would not, and indeed, in most cases, could not have used the paper on which his paintings were executed. In addition to this scientific evidence, the scholars maintained that the painting technique was wrong.

Not satisfied, Kemper hired his own paper conservator, Mark Stevenson, who confirmed to Kemper that his 28 paintings that consti-

tute the "Canyon Suite" were not by Georgia O'Keeffe. Kemper demanded his $5,000,000 back from art dealer Gerald Peters. After intense
negotiations, a settlement was reached, the terms of which were to
remain secret. (Both parties fabricated and/or leaked parts of the settlement that made himself look good.) One element of the agreement is
confirmed: Kemper agreed not to criticize Peters.

Reaching a settlement was complicated by the fact that a portion of
the purchase price was land in Colorado that Kemper owned. Peters
claimed that the land was appraised too aggressively, resulting in an
appraised value that was much too high.

NOTE THE DELICIOUS IRONY: At the same time (seller) Peters
was hyping the value of the fake O'Keeffe's to (buyer) Kemper, (buyer)
Kemper was cooking the purchase price he agreed to pay (seller) Peters.

In the midst of the O'Keeffe/Kemper debacle, Gerald Peters was
wheeling and dealing elsewhere. To make fees, he arranged secret deals
with both the Colorado Springs Fine Arts Center and the Denver Art
Museum for them to sell important artworks and artifacts to private individuals at fire-sale prices. Gerald Peters and his wife Kathleen donated
four watercolors to Kemper's museum (and one oil painting to the
O'Keeffe museum) and took a tax deduction of $1,130,000. The IRS dis-
allowed the deduction and Peters was forced to pay almost $250,000,
which included fines and penalties. He sued to recoup the money but
his case was dismissed in 2006.

CLEVELAND MUSEUM OF ART

Founded in 1913, the Cleveland Museum of Art is one of America's
premier cultural institutions. In 2004, it purchased a life-size bronze
statue called Apollo Sauroktonos (Apollo the lizard slayer) which it
considered a coup.

The piece was acquired from Ali Aboutaam, 42, and his brother Hicham, 40, owners of Phoenix Ancient Art of Geneva and New York. (Their
father started the business in 1968 in Beirut, Lebanon.) The brothers are
known in the shady world of antiquities dealers to be in the forefront of
selling illegally excavated and smuggled artifacts. (The day after the
breathless announcement of the acquisition by the Cleveland Museum,

The Unscrupulous

Hicham Aboutaam pled guilty in New York to the federal charge of falsifying a customs document to hide the origins of an ancient silver drinking vessel.) This is the same pair that was convicted (in absentia) in Egypt a year earlier on charges of smuggling antiquities. They were sentenced to 15 years in prison.

The Cleveland museum claims the Apollo statue is the work of the great ancient Greek sculptor Praxiteles, (considered the best, along with a handful of others, who worked from 375 B.C. to 340 B.C.), and not a later less valuable Roman copy. The main argument advanced by the museum to establish this position is that Pliny the Elder mentioned (in his numerous writings) that Praxiteles who normally worked in marble, sometimes worked in bronze and created an Apollo. Talk about self deception.

Why didn't it occur to any of the museum staff that most educated people, including unscrupulous forgers and dealers, have also read Pliny the Elder? (The Italian, who perished in 79 A.D., suffocated by the fumes from the historically famous Mount Vesuvius eruption, wrote the world's first encyclopedia.) There are gaps in the provenance large enough to drive a semi through. There are also several coincidences, leading many to conclude that the piece is a fake.

Let's review the bidding. So far, we have the coincidence of 1) no compelling provenance for the statue, and 2) questionable dealers. There is another significant coincidence that cries out fake.

Michael Bennett, curator of Greek and Roman art at the Cleveland Museum, says he came upon the statue accidentally in Geneva in 2003 where it was being displayed in the Aboutaam's gallery in that city. Bennett states he called director Katharine Reid who requested that the statute be shipped to Cleveland forthwith.

You have to believe the coincidence that a priceless life-size statute (called the finest piece of classical sculpture purchased by a North American museum since WW II) just happened to be on display when the curator from the Cleveland Art Museum just happened to be visiting the gallery.

Ask yourself, if the work is for real, why in the world would a classic statute of this importance (it cost the museum about $5,000,000) merely be exhibited on the gallery's showroom floor. Dealers in antiquities that are truly masterpieces sell them one on one to key clients.

103

In a telling move, the Louvre withdrew a request to borrow the statute from the Cleveland Museum for an exhibition after the Greek government threatened a boycott. The museum held an international symposium in 2006, ostensibly to clear the air regarding the provenance of the masterpiece. Of course it did no such thing.

In the unlikely event the statute is not a fake, both Greek and Italian authorities are certain the piece was looted and smuggled out of their countries and want the statute returned. There are other disturbing matters regarding the Cleveland Museum of Art. In 1927, when Frederic Allen Whiting was director, the museum purchased a Dossena fake called "Pisano Madonna and Child." Not until two years later, in 1929, did Whiting admit that they had been duped and returned the piece to the dealer. What the Cleveland museum didn't admit, was that in the same month they returned one Dossena fake, they bought another Dossena fake named "Athena."

James Ferrell, the financier and mastermind behind a massive gang of looters of Middle Eastern artifacts, whose specialty was bribing public officials, placed a number of antiquities with the Cleveland Museum in order to give the pieces credibility in the marketplace. The tactic worked for Ferrell.

In 1948, the museum admitted it had been displaying a fake Joni painting as an authentic Sano di Pietro (1406-1481). The craquelure, which was produced by baking, gave it away. Between 1950 and 1990 the museum purchased eight antiquities from the notorious Robert Hecht, none of which have satisfactory provenance. In 2000, it was determined that almost 400 artworks owned by the museum had questionable provenance. In 2007, the Italian government began to move on the Cleveland Museum. The raids on the Medici warehouses confirmed that the museum owned a lekythos (oil jar) that had been looted from Italy.

Sounding like the MFA, director Timothy Rub indicated he was willing to speak with the Italians, "Once official contact is made." In the meantime, Rub refused to responded to three E-mails sent by the Italian authorities. Instead, the Cleveland Art Museum embarked on a major PR campaign that indicated (in strong language) that it had no intention of rolling over and would fight Italy tooth-and-nail, yadda, yadda, yadda.

In early 2008 the Cleveland Museum of Art bowed to the inevitable. Italy announced that a verbal agreement had been reached with Cleveland wherein the museum agreed to return 16 of the 27 works the Italians had targeted. Whether the brass was worried about hard time in an Italian jail, or was playing follow the leader, or was concerned about an embargo, (or what?), the tight-lipped museum isn't talking. The Apollo is still under discussion.

Christian Goller

Christian Goller, born in Lower Bavaria, admits he forged the painting of the German Renaissance painter Matthias Grunewald (c. 1470–c. 1528), which the Cleveland Museum of Art purchased in 1974 for $1,000,000. When doubts about the painting were raised, the museum hired the German art historian Hubert von Sonnenburg to check it out. After a series of scientific tests showed materials were used that had not been invented in the 1500s, Sonnenburg proclaimed the painting of Saint Catherine a fake.

Goller was tracked down and readily admitted he painted the Grunewald, which he said was inspired by a drawing for a lost painting. The fake took him a week to paint. He then added patina and crackle (as he calls it) and finished the process by rubbing the work with dirt.

When asked if he was a forger, however, Goller is in denial. "Whoever calls me a forger is lying. I only paint in the style of the Old Masters. I add patina and crackle for decoration." Goller calls his fakes reconstructions and has convinced himself that because he does not forge the original artist's signatures to the reconstructions, they are not forgeries. Evan Turner, director at the time and the man responsible for the purchase (and who had been defending the authenticity of the work), after it was confirmed to be a fake, disavowed the painting, saying it now was a very boring picture.

READY FOR A REAL, MIND-BOGGLING COINCIDENCE?

Eli Sakhai

Eli Sakhai, born in 1952, conceived of an ingenious scam which netted him some $25,000,000 over a 20-year period. Sakhai immigrated to

America from Iran in 1965 when he was 13 years old and eventually started an art gallery in New York. To establish credentials, he visited the major auction houses regularly and would occasionally purchase Impressionist and Post-Impressionist works. Sakhai would buy little known, relatively inexpensive paintings by modern masters; minor works. He would then hire artists to forge the paintings he'd purchased. (While it has never been determined who painted the fakes for Sakhai, the best guess is that he had them produced in China, which has a booming art fraud industry.) In any case, Sakhai would then take the original certificate of authenticity that came with his auction house purchase and attach it to the fake. He would then sell the fake to Asian collectors and dealers who relied on the legitimate certificates of authenticity. Years later, Sakhai would sell the original paintings far from Asia, through the very same London and New York auction houses from whom he made the original purchase.

The auction houses didn't ask for certificates of authenticity at this time because when they checked their records it was clear that they had sold the painting to Sakhai some years earlier. The Asia aspect of the scam was significant because, before the era of instant communications via the Internet, it was much easier to peddle fakes there, particularly in Japan, where a certificate of authenticity was revered. Also, since Sakhai had limited his fakes to minor works of major artists, he had a ready explanation as to why the painting wasn't in the artist's catalogue raisonné. Furthermore, in the mid-twentieth century, Asians were unlikely to spend their time or money on experts from the other side of the world. The original certificates of authenticity would seal the deals for Sakhai. How did Ely Sakhai's ingenious scam come to an end?

Sakhai purchased a minor work of Gauguin named "Lilas" at a Sotheby's auction. Working the scam he had perfected, Sakhai had the painting copied, attached the original certificate of authenticity to it, and sold it as an original Gauguin to a collector in Tokyo. In 1997, the owner of the Gauguin fake placed it with Christie's, who accepted it as authentic, relying on the real certificate of authenticity. A private collector bought the fake at auction, but three years later, in 2000, he decided to place it for sale, again with Christie's.

In a stroke of bad luck (for Sakhai), this was exactly the same time

Sakhai decided it was safe to make his move on the Gauguin. He placed his authentic Gauguin for sale with Sotheby's, from whom, you will remember, he purchased the painting many years earlier. In a coincidence you wouldn't believe in a movie or novel, in their May, 2000 catalogues, both Christie's and Sotheby's offered the same painting by Paul Gauguin for sale.

The embarrassed Christie's had their Gauguin vetted and withdrew the painting when it was determined by the experts to be a fake. Sotheby's proceeded with their sale and Sakhai gathered in over $300,000 from the auction. The fiasco caught the eye of the authorities. The FBI traced the history of the fake Gauguin and pieced together Sakhai's scam. He was arrested and charged with eight counts of wire and mail fraud. Proving that he still had his touch at the con, Ely Sakhai made a deal with the Feds in 2005. He pled guilty to conspiracy, agreed to pay $25,000,000, surrender 11 authentic paintings (at least the authorities believed them to be authentic), and agreed to serve a mere 41 months, instead of the 20 years for each of the eight counts, which would have meant prison for 160 years.

WHEN YOU'RE UP TO YOUR ASS IN ALLIGATORS, IT'S HARD TO REMEMBER WHY YOU WENT INTO THE SWAMP

Steven Straw

It was well-known in the insular art world that Steven Straw was a golden boy who had it all. While still in his twenties he owned Newburyport, Massachusetts' finest art gallery and all of the toys that go with the game, including a private airplane.

The son of a successful art auctioneer, Straw touted the relationship, and the expertise it gave him, and parlayed that into deals across the country. What the art world did not know was that the deals were bogus. Straw was selling partial interests in paintings he didn't own. Graduating from single painting scams, Straw started to put paintings into (nonexistent) packages and selling pieces of the partnerships.

Straw laced one partnership with 31 phantom paintings by artists such as Rembrandt, Titian, Renoir, and other masters. In 1978, a New York dealer who had invested over $3,000,000 in three of these partnerships became suspicious when he couldn't pin Straw down to give him documentation about the deals. He filed suit, which, as is usual in cases such as this, triggered the collapse of Straw's empire.

Straw's life spiraled down. He filed for bankruptcy, turned to drugs and served several terms in jail for offences as diverse as art fraud, check bouncing and possession of cocaine.

In 2003, former boy-wonder Steven Straw was found floating in the Merrimack River. He had taken his own life at the age of 51.

FISH OUT OF WATER

Peg Goldberg

In mid 1988, Indianapolis art dealer Peg Goldberg, a large woman with an ego to match, bought four sixth-century mosaics that had been looted from a church in northern Cyprus. Goldberg claimed she purchased the antiquities from Aydin Dikmen, at least she thought it was Dikmen. The mosaics, which measured about two feet square, had been ripped from the walls of the church of the Virgin of Kanakaria in Lythragomi. Goldberg paid a touch over $1,000,000 for the treasures. (She borrowed $1,200,000 from a local bank and pocketed the difference.)

At this point, Goldberg was a fledgling art dealer who knew nothing about the shadowy world of antiquities. (There is a real question, therefore, whether Goldberg knew she was buying looted antiquities or was finessed in a short con. Either way, it's clear that she was in way over her head in the world of looted and smuggled antiquities.)

The end came when one of Goldberg's partners offered the treasures to the Getty for $20,000,000. Marion True, curator of antiquities at the Getty museum in Los Angeles at the time, informed her friends in Cyprus where the stolen mosaics were located.

As we will see, Marion True is one of the most duplicitous individuals in the sordid, secret world of artifact looting, smuggling, and collecting. While we'll probably never know, True's motive to squeal on Goldberg may have been that Goldberg was invading the territory of one of her (True's) favored antiquity dealers. The authorities easily traced the artworks to Goldberg. Cyprus requested the return of the mosaics but she refused. Frustrated, Cyprus sued Peg Goldberg for the mosaic's return.

In 1989, a Federal Court ruled that Goldberg had not obtained legal title to the mosaics and ordered their return to Cyprus. Goldberg appealed the verdict to the Seventh Circuit Court of Appeals. She lost again. Determined as ever, Peg Goldberg spent the next several years trying to obtain information about the mosaics that would help her get the case reopened. She failed.

Since late 1991, the mosaics have been on display in the Byzantine Museum in Nicosia.

Aydin Dikmen

Aydin Dikmen, born in Turkey c. 1938, has lived in Germany since 1961 and has been selling looted antiquities all of his life.

Dikmen was well-connected to the Turkish government. For example, following the 1974 Turkish invasion of Cyprus, Dikmen coordinated the stripping of the cultural heritage of northern Cyprus, obtaining for himself (to sell) mosaics and other icons from the churches and religious buildings of the occupied area.

Dikmen always kept a low profile, primarily dealing through other dealers, so the authorities could never pin him down as a dealer in plundered and smuggled artifacts. In the 1989 Peg Goldberg case, however, it was revealed that Dikmen was the dealer who sold Goldberg the four mosaic pieces that had been ripped from the walls of a church in northern Cyprus.

Dikmen, posing as a state archaeologist, would hire local Cyprus diggers to obtain his booty, paying them a pittance. Although it took the Bavarian police almost nine years to move on Dikmen (they videotaped him selling stolen goods), when they finally raided his residences in 1997 (or 1998), they struck gold.

The authorities found more than 4,000 looted works worth an estimated $40,000,000 in the three apartments rented by Dikmen, including over 400 artifacts looted from Greek Orthodox churches in Northern Cyprus, two of which complemented the four he sold Goldberg.

The elusive Aydin Dikmen was arrested.

Marilyn Karos

When art dealers stay within their expertise, smuggling, double dealing, and passing fakes can be expected. When art dealers move out of their range of specialty, however, more exotic things have been known to occur.

For about 20 years, Marilyn Karos, dealt in paintings out of the gallery she maintained in her home in Whitefish Bay, a high end suburb of Milwaukee, Wisconsin. She was well liked and modestly successful.

In the mid-1980s, a man who owed Karos money paid her with three astrolabes and an armillary sphere. These are instruments that measured time and motion of stars and planets in ancient times.

The man who paid her didn't realize their true value, but when Koros checked she learned two startling facts.

First, they were part of a haul of 85 items thieves made off with from an astronomy museum in Rome. The loss was so devastating, the museum was forced to close. Second, Karos learned they were of inestimable value, worth up to $1,000,000 each, maybe more, depending on whom you ask. When Karos discovered that the items were stolen, did she call police or offer to return them to their rightful owners? Of course not, she's an art dealer. What she did was try to sell them. Since the market for astrolabes and armillary spheres is limited in Wisconsin (to put it gently), Koros still had the priceless items in her possession when she met a man named Richard O'Hara (born c. 1942), an antiques dealer with a shop in Chicago. Karos and O'Hara developed a personal and business relationship, so the stolen pieces ended up in his shop. O'Hara was also unable to sell them.

Enter Zakria El-Shafei, born c. 1966 in Libya. He had previously sold some items on consignment for Karos, so she gave the astrolabes and armillary sphere to him to sell on the same consignment basis. One problem. El-Shafei couldn't move the goods either. A worried Karos started to harass him for the return of the four pieces. (At the time, the duplicitous El-Shafei was trying to pawn the priceless treasures and/or receive a reward for their return.)

On a pretext Karous lured Zakria to her home where her lover/business associate O'Hara waited with two friends (Kosi and Williams). The friends proceeded to beat Zakria with their fists, but the masked O'Hara used a baseball bat. He also threatened to inject a deadly fluid into the belly of Zakria's pregnant wife.

Arrests followed. Early in 2001, Marilyn Karos pled guilty to one count of receiving and possessing stolen property and served seven months in prison. The ringleader, James O'Hara, was sentenced to ten years. There's more.

After getting out of jail herself, Karos hatched a plan to spring her lover O'Hara out of jail. In 2004, after searching for several years, Karos found James Kosi, 56, the key prosecution witness. She offered him $56,000 to sign an affidavit changing his story. Kosi went to the FBI who wired Kosi and recorded Karos' latest scam. Marilyn Karos, the art dealer who plunged into the shady world of looted artifacts, was charged with the federal crime of obstruction of justice. She pled guilty in 2005 and was sentenced to 20 months in prison and fined $30,000. But wait, believe it or not, there's more.

In 2004, 63 at this point, Karos teamed up with Majed Ihmoud, who posed as a Saudi sheik, to sell a fake Rembrandt entitled "Man with Golden Helmet" for $2,800,000. Karos forged a certificate of authenticity for the fake. Unfortunately for the pair, the supposed buyer of the painting was an undercover FBI agent. Karos admitted to the authorities that she had attempted to sell fake art and other bogus items many times, including a pair of ordinary brass doors that she claimed were once owned by boxer Muhammad Ali for which she had forged certificates of authenticity. In 2006, the 54-year-old Ihmoud pled guilty to conspiring to commit mail fraud and was sentenced to five months in federal prison and five months house arrest. Sixty-five-year-old Marilyn Karos also copped a plea in 2006 and was sentenced to one-year in federal prison.

You want irony? Here's irony. In 1986, art experts determined that "Man with Golden Helmet" was not pained by Rembrandt. It was a fake Rembrandt. Karos and her associates had selected a fake Rembrandt to fake.

Lawrence Salander

Lawrence Salander was a highly successful art dealer with a first class gallery on New York's Upper Eastside (79th Street). The Salander-

O'Reilly Galleries were established in 1976. With striking rooms, it enjoyed a top-notch reputation, paid its bills, mounted shows which were usually reviewed, and represented an impressive roster of collectors and artists. Salander loved to brag to the world that in 2003 the Robb Report called SOR (as it was known) "the best gallery in the world."

In 1995, the balding, intense, dynamic 46-year-old Salander made what he thought was the deal of his lifetime. He sold 50% of his gallery (O'Reilly was long gone) to Myron Kunin, a wealthy Minneapolis businessman/collector. Salander retained control, received a hefty salary of $500,000 a year, and access to a $3,500,000 line of credit. With stars in his eyes, Salander began planning what would turn out to be his downfall. He conceived the grandest private gallery in New York, the capital of the art world.

Salander found a five story townhouse at 22 East 71st Street, around the corner from the celebrated Frick Collection. The rent was a mind-boggling $154,000 a month. In addition, taxes on the space ran almost $20,000 a month. The costs translate, for starters, into over $2,000,000 a year in fixed expenses. After a $2,000,000 renovation, the new Salander-O'Reilly Gallery, which was planned as an adjunct to the original a few blocks away, opened to great fanfare in late 2005. But the clouds were already forming on the horizon.

The problem was that Salander didn't stick to what made him famous and (relatively) successful. Instead of stocking his new gallery with twentieth-century American art, he filled it with Renaissance and Baroque art. Old Masters is a highly specialized market that has a limited number of potential customers, almost none of which are collectors of twentieth-century American art.

In any case, the art world was flabbergasted when they saw the size of the space and the opulence of the expansion. Everyone questioned Salander's change in direction. In what might be the cleverest analogy of the year, a prominent dealer told the *New York Times* what the art world was thinking about Salander's switch from twentieth-century American art to Old Masters. He said, "It is as if a talented, successful pop singer decided to go into opera and then build himself La Scala."

With stagnant sales and sky-high expenses, Salander was on the ropes before he knew what hit him. His original, successful, gallery was shuttered within a year. He raised new money in 2006 from several partners, but ran through that money in record time. In the summer of 2007, Salander started to cut the well-known corners to stay afloat. Among other frauds, Salander borrowed almost $1,000,000 from Sotheby's, pledging 20 paintings he didn't own as collateral; he started selling the same painting to more than one buyer; he sold consigned paintings without the owner's permission and pocketed the money. And so, and so on, and so on.

Although he had no formal art education, Lawrence Salander never did think small when it came to art. For example, Renaissance Art Investors had over 600 works in his hands, and Benucci, a Roman gallery, sold Salander over $9,000,000 of art which he used to stock his new gallery. (Benucci collected less than $2,400,000 of the $9,000,000.)

Once the dam burst in 2007, over 40 lawsuits from defrauded parties were filed within two months, Salander's passive, silent partner, Myron Kunin, sued to terminate the partnership, and in late 2007, New York State Supreme Court Judge Richard Lowe III ordered the gallery closed indefinitely, even ordering the locks changed.

Lawrence Salander and his wife filed for Chapter Eleven (voluntary) bankruptcy, listing 53 creditors, of which the 20 largest were owed some $43,000,000. The full extent of Lawrence Salander's financial scams will not be known for some time. In any event, in 2008 the case ended up as a Chapter Seven (involuntary) bankruptcy in which the Salanders lost control of their assets and finances and stand to lose everything except what the court rules are exempt assets. The Manhattan District Attorney is conducting a criminal investigation.

TWO TRIALS THAT ROCKED THE ART WORLD

Frank Lloyd

Frank Lloyd (nee Franz Levai) was born in Austria in 1911 into a family that dealt in antiques. After World War II, Lloyd moved to London and, with partners, opened an art gallery, which he grandly named Marlborough, after the Duke. In the 1960s, the diminutive businessman, known for his intellect and toughness, built the preeminent art gallery empire in the world.

What the civilians and tight-knit art world didn't know was that behind everyone's back the dapper smooth-talking Lloyd was cheating and exploiting the artists he represented on a regular basis. Through a combination of sweet talk, hidden contract advantages, and double crossing, Lloyd built the massive Liechtenstein headquartered Marlborough, which had, at its zenith, over 20 associated companies throughout the world. Contrary to what Lloyd publicly maintained, he and his family were the sole owners of the fantastically lucrative empire. Not satisfied with being considered one of the pillars of the art world, in the 1960s Lloyd got excessively greedy, even for an art dealer, and his life and empire crashed. Vindication for the aggrieved did not come easy, however. Before going down, the pugnacious Frank Lloyd waged the most tenacious, but questionable and expensive, legal fight in the history of the art world.

Scamming the artist Mark Rothko (1903-1970), born Marcus Rothkovich in what is called Latvia today, began as soon as the Abstract Impressionist artist became a client of Marlborough in 1963. Lloyd (as he did with all of his artists) bought Rothko paintings at low, low prices and sold them at high, high prices. Nothing wrong with that, that's what dealers do. The problem was, in order to keep the portion of the sales price he paid Rothko down, and to keep the prices down for future purchases of paintings from Rothko, Lloyd lied to the artist about the amount he was selling the paintings for, routinely understating the sales prices.

In 1969, Rothko (whose professional standing was solid at this point) sold 26 oils and 61 smaller works to Marlborough for a touch over $1,000,000. That's the good news. The bad news is there was only $100,000 down, with the remainder, with no interest, to be paid over 14 years. While there were other terms, the significant one was that in return, Marlborough exacted from the artist the exclusive rights to represent him worldwide for eight years. The other bad news was that shortly thereafter, in 1970, Marlborough informed Rothko that the gallery would now decide which of his paintings would be shown in exhibitions. This demand stunned Rothko, who had always been protective of his work and had never even allowed anyone into the warehouses where he stored his paintings. (During his life Rothko consistently maintained that he wanted his works to be displayed in logical groups in museums and collections.)

Shortly thereafter, in the same year of 1970, Rothko committed suicide. At least that was the official police verdict of the death. (It will never be known whether it was Rothko's lingering illness and bouts of depression, or Marlborough's ultimatum, or both, that triggered the overdose of sleeping pills and the slashing of the veins in both arms. What is known is that the cause of Rothko's death will be speculated upon for generations to come.)

When Mark Rothko died in 1970, he was only 66 years old. His will left almost 800 paintings to the charitable Mark Rothko Foundation, which he had established to hold and disburse his paintings in an orderly fashion for exhibition and promulgation in museums. Rothko appointed what he considered three close friends as executors of his will and as three of the five trustees of his foundation. They were Bernard Reis (a secret director, secretary and treasurer of Marlborough), Theodoros Stamos (a fellow abstract painter who negotiated a sweetheart deal for himself from Marlborough almost immediately after Rothko's death) and Morton Levine (an anthropology professor who pretended not to see what was going on.)

What was going on was this. Since the contract in effect between Marlborough and Rothko at the artist's death was not binding on his heirs or estate, Lloyd switched to the big con, the charade that was to be his downfall. The first step in Lloyd's carefully orchestrated plan was to cement his relationship with Bernard Reis. Lloyd gave Reis favors, duties, and compensation in the Marlborough organization, all of which the egocentric Reis (and his phony socialite wife) ate up. An elderly, soft-spoken attorney/accountant, Reis's greatest thrill was sucking-up to artists and integrating himself into their professional and personal lives. Unknown to the artists, Reis was steering them to Marlborough because he was on Lloyd's payroll. (Reis was an inveterate collector who would accept paintings in lieu of fees from his artist friend/clients. While barter is a time-honored device, two problems arose with Reis' tactics. Reis would demand from the artists a larger, more important painting than his services warranted. And, Reis neglected to tell his partners about his acquisitions for services rendered, forcing a number of his accounting partners to sue him for their share of his hidden income.)

During his lifetime, Mark Rothko thought Bernard Reis was his dear, close, personal friend. Reis ingratiated himself into every aspect of Rothko's life, advising him on taxes, studios, legalities, and exhibitions. He advised the artist to drop close friends who were suspicious of him (Reis), and, even advised Rothko that he should dump his mistress. It was Reis who drew up Mark Rothko's will and the corresponding foundation, which was Rothko's chief beneficiary. The artist never suspected the duplicitous Lloyd and Reis were setting him up for one of art's greatest scams. Lloyd's next move was to have Bernard Reis (now his employee) rush a change through the foundation's objectives.

Reis delivered. He excised Rothko's intentions (which were that the foundation hold his paintings and see that they went to the right museums and collectors, with the proceeds put to charitable and educational purposes) and substituted language that the foundation's purposes were simply to help needy and elderly artists. With this change, Reis was able to claim that money was needed to fulfill the new (his) terms of the foundation. At roughly the same time, on Lloyd's behalf, Reis obtained a ridiculously low appraisal of Rothko's works. The appraisal was made by a Lloyd insider. (The supposedly independent appraisal was typed on Reis's typewriter.)

Within five weeks of Rothko's death, Reis saw to it that Rothko's studio was turned over to Marlborough. In fact, Reis signed the lease and rent checks for Rothko's studio on behalf of Marlborough.

Completing the scam, in order to gain control of Rothko's entire oeuvre, Lloyd had Reis quarterback two grotesque contracts. In the first, the three executors (who were also trustees of the foundation) sold Marlborough 100 Mark Rothko paintings for a paltry $200,000 down, and $1,600,000 to be paid over 12 years, interest free. In the second, the three executor/trustees consigned the remaining 698 Rothko paintings to Marlborough, granting the gallery the exorbitant commission rate of 40% to 50%. (The firm was receiving 10% during Rothko's life.) Because of these agreements, the foundation gave up all rights to Rothko's lifetime painting collection for an embarrassingly low price and on ridiculous terms.

In 1971, Rothko's heirs (his under-aged daughter Kate and son Christopher) sued the executor/trustees and Marlborough in New York's Surrogate's Court (known as the widows and children's court) for wasting the assets of the estate. Not long thereafter, because the case was so obviously heinous and hatefully evil, New York's Attorney General's office entered the case in the person of Assistant Attorney General Gus Harrow. Harrow was the best friend the Rothko children and the public could have had. His truthfulness, dedication, and tenaciousness stood in stark contrast to Lloyd's total disregard for honesty or the rule of law.

In 1972, the Surrogate Millard Midonick ordered a halt to Marlborough's sale of any Rothko paintings. Too late. Lloyd had made his moves. Before the court imposed the injunction, Marlborough claimed to have already sold 71 of the 100 paintings it purchased, and 69 of the 698 consigned. The estate received $1,500,000 of this take, while Marlborough kept a whopping $3,500,000.

But that wasn't the worst of it. Frank Lloyd continued to sell Rothko paintings despite the court's ruling banning such sales. To make it appear paintings were sold prior to the ban, Lloyd falsified sales dates, and in a further act of deception, hid the exorbitant profits in secret bank accounts. In addition, Lloyd parked a number of Rothko's paintings with friends (and claimed they were sold) in order to place them outside of the jurisdiction of the court.

In 1974, the case, which is one of the most famous breach of fiduciary cases in history, went to trial. At the trial, there were 16 attorneys (plus assistants) seated in the courtroom. This clearly underscored Frank Lloyd's actions of the previous three years, which included suits and counter-suits, claims and counter-claims, and other lawyerly shenanigans. When the trial ended eight months after it began, there were almost 900 exhibits and some 20,000 pages of evidence produced by Lloyd's seven teams of lawyers.

Some of the testimony by art experts was laughable and bordered on the indecipherable. Here's a great example. Arnold Glimcher, president of Pace Gallery, testified during the trial: "When you can point to an artist's ancestors and antecedents, and you can, with strong judgment, say that the antecedents [sic] would not have come after him had he not existed, he's inextricable from the history of art."

In 1975, an 87-page judgment was issued in favor of the children and against Marlborough, Lloyd, Reis, Stamos and Levine. In strong language, the court set aside the Marlborough deals. The three executor/trustees were held to have breached their duty of loyalty by making two agreements that were patently unfair to the estate. They were removed from office. Marlborough was held to have knowingly induced and participated in the disloyalty. The defendants were fined almost $10,000,000, which included a $3,800,000 penalty against Lloyd and Marlborough for tampering with evidence and contempt of court for shipping 62 paintings out of the country in violation of the court's order.

The court's ruling should have ended Frank Lloyd's con, but it did not. Lloyd had yet another trick up his sleeve. Following the judgment, Lloyd arranged for his man in Liechtenstein to fly to Toronto to remove all of Rothko's artworks to Zurich to avoid paying the Rothko judgment. A tip from Howard Eisenberg (obviously a conscientious attorney who understands that lawyers are officers of the court) allowed New York Assistant Attorney General Gus Harrow to squelch the plan and freeze multi-millions worth of artworks.

Following the verdict, the New York County District Attorney turned up the heat in his quest to determine if Lloyd and Marlborough had committed any crimes in regard to the Rothko case. Sadly, the criminal investigation of Lloyd's activities brought out the dark side of one of Lloyd's lawyers. The lawyer (and former judge) named David Peck, of the Sullivan and Cromwell law firm, engaged in highly questionable activities. In an attempt to skewer the District Attorney's investigation, Peck went directly to the New York Attorney General and the Surrogate judge (as well as others).

Attorney Peck's pitch was simple, to the point, and probably illegal (it certainly was unethical). Lloyd would not post a bond in the civil case unless the criminal investigation was abandoned by the District Attorney. Why was Lloyd posting a bond in the civil case critical? Peck explained that since Lloyd was sequestered in the Bahamas, it would be impossible for Rothko's heirs to collect on their judgment. The bribery attempts of David Peck hit the papers and not only emboldened the District Attorney to pursue criminal charges against Lloyd, they inspired the Appellate Court to deny Peck's request on behalf of Lloyd and Marlborough for a stay of monetary enforcement.

In 1976, in order to gain the return of his art frozen in Toronto, Lloyd posted bond. The interesting thing about this move was that Lloyd returned 41 paintings (for a credit of $3,400,000). These were paintings that, throughout the trial, Lloyd had strenuously maintained had been sold. In 1977, the New York Court of Appeals unanimously upheld Surrogate Midonick's decision, calling the conduct of the three executors and Lloyd "manifestly wrong and indeed shocking."

Also in 1977, the seemingly endless civil battle turned into a criminal case. Lloyd was indicted on two counts for the crime of tampering with evidence. And a warrant was issued for his arrest. This battle lasted 11 years, during which time the mesmerized art world was shocked time and time again by the revelations of greed, abuses of power, and conspiracy. The art world was also intrigued and fascinated (why didn't I think of it, they said to themselves) to learn of Lloyd's intricate network of bank accounts in Switzerland and shell corporations in Liechtenstein which enabled him to hide both art and profits.

While Lloyd's criminal trial was in progress, Bernard Reis sold off his art collection piece by piece, and after the verdict, filed for bankruptcy. He died 11 months later. Theodoros Stamos signed over his home to the estate but was granted life tenancy.

In 1982, Frank Lloyd turned himself in to the New York County District Attorney to answer the indictment for two felony counts; destruction of evidence and forgery. He was convicted by the jury. The judge could have sentenced Lloyd to four years in jail. In an obvious deal, however, the judge merely ordered Lloyd to establish a scholarship fund and present a series of art lectures and showings for local high school students. There is no evidence that Lloyd complied with these innocuous conditions.

Frank Lloyd died in the Bahamas in 1998 at the age of 86, a pathetic shell of a man, his reputation in shambles. What brought Lloyd down? Almost unprecedented greed. Lloyd repeatedly expressed his philosophy, "I collect money, not art."

This from the number one art dealer in the world.

During the period the Rothko scandal was unraveling at Marlborough, the case of Francis Bacon and his relationship with Marlborough burst into the news.

Bacon, who was 82 when he died in 1992, was born in Ireland, but spent most of his life in London. At the time of his death, he was the leading living artist in England. Bacon was also the classic bohemian artist portrayed in literature, movies and plays, a swashbuckling, hard-drinking, hard-playing, gambling rascal who lived (in the world's most modest flat) only for his art, when he wasn't enjoying life to the fullest.

Marlborough was Bacon's agent for most of his life, beginning in 1958, and Lloyd would stop at nothing to keep him in its camp, including blackmail. Professor Brian Clarke, who was executor of Bacon's estate, filed a lawsuit against Marlborough, claiming, among other things, that Marlborough systematically defrauded Bacon out of hundreds of millions of dollars, stole over 30 paintings from the artist, and secretly produced prints of his work without giving Bacon any of the income. Clarke also maintained that Marlborough purchased paintings directly from the artist for nominal sums and then resold them for significantly higher amounts, and that they charged the artist up to seventy percent commission for some paintings they sold. Clarke also alleged that Marlborough blackmailed Bacon to stay with the firm.

Even though it appeared he had an open and shut case, Clarke eventually figured out that he would have serious problems winning the lawsuit. His problem was that when Marlborough realized the executor was going to file a lawsuit, the firm moved all of the relevant damaging documents out of the country. With the evidence hidden, and the estate's legal costs becoming astronomical due to Marlborough's delaying tactics, Clarke dropped the lawsuit.

Marlborough Galleries continues in the art business to this day.

Otto Wacker

In 1925, Otto Wacker (1905–1976) set up shop as an art dealer in Germany. Prior to that, Wacker appeared in his native city of Dusseldorf as a Spanish dancer named Olindo Lovael. With confidence and a trickster's charm, Wacker ingratiated himself with, and gained the confidence of, the world's top van Gogh experts (J. Baart de la Faille and Julius Meier-Graefe) and convinced them to issue certificates of authenticity for the fake van Gogh paintings he wanted to sell. Dealers and collectors were happy to accept the expert opinions of de la Faille and Meier-Graefe. After all, de la Faille wrote the first catalogue on van Gogh. Wacker's cover story was that the original owners of his van Gogh's was a titled Russian, blah, blah, blah.

The scheme worked. With major league certificates in hand, over a relatively short time (approximately three years) Wacker was able to sell 29 fake van Gogh paintings to the most prominent art galleries in Germany. Moving right along with his scam, the bold Wacker planned a major exhibition of van Gogh paintings (to include his fakes) in the Paul Cassirer Gallery, the top dealer in Berlin. Wacker's idea, of course, was to legitimize his fakes. Fate, however, intervened in the form of Grete Ring, an employee of Cassirers. Otto Wacker's con would never recover.

The exhibition was about to open, but three (or four) of Wacker's paintings were not yet delivered, so space was left for them on the walls. When the paintings arrived they stood out from the others which had already been hung. Grete Ring spotted them as fakes and they were returned to Wacker. In the tight little world of art in Berlin, the word spread, and a total of 33 van Gogh paintings in Germany were determined to be fakes, and all of them came from Otto Wacker. In 1928, Wacker was sued by one of the galleries. Four years later the government got involved and Otto Wacker was finally, officially charged.

The Wacker trial ranks with the Rothko/Marlborough trial as one of the most notorious art orientated cases in history. Every art expert in Germany testified at the highly publicized trial. The only fact determined with any certainty was that the Russians had never purchased any van Gogh paintings, much less 33 of them. After that, the testimony bordered on the ludicrous. The public, which was closely following the scandal, loved seeing the supercilious art experts sometimes humiliated, and always embarrassed. For example, based on the conflicting (and changing) expert testimony, the entertained public was able to draw several conclusions: All 33 of the paintings were genuine; all 33 of the paintings were fakes; certain of the paintings were forgeries and certain ones were not. And vice versa.

In 1932, after two trials, the court found Otto Wacker guilty of cumulative fraud and falsification of documents and sentenced him to 19 months in jail and imposed a monetary fine. After getting out of jail, Otto Wacker, the ex-cabaret performer turned art dealer, retired from the art business. He died in 1970 at the age of 72.

In some ways, the most interesting aspect of the Wacker case is that today all art experts agree that the 33 Wacker van Gogh's are fakes, but it has never been determined who painted the forgeries. Claude-Emile Schuffenecker is the prime suspect.

Claude Emile Schuffenecker

Frenchman Claude Emile Schuffenecker (1851–1934) was not only a forger, he was a serious collector whose collection consisted of over 100 works of van Gogh, Paul Cezanne (1839–1906), Paul Gauguin (1848–1903), and several other contemporaries. Like most forgers, Schuffenecker wanted to be a famous artist, but his lack of talent blocked his dream. He taught art to keep his hand in the business, and made it a point to befriend, and run with, many of the best artists of the day. He was particularly close to Gauguin.

In 1903, to settle a bitter divorce, Schuffenecker "sold" his entire impressive art collection to his brother, Amedee, who was a wine dealer. A fast study, Amedee realized that there was a lot more money to be made in art than wine, so he reinvented himself as an art dealer. Amedee focused on the fact that his brother, who resented that he had achieved no recognition as a painter, had been copying van Gogh, and others, to prove that so-called connoisseurs were mistaken about his talents. The light went off for the newly minted art dealer; even more money could be made selling fakes.

Amedee put his brother to work full time copying works from what was now his (Amedee's) collection. Since Emile had already begun to copy van Gogh, and since van Gogh was the easiest artist in the collection to copy, and since the value of van Gogh paintings had begun to escalate after his suicide in 1890, and since their extensive number of legitimate van Goghs was the perfect cover for their clandestine activities, that is where the brothers concentrated.

As of today, the estimates of van Gogh fakes painted by Claude Emile Schuffenecker (and sold by his brother to top museums and collectors all over the world) range from 30 to 60. Experts continue to examine the evidence: Additional van Gogh fakes painted by Schuffenecker are sure to be uncovered.

For now, scholars are concentrating their efforts (and venom) on the painting known as the "Yasuda Sunflowers," which became famous when it sold for a record amount in 1987 to the Japanese insurance firm of the same name. Numerous curators and auction houses, either in an effort to justify their judgment or too timid to accept the fact that a painting that sold for almost $40,000,000 could be a fake, call it authentic. (A record at the time, the sales price was about three times more than had ever been paid for a painting.) Listen to what one of "Yasuda Sunflower"'s greatest defenders said in 1997: "Thus, while Schuffenecker may have produced copies after van Gogh there is no evidence that he *actually* forged works." (Italics courtesy of the author.) Talk about being in denial.

On the other hand, numerous other experts in the world of art call the "Yasuda Sunflowers" a fake Van Gogh, painted by Schuffenecker. Jill-Elyse Grossvogel, the world's leading expert on Schuffenecker, has written the catalogue raisonné on the artist and curated several of his exhibitions. She states categorically "I see no way that they [the "Yasuda Sunflowers"] can be Vincent's."

Bottom line. In addition to the stylistic problems with the painting, its hazy provenance leads straight to the Schuffeneckers, as do so many, many, many other van Goghs. Common sense tells us that when the provenance of large numbers of an individual artist's works begins with one artist or dealer (as it did in the Otto Wacker case) coincidence is not only out of the question, it is absurd.

Jean-Claude Binoche

In his 1992 sales catalogue, French auctioneer, Jean-Claude Binoche, stated that a "van Gogh" painting to be auctioned entitled "Garden in Auvers" was painted by van Gogh and first belonged to the artist's sister. The painting was purchased at the auction by a Jean-Marc

Vernes for $10,000,000.

In 1998, Vernes' heirs sued to cancel the sale, alleging that the painting was a fake and therefore the sale was a fraud. For evidence, they pointed out that the auction catalogue was false. The painting had been in the possession of notorious van Gogh forger Claude-Emile Schuffenecker, not van Gogh's sister as Binoche claimed.

SNAPSHOTS

Dennis Anderson

In 1984, 37-year-old Dennis Anderson was arrested and indicted for perpetrating a multi-million dollar swindle. Anderson was a runner, that is a dealer working as a middle man between sellers and buyers. What he did was go to the top galleries in Manhattan and borrow paintings, claiming that he had buyers ready to purchase the works. To obtain the valuable paintings, all the con man Anderson had to do was sign his name to a receipt. He had such a good reputation, having been a curator at the Chrysler Museum in Norfolk, Virginia, holder of two master degrees in art (or so he said) and having penned three art books, that's all that was asked of him

What Anderson did was sell the artworks and pocket the money. His scam, which lasted less than a year, netted him over $2,000,000 from the 50 or so paintings he borrowed. Anderson copped a plea.

David Bowen

Working out of his home in suburban Cincinnati, 67-year-old David Bowen agreed to sell eight paintings owned by the Board of Education. For no fee. Bowen sold the paintings all right, but kept most of the proceeds for himself. After being charged, in 1999, Bowen worked a deal with the prosecutor. He pled guilty to one count of mail fraud and agreed to turn over approximately $10,000.

Even though the numbers scammed are small, there are three sad dimensions to this story. One, the Board believes Bowen scammed about $25,000. Two, Bowen served on the Board he scammed. Three, and most important, the eight paintings he sold were originally purchased with the pennies, nickels, and dimes donated by school children. So essentially, Bowen scammed the kids rather than the Board.

Leo Castelli

Leo Castelli opened his gallery in New York in 1957. He became wealthy and famous for discovering and supporting pop artists

In 1964, Castelli bribed the judges at the 34th Venice (Italy) Biennale on behalf of his client Robert Rauschenberg. It worked, and much to the consternation of the European critics and press, Rauschenberg was awarded the Grand Jury Prize. It is generally agreed that the effect of the award (and Castelli's maneuver) was to shift the focus of pop art from Europe to America.

Douglas Christmas

Canadian-born Doug Christmas, 65, has been an art dealer since 1961. He has moved his operations from Vancouver to Los Angeles, from New York to Paris and Mexico City. At least that's what he claims. One thing is for sure. Christmas thrives on exhibiting huge contemporary artworks (and is considered a maverick for it) and his galleries certainly reflect that. His relationships with artists have been complex and tempestuous, best categorized as love/hate in nature.

In a field where lawsuits are everyday occurrences, the secretive, flamboyant Christmas may be the all time champ. According to a lengthy profile in *LA Weekly* in 2003, court records in Los Angeles show that Doug Christmas has been sued 55 times by artists, collectors, investors, landlords, service industries, former friends and other dealers. He has been sued under three different spellings of his last name and nine different business names. Since the early 1980s, Christmas has filed for bankruptcy on a regular basis. His problems are not only civil; Doug Christmas has also been dogged by criminal charges.

And that's only in LA.

Costco

Believe it or not, Costco, the big box retailer, has become an art dealer. Quick studies, one of the first thing they did was sell fake Picasso drawings on their website. The purchaser of the fake Picasso checked with 70-year-old Maya Widmaier-Picasso (the artist's daughter who authenticates Picasso's works). She stated the drawing sold by the giant retailer was a fake. Not only that, she said that the certificate of authenticity bearing her name was also a forgery.

Acting like they've been art dealers for decades, while continuing to deny that the 2005, $40,000 sale (and others) were fakes, Costco quietly removed certain other drawings and lithographs from their website. In conjunction with the denials, Costco pounded away at the fact that purchasers of fakes could receive a full refund of the purchase price, just as they can for toilet paper or bug spray. No questions asked. So why the denials?

Frank De Marigny

Manhattan Beach, Californis dealer Frank De Marigny tried to sell a fake Renoir to an undercover agent for $3,200,000. He pled no contest and was sentenced to 30 months in jail for the crime.

Charles Merrill Mount

Mount is a biographer of John Singer Sargent (1856–1925), Gilbert Stuart (1755–1828), and Monet. He is also a notorious thief who served time for stealing historical documents. In 1964, Mount placed a bundle of fake Sargeant watercolors for sale at Christie's. The works slid right through.

Paul Durand-Ruel

The Parisian was caught in 1902 with two fake Renoirs he was trying to sell. Renoir himself uncovered the forgeries.

Jerome Eisenberg

Owner of Royal-Athena Gallery in New York, Eisenberg admits to buying almost 30,000 Egyptian artifacts in the early 1960s. Of the 30,000, he says, only about eighty had a trustworthy provenance.

James Edward Little

Englishman James Little (1876–1953) forged and then sold Maon (Polynesian) artifacts that fooled scholars, museums and collectors in every part of the world. Little also forged the documentation of the fakes.

Little learned about the specialized artifacts by going to museums in England. Little came up with a pretty good scheme: He would steal the artifacts, replace them with fakes, and sell the originals. As his business grew (he would place advertisements in scholarly publications) he skipped the theft part and just forged the antiquities. The end came when Little botched a museum burglary and was sent to prison for theft.

David Ramus

Ramus had a short but volatile career as an art dealer. Ramus rode the art boom of the 1980s and got busted (along with the art market) in the 1990s. He served a year for interstate transportation of stolen art and has turned into a decent novelist. He wrote his first novel in 1994 "to exorcise demons," and wrote his second while in prison. Ramus makes a rare admission. "I failed miserably in the art world."

David Holland Swingler

David Swingler was a food importer, specializing in Italian goods. During his trips to Italy, ostensibly for his food business, Swingler would visit archeological sites and chat up the tomb raiders. Incredibly, it was that easy to buy looted artifacts. Swingler worked with an Italian partner, Lucio Di Luzio. Di Luzio would slip the looted artifacts in pasta containers he was sending Swingler from Italy to America.

The conspirators, who specialized in ancient vases, had a thriving business in the smuggled artifacts. But to Swingler's eternal chagrin, his partner made a typical but serious mistake: Di Luzio dumped his wife, Sandra. Incensed, Sandra went to the nearest police station and squealed on her husband to the Italian authorities. When the Italian police searched Lucio DiLuzio's home, they uncovered a cache of illegal artifacts in his basement.

In the early 1990s, when the US Customs officials searched David Swingler's home in Laguna Hills, California, they found 230 Apulian and Etruscan vases in the Orange County home. The antiquities have an estimated value of over $300,000. In 1996, David Swingler was sentenced (in absentia) by an Italian court to four years and eight months in prison. He was also fined. In 2000, the vases seized from Swingler's home (which date from 330 BC) were returned to Italy.

Want a laugh? The authorities also discovered Swingler was advertising his plundered antiquities for sale by placing advertisements on car windows under the windshield wipers in his neighborhood.

Julien Tavener

In 1990, Englishman Julien Tavener purchased Boston's redoubtable 90-year-old art gallery Haley & Steele. Tavener continued Haley & Steele's traditional art dealer business and also retained the firm's historic emphasis on rare prints.

In 2005, the 43-year-old Tavener was awarded a contract by the Friends of the Commonwealth Museum Foundation to produce and sell prints of three rare state-owned Paul Revere engravings. The sets were to sell for $1,200 each, with 75% of the proceeds to go to the Foundation. Tavener sold 182 sets of the prints, but made only a nominal payment to the foundation. Tavener pocketed the money, abruptly closed the gallery he had owned for 15 years, bundle up his wife and children, and skipped town under cover of darkness, abandoning his house, cars, business and life.

Scores of customers lost thousands of dollars (and artworks), their total losses have been estimated at $3,000,000 by investigating authorities. When reached at his brother's home in England, Julien Tavener insisted he would return to America someday to stand trial. And pigs can fly.

CHAPTER SIX
KINGS OF UNSCRUPULOUS DEALERS

Bernard Berenson & Joseph Duveen

If you interview a room of people who are knowledgeable about art and ask them who was the greatest art dealer of all time, 99% will answer Joseph Duveen (1869–1939). Ask that same group who was the most unscrupulous art dealer of all time, 99% will again answer Joseph Duveen. The group would be only half right. While Duveen was unscrupulous, compared to Bernard Berenson he looked like Saint Teresa.

In a great part due to Harvard University's spin doctors, Bernard Berenson (1865–1959) is referred to as "the eminent art historian and critic," or "a connoisseur of Italian art and arbiter of taste," or "the world's foremost expert on Italian Renaissance art," or "a collector for others," or even "the greatest humanist of the early 20th Century."

While Berenson could fairly claim some of these accolades, nobody categorizes him as an art dealer. They should. Because that is what Bernard Berenson was his entire adult life. An unscrupulous art dealer.

Berenson is one of the champion unscrupulous art dealers of all time for two basic reasons. First, his life was one huge lie, so his dealing takes on a pathetic dimension. Sort of like the little boy who commits a no-no and then hides behind his mother's skirts. Second, Berenson's secret attributions for over 30 years were instrumental in making his partner, Joe Duveen, the Number One art dealer in the world.

Bernhard Valvrojenski was born in Lithuania in 1865 to a Jewish family. His father changed the family name to Berenson and moved to Boston when Bernhard was nine-years-old. Young Bernhard, mother and family, followed the next year. The exceptionally bright Bernhard studied assiduously, graduating from Harvard in 1887. While at Harvard, in order to be accepted into the closed societies of Harvard and Boston, the socially ambitious, class conscious 20-year-old Berenson was baptized as an Episcopalian, the most acceptable label in Boston at that time. (When it was advantageous to him, Berenson even spouted anti-Semitic slogans.)

Anxious to keep his humble upbringing and Jewish heritage secret, in his school years Bernhard never once invited one friend or classmate to his family's modest home in the North End of Boston. Not once in a period of twelve years.

After moving to Italy in 1891, Berenson converted to Catholicism, the most acceptable label in Italy at that time, or any time. This move was a mere five years after his Episcopal conversion. (Always alert to anything that could help his persona, no matter how small, during World War I Berenson dropped the Germanic "H" from his first name: Bernhard Berenson became Bernard Berenson.)

In 1894 Berenson began publishing various studies on art, expanding on the writings of his hero, the Italian art connoisseur Giovanni Morelli (1816– 1891), who believed in the minute examination of a work, and gave much more attention to the smallest details than had previously been the case. Morelli believed that the identity of a painter could be determined by studying the unconscious or unimportant parts of a picture. He believed that ears, eyebrows and even ankles (places where the artist is generally not focusing) betray the artist's identity because the artist maintains consistency in these areas throughout his life. Morelli's system, which is much like handwriting analysis, became known as scientific connoisseurship.

Berenson read Morelli's book "Italian Pictures: Critical Studies of the Works in the Galleries of Munich and Dresden," sought out the master, picked his brain, and finally adopted Morelli's theories. And improved on them. Berenson became famous through his writings on this style of connoisseurship of art as well as through his categorizing of Italian Renaissance painters. His Lists became so celebrated they were referred to as The Four Gospels. Berenson was assisted in his major literary works by his lover, Mary Smith Costelloe (whom he married in 1900, after her husband died.) Mary was a respected writer of art history who often wrote under the pseudonym Mary Logan. Most observers say Mary wrote a good portion of the books Berenson is credited with, but there is no agreement among scholars on this point.

In 1894, Bernhard began advising Isabella Stewart Gardner, a Boston socialite he met in his Harvard days. Initially, Mrs. Gardner, the experienced collector, would tell the young, inexperienced Bernhard what to buy and he would acquire the painting for her in Italy. He received a 5% commission of the purchase price from Mrs. Gardner. In order to keep the price he paid for paintings as low as possible, Berenson's deal with Mrs. Gardner was a well-guarded secret when he negotiated for her. Since he was receiving a percentage of Mrs. Gardner's purchase price, however, it was in Berenson's best interests to make the price she paid him as high as possible. Berenson never told Mrs. Gardner what he paid for a painting, and whenever possible, he received a double-dipping commission from the art dealers from whom he purchased the work for her. Right from the start, Berenson urged inferior imitations and even fakes on Mrs. Gardner in order to obtain his coveted 5%.

As his celebrated eye developed, Berenson gradually was able to shift things around; he began recommending paintings to Mrs. Gardner, who usually took his advice. At this point, Berenson worked with various dealers, although most of the pieces (16 in all) were from Colnaghi's, an arrangement of which Mrs. Gardner disapproved. Since it was an advantageous relationship for him (he was also getting paid by Colnaghi's), Berenson disregarded her wishes and continued to deal with Colnaghi's.

As might be expected, when the disparity in price between what Berenson bought the painting for and what he charged Mrs. Gardner was discovered (or suspected), squabbles between the collector (who had a husband knowledgeable about art) and her advisor ensued. Berenson consistently, and smoothly, told Mrs. Gardner (and everyone else in his 70 years of dealing) that he had no financial stake in the deal at hand, but he always did. Worse, if he didn't stand to make money on a deal, Berenson would do his best to kill it.

One final note regarding Berenson's actions for Mrs. Gardner. If he couldn't deliver a work of art to her, he wouldn't get paid. At this time, Italy was attempting to keep its artistic treasures in the country. So what's a poor fellow to do? No problem. To insure his fee, Berenson, with the help of others, smuggled works out of Italy for Mrs. Gardner via England and/or Switzerland. Berenson's dealing for Mrs. Gardner helped in the establishment of The Isabella Stewart Gardner Museum in Boston, called Fenway Court. Of the 290 paintings in the Gardner Museum, Bernhard chose over 60, many of them acknowledged masterpieces. His writings and Fenway Court dealings established Berenson's reputation in America and Europe, and he was on his way to immortality.

In 1889, B.B. arrived in Florence, eventually renting Villa I Tatti, which was a short distance from town.

The first tipping point came in 1895, when Berenson was 30 years old. Berenson published an alternative catalogue for an exhibition of Venetian paintings being held in London at the New Gallery on Regent Street. He was smart enough to know that he needed scholarly credentials to achieve the personal recognition and acclaim he craved. Berenson was familiar with all of the 300 works in the show, so he was able to produce his catalogue and make it available for distribution only a few days after the exhibition opened. Berenson's catalogue was a bombshell.

Going right for the jugular, in commanding and imperious language, Berenson challenged almost every attribution in the exhibition. For example, he said that of the 33 Titians, only one was by the master, and of the 21 paintings attributed to Veronese, none were by him. And so on. Displaying an innate sense of public relations, instead of writing only negative comments, Berenson brilliantly reattributed all of the works in the exhibition, at least wherever he felt that was possible. Berenson's bold maneuver was the talk of the art world and established him as the authority on Italian Renaissance paintings. The incident caught the eye of Joe Duveen, who ordered his people to make an in-depth investigation into Berenson's life.

It was in I Tatti that B.B. hit his stride: He had a supportive wife, a brilliant and understanding live-in lover, a beautiful villa overlooking Florence, and a growing reputation as the Number One art connoisseur in the world supplanting the German, Wilhelm von Bode, who believed in the now obsolete, heavily theoretical, strict academic approach to authentication.

One thing was missing: Money. For the lifestyle B.B. craved, he needed lots and lots of money. Enter Joe Duveen. In 1906, Duveen was introduced to Berenson by Lady Sassoon, one of a life-long string of Berenson lovers. Duveen (who had done his homework) hired Berenson on a handshake. (At this time, Berenson was taking secret commissions from Agnew's for recommending their paintings to purchasers.)

Duveen's instincts were golden. Berenson was a perfect fit. As was the case with most of the robber barons of the era, timing and luck played a significant part in both lives.

Duveen, a dealer who was born into his family's art business, had purchased several first-class collections that included numerous Italian paintings. Duveen needed someone to authenticate these works, as well as someone to unearth other Italian paintings he could sell. Duveen knew that Berenson had an impeccable reputation as a connoisseur of Italian Renaissance paintings, and learned that Berenson had made it his business to know where in Italy the art was located. Duveen had also discovered that Berenson was an unusually greedy man who needed tons of money to lead the life-style he dreamed about.

Bernard Berenson and Joe Duveen were made for each other. Both men were vain and had gigantic egos; both were obsessed with the art business; both were avaricious and desperate for personal recognition and acceptance in society. And, they both played the art world like symphonies, reveling in the field's almost paranoid need for secrecy.

Duveen knew a good thing when he saw it, so informality flew out the window. Anxious to place Berenson under his control, in 1907 Duveen offered Berenson a five-year written deal. This initial written agreement provided for Berenson to authenticate paintings Duveen owned. In return, he would receive 10% of the profits (twice what Mrs. Gardner paid him) of any painting sold that he had authenticated. Berenson was to work exclusively for Duveen, and secrecy was demanded. This contract gave B.B. (who was constantly in need of more and more money) so much confidence he began negotiations to purchase his beloved Villa I Tatti.

Within a year, because of Duveen's constant pressure, Berenson was working full time for Duveen. (Or so Duveen thought: B.B., as always had secret side deals.) B.B. had switched sides. Now, instead of secretly representing the purchaser (Mrs. Gardner), he secretly represented the seller (Duveen). Suddenly, his standards slackened. Some old attributions were changed from a lesser to a greater hand. Optimism now ruled. Example: At Duveen's request, Berenson labeled so many paintings Bellini Duveen was selling them in quantity, and once boasted to a client, "I can assure you that the stock of Giovanni Bellinis is absolutely inexhaustible."

The contentious secret deal lasted some 30 years and was immensely profitable for both Duveen and Berenson (who took in tens of millions of dollars from Duveen in that period). Inevitably (remember, we're talking about art dealers here) the terms of the deal changed numerous times. Berenson pressed his advantage whenever Duveen demanded a higher attribution. By 1912, Duveen was so dependent upon Berenson and his attributions, he agreed to pay Berenson a phenomenal 25% of the net profits on all Italian works that were bought by collectors based on his attributions, plus an annual retainer.

Berenson was worth every cent because he was a money machine for Duveen. From wherever he was in the world, Duveen would send Berenson photographs of paintings. Without seeing the actual paintings, B.B. would scribble his comments on the back of the photos (which were mostly in black and white), sign and return them. Duveen then used these Berenson authentications as certificates of authenticity to make his sales.

All was not smooth in those salad days however. For one thing, Duveen continuously badgered Berenson to write articles for prestigious publications which were favorable to his inventory. The larger-than-life Duveen bullied B.B., pressing for the highest possible attribution because the greater and rarer the master, the more the painting would fetch. The highest possible price was advantageous to both parties so B.B. routinely obliged. Example: Duveen would demand B.B. label a painting a rare Giorgione instead of a painting by his prolific student Titian.

Because their styles were so different, the reserved Berenson and the out-going Duveen disliked each other on a personal basis. Deep down, Duveen felt he owned Berenson (which in a way he did), while Berenson blamed Duveen for being the devil who fueled his sinking deeper and deeper into a big, black hell hole of deceit, out of which, as the years flew by, he saw less and less chance of escaping. Since both parties were getting filthy rich from the scheme, however, they got along, finally using intermediaries to communicate.

A secret ledger, the X Book, was established by Duveen to keep track of the paintings he sold based on Berenson's attributions. Both parties were extremely busy. For example, in 1926 there were 242 paintings listed in the X Book of which 173 had been sold. In true art dealer fashion, however, neither party trusted the other. Berenson was confident that Duveen was not acknowledging all of the sales his attributions were responsible for, and Duveen was equally confident that Berenson wasn't working exclusively for him, which was a condition of the deal. Both were right.

In 1928 Berenson negotiated a new five-year agreement with Duveen, which, as always, was even better than the previous one. In addition to a retainer and other payments, Berenson was now to be paid 10% of all purchases Duveen made on Berenson's recommendation. Got that? Berenson was to be paid whether or not Duveen sold the paintings he recommended. That's a hustler hustling a hustler.

In the art industry, where snobbery reigns supreme, Berenson had all of the tools to rise to the top. Berenson was slim and handsome with delicate features, always impeccably groomed, well mannered, well read, fluent in a handful of languages, a brilliant conversationalist and wit. He was arrogant, but charmingly arrogant. He spoke English with a practiced accent. In addition to being a social snob, B.B. was an intellectual snob, who felt his method of judging paintings was the only valid one. B.B. was also imperious, considering ordinary mortals beneath him and made it a point all of his life to only deal with individuals who were in a position to help him in some way. If that changed, or they crossed him (say with a critical article), he dumped them.

Even Berenson's many lovers and mistresses were selected for what they could do for him. Most of his life he flaunted his amorous escapades (even to his wife, who reciprocated in kind), but he was much more discreet when he was young. Example: From 1908 to 1912, B.B.'s tumultuous four-year affair with the mysterious and glamorous Bella da Costa Greene was kept secret by both parties so her boss wouldn't be angered and turn on B.B. After all, Greene was the curator of rare books and manuscripts in the library of J.P. Morgan. Berenson's long-time secretary, assistant and lover at I Tatti, Nicky Mariano, was, in many ways, more influential to him than his wife.

With this inherent instinct of courting the right people (plus a lifetime of practice), B.B. made his magnificent residence just outside of Florence, Villa I Tatti, the place where intellectuals gathered in Europe. And Berenson knew how to play the role and enhance his façade in his sumptuous Italian villa. He entertained creative, titled and wealthy people, always making an entrance at his nightly dinner parties at just the right moment (for example), dressed to the nines in dinner jacket and boutonniére. When he entered the room, his very presence (abetted by both his secretary/lover and wife) caused the guests to rise in his honor. Lord of the Manor. Above the fray.

Berenson was as clever and duplicitous as Duveen in the politics of dealing in art, and in the politics of life as a surreptitious dealer. Consider: Count Alessandro Contini-Bonacossi (1878-1955) was a collector/ dealer whom Berenson artfully dodged when first approached for attributions. But then the Count became more influential as a dealer. Berenson saw him begin to sell millionaire collector Samuel H. Kress various works of art in 1927, so he took the Count on as a client and began authenticating his paintings, many of which were fakes. (Joe Duveen eventually got Kress as a client and sold him the bulk of his collection, which totaled an astounding 3,210 artworks.) If the name sounds familiar, it's because Count Contini-Bonacossi is the Italian art dealer who sold Hermann Goering (Hitler's right-hand man) Italian art treasures. Approximately 50 pieces were confirmed to have been a part of the Count's secret arrangement with the Nazis. After World War II, Berenson testified as a character witness for the Count before the commission investigating his dealings with the Nazis. Contini-Bonacossi used his business partner Berenson's script when interrogated by the Allies: "I'm not a dealer," he insisted. "I'm a connoisseur."

In 1895 (those heady, Pre-Duveen days), Berenson wrote that Giorgione's "Portrait of a Man" (the so-called "Ariosto") was in "deplorably bad preservation." About 1912 (Post-Duveen), some 17 years later, the very same painting was, he wrote, "in a miraculously fine state." Based on Berenson's updated attribution, Duveen now was able to sell the painting to collector Benjamin Altman for an elevated price.

Joseph Duveen became sick with cancer in 1934; the partnership blew up in 1937 over an attribution. Duveen died two years later. After the split, Berenson moved right on, establishing (continuing) a relationship with the Wildenstein Gallery, and others. He continued dealing for 22 more years until his death in 1959, ruling on some 1,000 paintings for Wildenstein between the time of the split with Duveen in 1937 and his death in 1959.

Under the circumstances, it's axiomatic that the survival rate of Berenson's attributions borders on the abysmal. For example, experts now say that of the 20 Bellinis he authenticated, only half are considered autograph works. Worse, of the 17 Titians, only four are so considered.

In a class report sent to Harvard in 1897, Berenson described himself as "a disinterested scholar and aesthete," but the reality was that even at this early age he was an art dealer working hard for the almighty buck. AESTHETE: One having appreciation of, responsiveness to, or zealousness of the beautiful. Berenson's beautiful dream: Beauty for beauty's sake.

Hiding his dealings (just as he hid his heritage), B.B. advanced this aesthete and gentleman scholar myth all of his life: This is the big lie that made Berenson a legend in his own time. Whether in denial or just a congenital liar, or both, Berenson never, ever, referred to his secret, tension filled 30+ year deal with Duveen, even when talking or writing to close friends.

George Santayana (1863–1952), who knew Berenson from their days together at Harvard, after meeting with B.B. in his later years, offered this caustic take on his life-long acquaintance, " . . . I can't help feeling that it [his continued enthusiasm in art] was lighted and is kept going by forced draught, by social and intellectual ambition and by professional pedantry."

Near the end of his life, like many before him, B.B. confronted himself. He became melancholy and jotted down some observations of his behavior, insufferable and otherwise, in a slight volume entitled "Sketch for a self-portrait." "I soon discovered that I ranked [with the public]," he wrote, "with fortune tellers . . . astrologers . . . and not even with the self-diluted of these, but rather with the deliberative charlatans. Yet I repeat that I took the wrong turn when I swerved from more purely intellectual pursuits to one like the archaeological study of art, gaining thereby a troublesome reputation as an expert. My only excuse is . . . I needed a means of livelihood."

Bernard Berenson never acknowledged (even in his advanced years, even to himself) that he had been dealing for his entire lifetime. "I wasn't an art dealer, I was a connoisseur." Rene Gimpel, the Parisian art dealer and Berenson's brother in law (he married B.B.'s sister Florence), knew Berenson intimately and saw things differently. In his now famous diary Gimpel wrote, "I went to see Berenson at the Ritz, at ten in the morning. He was laying down, a manicurist was with him; but she'll never round off those claws." (Gimpel also wrote that France had a system of experts associated with the major auction houses who provided fake certificates of authenticity on a regular basis, as needed.) Displaying a rare lack of common sense, in 1922 Berenson tried to sell Gimpel a number of fakes. No sale.

Bottom line? Lord Kenneth Clark, one of England's (and the world's) most revered art historians and Berenson prodigy (almost) let Berenson off the hook when he wrote, "And then we may charitably suppose that when he began working for dealers, Berenson did not realize what kind of jungle he was entering . . . He could not have foreseen the density of the forest, the hidden pitfalls and the poisonous tendrils that were to enmesh him and make freedom of action almost impossible." Clark added, "The fact is that for about 40 years after 1900 he [Berenson] did practically nothing except authenticate."

In 1959 (two months after B.B's death), after equivocating for a full 20 years, Harvard accepted Berenson's gift of Villa I Tatti, its grounds and out buildings, its remarkable contents of period furniture, its art, its library and its fototeca. Today the villa is known as the Harvard University Center for Italian Renaissance Studies and is renowned as the premier facility of its kind in the world. Nowhere in Harvard's extensive and beautifully prepared publications regarding Berenson and Villa I Tatti is Joseph Duveen even mentioned.

The Harvard University Press did publish two well-researched, excellently written books by award winning author Ernest Samuels. Sadly, the volumes subtly skewer Duveen and glorify Berenson. In 1987, the legendary writer John Updike defended Berenson when he reviewed "Artful Partners" by Colin Simpson and one of Samuels' books on Berenson. Here's a big surprise: Updike went to Harvard.

Who was this Joseph Duveen everyone calls the greatest, most spectacular, most famous art dealer of all time? Who would know better than Bernard Berenson? After Duveen died, here's what B.B. said, conveniently disregarding the fact that he was Duveen's partner for 30+ years: "Duveen was at the center of a vast nexus of corruption that reached from the lowliest employee of the British Museum right up to the King."

Joseph Duveen was born in Hull, England in 1869 to a family that was in the antiques business. As a youth Joe learned the business from his father and uncles. He also learned some of his most helpful lessons from them. He was taught that information is not only valuable, it is worth paying for; always offer to buy back a work of art for the same price you sold it for, minus ten percent; never hesitate to give your multi-millionaire (billionaires in today's money) clients credit with no time limit. And, finally, price is not consequential to the American robber barons if they feel they are getting something extra for their money, something that is significant, or they think is significant, to their lives.

At the turn of the last century, Joe Duveen was sent to work with his uncle Henry in the firm's New York office. (Henry Duveen had arrived in New York in 1886.) S.N. Berhman famously observed, "Early on, Duveen noticed that Europe had plenty of art and America had plenty of money." Joe Duveen figured out how to connect the dots. The first thing he did when he arrived in New York was concentrate on paintings, where the big money was. He opened a new, sumptuous gallery in a swankier location, and displayed the paintings with velvet and muted lighting.

Duveen courted the rich and famous with zeal matched only by Berenson. He knew instinctively how their minds worked. For example, he took to explaining to his clients that even though they were multi-billionaires, they could never be a part of nobility, due to the unfortunate structure of America's political system. But, Duveen would stress, even though they lacked tradition and family renown, by buying family portraits and other works of art that belonged for centuries to British nobility and the nobility of Europe (the Renaissance in particular), they could, in essence, become Lords and Ladies themselves. And thereby achieve immortality.

To put it another way, Duveen knew instinctively that these billionaires saw themselves as America's aristocracy (and in a way they were.) He would patiently explain that there was no better way to align themselves with European aristocracy than to hang the paintings of real aristocracy on the walls of their various mansions. In essence, Duveen convinced his robber barons that their social status was more meaningful than money.

On the other side of the Atlantic, in Europe, Duveen knew how to exploit the snobbishness of the nobility. He was truly a great judge of character (and therefore a great salesman) who understood the psychology of both his billionaire buyers and noble sellers better than anyone before or since. Lord Kenneth Clark, talking about the cherubic-looking, robust Duveen, who had a florid complexion, full lips and a natty mustache, said it beautifully when he wrote, "He [Duveen] was irresistible. His bravura and impudence were infectious, and when he was present everyone behaved as if they had had a couple of drinks. He worked entirely by instinct . . . and he had rightly seen that, whereas in America it paid him to be very grand, in England he could get further by bribing the upper classes and playing the fool."

Duveen Brothers tried every imaginable tactic to corner the market on Old Masters. Joe was able to eventually accomplish this monumental goal in the 1920's, but there were bumps along the way, such as the famous Duveen Brothers smuggling case of 1910. The United States Government charged Henry Duveen with defrauding the US by undervaluing great works of art by as much as 90%. Henry had finagled the position as the official in the US Customs Office in New York City charged with the responsibility of evaluating art that came through the port. When Duveen Brothers works came through, Henry placed a ridiculously low value on them, and when his competitor's art-works came through, he placed sky-high valuations on them. The court fined Henry Duveen $1,400,000, which the firm did not have. J. P. Morgan, a client of Duveen Brothers, paid the fine, which settled the case. Joe Duveen's fingerprints were all over the caper.

In 1908 Joe's father died and he inherited 15% of the stock of the family business and a substantial sum of money. From then on, and for 31 years until he died in 1939, even while his uncle Henry was the technical head of Duveen Brothers with 35% of the stock, Joe was the real power. He solidified his position when his Uncle Henry died in 1918. Duveen purchased his uncle's shares and forced the other Duveens to sell their stock to him, keeping several family members on as salaried employees. When one of the family wanted to go into the art business, Joe wouldn't allow him to use the Duveen name.

Why is there no Duveen Brothers art gallery today? Joe wouldn't allow it. "I don't want any Duveen to come after me," he once said. After Duveen's death the company was sold lock, stock, and barrel to Norton Simon in 1964. What did the others in the family think of Joe Duveen? Discussing his cousin, Jack Duveen said, "with Joe the end justified all and every means." What were some of these all and every means?

Duveen created an intelligence network that countries envied. Through his employee, Bertram Boggis, he bribed every level of servant his clients and potential clients had. Housekeepers, maids, chauffeurs, butlers, chefs, elevator operators and secretaries in homes and hotels all over the world were on Duveen's payroll. The art critic, A.C.R Carter was practically the official mouthpiece of Duveen. The stratagem paid off in spades.

Duveen also had a coterie of restorers on his payroll. Their primary job was to make the paintings look nice for his guileless American clients. Many times restoring evolved into out-and-out fakery. In addition to selling fakes (Duveen sold banker Jules Bache [1861–1944] a fake Bellini's, a fake Botticelli and a fake Vermeer), repeated smuggling, the bribing of auctioneers and custom officials was routine for Duveen.

When Duveen saw, or was asked about, a rival dealer's painting, he would sniff and call it a copy, fake and fraud without hesitation: "I smell fresh paint." This tactic often resulted in expensive lawsuits, but Duveen seemed to revel in the action.

In the late 1920s, Duveen called two of con man/collector Carl Hamilton's paintings "worthless, retouched, ruined," before their auction. Duveen was such a famed presence in the art world, his comments killed the value of the della Francesca and Lippi paintings. What motivated Duveen? Through a middleman, Duveen bought the two paintings for a song.

When the prolific and talented Sienese forger Joni's autobiography was translated into English in 1936, Duveen bought and destroyed all of the copies he and his associates were able to get their hands on because there were allegations in the book that his secret partner Bernard Berenson bought and sold fakes. Berenson's name did not appear in the book. On the other hand, Duveen secretly subsidized many of Berenson's publications.

Duveen would do anything for a client, including lying under oath for him in court. At the well-known Andrew W. Mellon (1855–1937) tax fraud case in 1934, the Government claimed Mellon owed over $3,000,000 in back taxes and penalties for artworks he had bought for his own personal pleasure. Duveen won the case for his client by testifying that Mellon bought the paintings with the intention of donating them to a public gallery in Washington, which he and his client had (supposedly) been planning for years. The National Gallery in Washington is the happy result of Duveen's chicanery.

In another famous case, Mrs. Andre Hahn sued Duveen for saying her Leonardo da Vinci "La Belle Ferroniere" was "a fake, a copy like hundred of others." Duveen was so powerful in the art world, his comment killed the value of Mrs. Hahn's painting. Duveen maintained the original was in the Louvre Museum in Paris. At the hearing, Duveen admitted he had never seen Mrs. Hahn's painting, only a photograph.

Berenson had previously (Pre-Duveen) written that, "The Louvre's painting of 'La Belle Ferroniere' showed absolutely no traces of Leonardo da Vinci's authorship." At the trial however (testifying in Duveen's defense), Berenson flip-flopped and maintained that the Louvre painting was the original and Mrs. Hahn's painting a mere copy. Berenson, under intense cross examination, was forced to admit publicly for the first time that he was on Duveen's payroll. Duveen settled out of court.

The Duveen Brother's organization was so secretive and complex it consisted, among other things, of multiple sets of books and code names which they used in correspondence and cables. Bernard Berenson, to his chagrin, was given the code name Doris, which provides a good indication of what the Duveens thought of B.B. For his part, Berenson felt that dealers were below him intellectually and should, at best, be merely tolerated. While this assertion contained a grain of truth, the fact that Berenson repeatedly said this publicly made many enemies for him.

In addition to having all of the con man's traits, the cherubic-looking Duveen was always perfectly tailored, even though he was on the portly side. He labored as hard at seducing rich people for friends as he did for selling them masterworks, so he had a client list that reads like a combination of who's who and the social registry in America at the turn of the last century. A small sampling: Benjamin Altman, the Department Store mogul; Jules Bache, the banker and financier; Mrs. Anna Dodge, heiress to the automobile fortune and the richest woman in America; Henry Clay Frick, the coal and steel (and notorious anti-labor) baron; railroad mogul H. E. Huntington, his nephew, Collis P. Huntington, and his wife Arabella, who married both; Samuel H. Kress, of five-and-ten-cent store fame; Andrew W. Mellon and his son Paul Mellon, the bankers; J. P. Morgan, the banker; Margaret Merriweather Post, the Post cereal heiress, who stated, "Joseph Duveen was the most important man in my life besides my father"; and The Wideners, who owned all of the streetcars in Philadelphia.

Duveen occasionally worked the other side of the Atlantic. He sold Arthur Lee, an obnoxious self-made English collector, a ton of paintings, almost all of which were fakes. Duveen once appealed to Berenson to attribute a dozen questionable paintings after he had made the sale. B.B. complied. At racetracks and roulette tables this is called past-posting, and, to put it mildly, is frowned upon.

Fortunately for Duveen and his billionaire collectors, Congress passed the Payne-Aldrich Tariff Act, which abolished the 20% import duty on works of art coming into America. As if in answer to Duveen's promise of immortality (and at Duveen's nudging), many of these art collections became the basis for museums across America.

Joseph Duveen was a generous man, as long as it served his ambition. He made numerous donations of paintings and money to the art museums of London and was made a baron in 1933, choosing the title Lord Duveen of Millbank. Duveen was a Trustee of the National Gallery in London (as well as numerous other art organizations in England), but was denied reelection because of conflicts of interest. Selling paintings that one owns to the institution on whose board one sits was considered an inexcusable no-no by the then director, Kenneth Clark.

Putting aside his nefarious tactics, what Joseph Duveen accomplished in the world of art has never been equaled. Why? Duveen moved more Old Masters from Europe to America than all of the other dealers combined.

As they say in baking, timing is everything. Duveen reached his maturity at the precise time America's robber barons were reaching their financial and social pinnacles.

The last word about these two colorful, hard working scoundrels (Duveen crossed the Atlantic by boat over 100 times) goes to Peter Lathan, who observed that Joseph Duveen and Bernard Berenson were, "Two ruthlessly unpleasant men who deserved each other."

CHAPTER SEVEN
UNSCRUPULOUS AUCTIONS & AUCTION HOUSES

When people buy [at auction] they are making their purchase
in pursuit of some extra validation for themselves,
[and] it is the newly rich who tend to crave
this validation more urgently than others.

— Robert Lacey

There's so much monkey business going on in auction sales
that nobody knows what has been sold, what are the reserves,
what are the conditions . . . One has to check every sale.

— Frank Lloyd

Since auction houses were established over 250 years ago, they have honed their skill of fleecing the public in innumerable ways. One little known but effective maneuver is to work with rings. Dealers get together and agree not to bid against each other for a lot, designating one member of the ring to buy the piece in at a fraction of its true value. Afterwards, usually at a pub, a second auction is held. The second winner of the private auction gets the work he wanted, and the original auction winner then splits the new money he receives (from the winner of the private auction) with the other members of the ring. What does this have to do with auction houses?

Rings almost always operate with the cooperation of auction houses, which use a number of tactics to pick up extra dollars from the ring for their cooperation. One trick is to omit the ring's designated piece from the auction catalogue and then introduce it at the sale as an additional lot. In other moves, the designated piece might be hung in a dark, inaccessible place, and sometimes the special piece is even "temporarily withdrawn" from the preview. Rings were made illegal in England in 1928, and are also illegal in America. They now operate underground and are most prevalent at small, country auctions.

Auction houses have many tricks. For example, say a naïve seller brings in what the auction house knows is a valuable artwork. Instead of notifying the customer, they place it in a different category. For example they might put a painting into the furniture group, and then label it broadly, say "Portrait, Italian School." The auctioneer then buys the piece for the low estimate. After a discreet amount of time (so the seller is less likely to catch on) the auction house sells the precious item at an enormous profit.

Auction houses have historically been guilty of what is called "chandelier bidding," which is a series of imaginary (phantom) bids placed by the auctioneer to raise the price of the item being auctioned. In these cases the seller wins (receiving a higher price) and the auction house wins (receiving a higher commission.) The buyer is the loser.

Since the advent of reserves, which is the secret price below which the work will not be sold, chandelier bidding is used to get the bidding up to the reserve. If the tactic is unsuccessful and the bids don't make it up to the reserve, don't fret for the auction houses, they never admit failure. The auctioneer will say something like, "sold to Mister X," using a name similar to that of a real client.

Auction houses have begun to employ a new tactic called third party guarantees. A dealer agrees to place the first (or multiple) bid in exchange for a lesser commission if he wins the piece. This gives the dealer (and the auction house, if they have given a guarantee) a financial edge over ordinary bidders and also skewers the reported price.

Other auction house scams include: colluding in smuggling items (using false identities, secret bank accounts, off-shore arrangements, and bribery) by moving items to branches most likely to produce the highest price, regardless of the law; collusion between auctioneer and bidder; giving potential clients super-high estimates regarding their potential consignments and then lowering the figure just before the sale; having a financial stake in the work without informing the bidders (or sellers) of their ownership position and therefore their conflict of interest; laundering money by turning a blind eye to cash transactions; placing low presale estimates on works to attract potential buyers who hope to snare a bargain; placing maximum imaginable prices on paintings to maintain the image of its market value (and to tempt the owner to sell); placing a valuable item into a mundane collection; pretending their catalogues are labors of scholarship instead of sales pieces; returning fakes (when exposed) to the seller, not the police; salting important lots with inferior items; selling fakes, either not caring about their provenance or not bothering to conduct a proper check; selling illegally plundered and smuggled items (since 1965, Sotheby's has sold over 2,000 Apulian vases, 85% of which were undocumented); shill bidding; substituting merchandise of lesser value into a lot after the sale; the quick knockdown by the auctioneer; undisclosed conditions that relate to both buyers and sellers; and, perhaps, most egregious of all, turning art into a market commodity (and nothing more).

There are hundreds of auction houses in the world, but the only two that really count are Christie's and Sotheby's. That's why their commission rigging was such a monster news story, and why their sins, even their peccadilloes, are so important.

CRIME & PUNISHMENT AT THE TOP

Christie's & Sotheby's

Sotheby's was founded in 1744 in London, while Christie's was founded in 1766, also in London. Originally, both houses were rather pedestrian affairs, used by sellers of merchandise as a last resort.

There is disagreement when this all changed, and auction houses became the place to sell important possessions. Whatever the year, by adding a snobby social aspect to the business of buying art (both society and the newly rich love to wear gowns and black ties) the cleverly structured role of Sotheby's and Christie's as social arbiters, as well as art connoisseurs, was enthusiastically embraced by collectors all over the world.

Over the years, both auction houses have been guilty of illegal activities. A few examples include Peter Wilson, the suave ex-head of Sotheby's, used inside information to sell his personal items at auction at inflated prices. Wilson also personally purchased pieces of the priceless looted and smuggled Roman silver service (known as the SEVSO Silver), and then, after the purchase, bought fake provenance from a dealer in Lebanon. (Speaking of inside information, when Sotheby's went public in 1977, insider trading was rampant.)

In 1997, following Peter Watson's expose in a book and on television, Sotheby's closed down its antiquities department in London, thereby admitting, in effect, that it was selling plundered and looted antiquities. Watson's evidence was largely gathered from disgruntled employee James Hodges, who was the administrator of Sotheby's antiquities department. By virtue of his position, Hodges had all of the relevant paperwork under his control. In addition, the hard-hitting investigating journalist wired a lady (who pretended that she had a painting she wanted to sell) for a meeting with Roeland Kollewijn, Sotheby's Old Master expert in Milan. Kollewijn told the potential customer that more money could be made by all parties if the painting was sold in London, and explained that he routinely smuggled artworks to London through Switzerland. "They [the bosses] don't want me to do it, but they want me to do it," he said into the hidden microphone, adding, "If I were in power, I would arrest the whole lot here."

In 2002, Sotheby's (and the owner of a Rubens' painting named "The Massacre of the Innocents") claimed to Austrian authorities that the painting was a mere bagatelle. At a subsequent London auction, the mere bagatelle sold for $117,000,000, more or less, depending on the exchange rate. The Austrian authorities are investigating.

In the 2005 an Italian court found Giacomo Medici, long considered the king-pin of the multi-billion dollar antiquity smuggling trade, guilty of receiving and exporting stolen antiquities. Judge Mutoni said, "selling and re-buying the same artifacts [at auction], Medici and his associates were able to trade in 'clean' works of art, sellable to whomever they wanted at the prices they themselves set at auction." Why the extensive laundering? It is done to prove that the items were bought on the open market, thereby giving them a respectful provenance, and a so-called fair market price. The judge also said (among other things) that Medici sold hundreds of stolen Italian antiquities at Sotheby's "thanks to the absolute absence of controls on the part of the auction house and the complicity offered by its employees." When Felicity Nicholson, controversial head of antiquities for Sotheby's, was questioned about this, she purred, "We assume our clients have title to whatever it is they are selling."

Both Christie's and Sotheby's have sold fakes over the centuries, many of which were, in auction house double-speak, "clumsy." In 1981, David Bathurst, chairman of Christie's International, after a disappointing sale in New York falsely claimed that two masterpieces had sold for millions of dollars, although they remained unsold. Following up on tips, the Department of Consumer Affairs investigated and a settlement resulted in a fine and banning Bathurst from conducting auctions for two years. In 1992, John Block, head of Sotheby's jewelry department, and Francois Curiel, his counterpart at Christie's, initiated a price fixing scheme.

In 2000, Sotheby's sold a fake del Sarto painting without giving notice in its catalogue, or otherwise, that there were challenges to the works authenticity, challenges the auction house knew all about but chose to ignore. Also in 2000, workers at Sotheby's accidentally destroyed a painting by Lucien Freud (born in Berlin in 1922), thinking its protective wooden case was empty. The auction house placed a value of $240,000 on the painting and agreed to reimburse the consignor for that amount. Sounds good, right? The problem is that art experts cried foul, pointing out, among other evidence, that a Lucien Freud was sold for $1,600,000.

In a similar case, in 2001 Christie's appraised a painting by the master Ludovico Carracci (1555–1619) for the paltry sum of $15,000. Shortly thereafter, a subsequent purchaser put the work up for auction at Christie's. The painting was hammered down for a whopping $5,200,000 to the Met.

The fact that auction houses have begun operating like banks, no, make that pawn shops, is particularly worrisome. The auction houses are loaning money to selected bidders of the art they are auctioning, making them partners with those bidders. Yes, the auctioneers are hawking their own artworks to themselves. but since there is, in essence, no disclosure, the other bidders don't know about this blatant conflict of interest. In this connection, the high profile Alan Bond and Japanese cases shook the art world.

Alan Bond

Seventy-one-year-old Australian Alan Bond was one of the art world's most famous collectors. Bond's fame came knocking in 1987 when he paid a record $49,000,000 at a Sotheby's auction for van Gogh's "Blue Iris," gaining a huge commission for the auction house and establishing the price for future van Gogh sales. Word leaked out that Sotheby's, without disclosing the fact, had loaned Bond half of the purchase price. Worse, the painting that Bond made famous was not purchased with his money but with money diverted from a public company. Worse yet, Bond then turned around and sold the painting, diverting the receipts to one of his personal companies.

This was not Bond's only fraud. In 1983, Bond bought Manet's "La Promenade" through one of his private companies. He then leased the painting to one of his public companies for $100,000 per month for five years, pocketing over $1,000,000. The fall of the Australian entrepreneur, who became a national hero when he won the America's Cup in 1983, was complete when he pled guilty in 1997 to defrauding Bell Resources out of $1,200,000,000. Alan Bond, whose empire ranged from breweries to hotels, gold mines to newspapers (and just about everything in between) served a little over three years of his four year jail sentence. He was released from prison in 2000. When Bond went belly-up, the auction house repossessed the van Gogh.

Also in 1987, the Yasuda Fire and Marine Company of Tokyo paid approximately $40,000,000 for one of van Gogh's Sunflower paintings, and in 1990, another Japanese, Saito Ryvei, paid over $82,000,000 at a Christie's auction for van Gogh's "Portrait of Doctor Gachet." Both paintings were repossessed when their owners went bankrupt. Yes, three of the world's most expensive paintings were repossessed. Between 1984 and 1992, of the top 20 Japanese buyers (who had spent between $20,000,000 and $100,000,000), 17 were either bankrupt, in jail, or under intense investigation. This is of no concern to the auction houses: They don't check things out because they don't want to know. Establishing record prices for artworks and reaping commissions from subsequent sales is the name of their game.

One last example. In 2007, Christie's was forced to withdraw a glazed ceramic sculpture from auction because the Turner Prize-winning artist, Grayson Perry (born in 1960 in England), said the piece was a fake of his work. Christie's claimed they had vetted the work extensively, but it turned out the auction house never checked with the 47-year-old artist, who was alive and well.

The most outrageous action of all was the Sotheby's/Christie's price fixing scandal. To understand the art world's most famous crime, one needs to go back to 1975, when Christie's announced to a disbelieving public that it would henceforth charge a 10% commission to buyers, whereas for hundreds of years their income consisted solely of commissions paid by sellers. Three days later, Sotheby's followed suit. The charge to buyers combined with the suspicious timing, raised an uproar in England, which at that time was the center of the art auction business. Dealers were incensed and sued. The British government investigated. The dealers and auctions houses settled, as they say, on the courthouse steps, and the government was satisfied with a small fine.

Not only did the unprecedented action completely change the dynamics of the auction business, the actions of the UK authorities vividly demonstrated that collusion is no big deal in England. Unfortunately for Sotheby's and Christie's, collusion to set prices and restrain trade are a very big deal in America.

In 1983, Alfred Taubman, born in 1924, the billionaire king of regional, covered shopping malls, bought control of Sotheby's. At the end of 1992, Sir Anthony Tennant was made chairman of Christie's International. In 1993, the two moguls began a series of 12 confidential meetings, with no one else present at the sessions. At these meetings, Taubman and Tennant agreed to stop waiving seller's fees to obtain the seller's business, to establish a sliding scale of seller's fees that would be non-negotiable, and to not compete with each other for major client's consignments. The bosses instructed their respective presidents to work out the details.

Sotheby's hired gun was Diana "Dede" Brooks, a five-foot ten-inch competitive (read ruthless) and competent WASP, who was in her forties and had risen through the ranks at Sotheby's through hard work and adroit moves. Dede Brooks was Taubman's prodigy and the first woman to run a major auction house, no mean accomplishment. Christie's gunslinger was Christopher Davidge, a clever man in his late forties, who had clawed his way, through hard work and blistering tactics, from humble beginnings to the top of Christie's, which was a classic English snobby good-old-boys club at the time. Also no mean accomplishment.

The pair started meeting in 1993, and did their work well, although satisfying their bosses without raising the suspicions of others in their companies took time. Unknown to Brooks, Davidge was keeping written records of his illicit meetings with her, documents that would one day destroy her fairytale life. By 1995, the deals were hammered out and Christie's announced a non-negotiable scale of fees for sellers. Sotheby's followed.

It wasn't long until law suits, claiming collusion, started to fly. The flurry of lawsuits caught the eye of the United States Justice Department, which started an investigation. The lengthy investigation was plodding along until a nervous Christie's fired Davidge in 1999. In retaliation, and to save his own hide, Davidge turned a bushel of documents over to his attorney. These were incendiary documents that, taken together, spelled out the scheme of collusion. In one of the smartest moves in criminal justice history, Ed Dolman, the new president of Christie's, threw the documents and company to the mercy of the US Justice Department, which granted Christie's immunity in exchange for the documents and Davidge's testimony for the prosecution.

In 2000, Taubman and Brooks retired from their positions at Sotheby's. In a plea agreement, Dede Brooks pled guilty to one count of conspiring to violate anti-trust laws prohibiting restraint of trade and agreed to testify against her former boss and mentor.

Dede Brooks, based on her plea deal, was spared hard jail time. The disgraced one-time queen of the art world, who over the years touted her honesty and integrity, was sentenced to three years probation, six months house detention, 1,000 hours of community service and fined $350,000.

On the criminal front, in 2001, after a four-year investigation, the US government indicted Alfred Taubman and Sir Anthony Tennant. Al Taubman was found guilty and sentenced to one year and one day (which made him eligible for time off for good behavior) and fined $7,500,000, which was about 5% of the $150,000,000 in business affected by the conspiracy. Taubman served 9 1/2 months in 2003. Sir Anthony Tennant refused to return to America to face trial, and the British government (taking care of one of its good-old-boys) refused to extradite him.

On the civil front, some 100,000 former customers who had filed suit against Sotheby's and Christie's were joined in a class action by judge Louis Kaplan. (Authorities figure the collusion cost clients of the two auction houses over $40,000,000.)

David Boies was named lead counsel in the class action case. Boies is a high-profile attorney who has had some important successes but has had even more spectacular failures, among them the tragically botched representation of Al Gore in 2000. (Or was Boies a double-agent as many suspect?) Over the years, the unctuous Boies has also been charged with several serious ethics violations. In this collusion case, Boise did a decent job, negotiating a settlement worth $512,000,000. His fee was $27,000,000.

Sotheby's and Christie's share of the settlement was $256,000,000. Taubman agreed to pay $156,000,000 of Sotheby's settlement cost. He also agreed to pay $186,000,000 to Sotheby's to help the auction house get back on its feet, to avoid future liability, and to protect his investment.

Christie's has come up with yet another way to scam the system. Sotheby's tried the tactic earlier, apparently without real success, when it bought the Andre Emmerich Gallery in 1996 and Noortman Master Paintings in 2006. Over the centuries, auction houses and art dealers have been at arm's length and compliment each other. Dealers nurture the careers of artists and sell their works (the primary market) and auction houses sell art that has been bought and sold before (the secondary market).

In early 2007, however, Christie's bought London and Zurich dealer Haunch of Venison (what a name for an art gallery). In late 2007, Christie's opened a Berlin branch, and in the fall of 2008 it opened a branch in New York City. Haunch specializes in contemporary and post-war art and bypasses dealers, Christie's traditional sources of these works. Reacting to a storm of criticism, Christie's denied that it had gone into the dealership business to acquire art to stock its contemporary sales, claiming the gallery is a separate operation. Besides, they insist, there is no conflict of interest because the employees of their galleries are not permitted to bid on items Christie's is auctioning; we, the simon-pure parent auction house, would never permit such a flagrant conflict of interest.

The art world was quick to point out that the 20,000 square foot New York gallery is located in the same building as the headquarters of the auction house; the galleries are wholly-owned subsidiaries of Christie's; the head of the gallery and the head of the auction house both report to the CEO of Christie's; and, Haunch employee bidding reportedly is occurring both above and below the public radar. Christie's shrugged off all of the dealer's concerns, insisting that it acquired Haunch to expand its private sale business for its expanding international clientele, particularly Chinese and Russian, and indeed, intends to open a galley in China. Christie's does not admit that they are intent on dominating the primary art market just as they, along with Sotheby's, dominate the secondary market. (Christie's has doubled its volume of private sales since acquiring Haunch of Venison.)

Dealers appear unable to stop or even slow this trend, a trend that threatens their existence, the same way the independent bookseller industry was ravaged by the giant chains. (Another threat to dealers has surfaced from the other direction. In late 2008, Damien Hirst, 43, the bad boy of British art, bypassed his dealers and took his 223 artworks directly to Sotheby's. The success of the two day auction, which raised over $200,000,000, sent the art world into spasms.)

EBAY SCAMS & CONS

Ken Fetterman & Kenneth Walton

Ken Fetterman and Kenneth Walton, who are both in their late thirties, perpetrated yet another hard-to-believe scam. Working out of Sacramento, the pair would scavenge garage sales and flea markets and then sell the pieces sight unseen by the buyers on eBay (the world's largest flea market) as original masterpieces. They became masters at listing and displaying the works, making clever, well-calculated mistakes in their descriptions to make it appear that they were dumb amateurs. Further, between 1998 and 2000, Fetterman and Walton established almost 50 fake identifications and, through shill bidding, bid against themselves to create interest and hook unwary legitimate bidders.

Even though the scam was extremely lucrative (attorney Walton gave up practicing law to concentrate on the con), naïve listing and shill bidding became too tame for the pair. So Fetterman and Walton began raising the ante. When a cheap painting they purchased resembled the work of a famous artist, they began to altar it by adding the well-known artist's signature or initials. The pair continued to play the dope in their descriptions of the paintings, or pretending not to notice key factors (like the forged signatures or initials). The scam worked so well, the pair believed it could go on forever. And maybe it could have, except for their excessive greed.

Fetterman and Walton bid up a fake Diebenkorn to the point that a European collector bid an astounding $135,000 for the painting. Remember, this is sight unseen. The transaction caused a media frenzy, which in turn caused the authorities to investigate. Ken Fetterman and Kenneth Walton were charged in a 16 count indictment, including mail fraud and money laundering. To avoid jail time, Walton pled guilty, which cost him the right to practice law, and turned state's evidence, implicating Fetterman. Fetterman fled but was picked up in 2003 on a routine traffic violation (a cracked windshield). A check of his fingerprints revealed he was a wanted man. Ken Fetterman was sent to prison for 2 1/2 years.

Richard Vitrano

Richard Vitrano (born Richard Rubin, he used a number of phony names) placed a unique spin on his eBay scam. Over several decades, Vitrano worked his cons in conjunction with Jerry Schuster and Charles Heller. Vitrano accumulated his cache of fakes from forger Manuel Marin. He then created fake provenances for the fake paintings, using catalogues of defunct art galleries to produce impressive looking invoices. The 59-year-old Vitrano made deals with over a dozen eBay sellers. He convinced legitimate sellers to list his paintings for him, without disclosing they were fakes. As part of the deal, for which he paid a few hundred dollars a month, Vitrano was granted access to the seller's ATM and debit financial accounts.

After that it was easy. Vitrano placed shill bids on his fakes to drive the prices up, and his phony bid always won the online auction. Sounds like he goofed, right? Wrong. Here's another clever twist in the scam.

After the bidding was over, Vitrano would contact the under bidder and claim that the sale to the winning bidder had fallen through so it was his or her lucky day. They could have the painting for their (lower) bid price.

When the buyers sent their payment, Vitrano withdrew the money from the account of the registered eBay seller with whom he had made a deal. By the time the buyer realized he had purchased a fake, Vitrano would have moved on, and the legitimate seller had the unenviable job of facing the purchaser and/or authorities. In late 2005, Vitrano pled guilty to wire fraud and to violating the terms of his parole. He had earlier convictions for interstate transportation of stolen property and, in New York and Florida, for selling fake art.

Jerry and Jill Schuster

The Jerry and Jill Schuster's con compares with the Fetterman/Walton eBay scam, except much less money was involved. In the mid-1970s, with childhood friend, Richard Vitrano, they opened an auction house in New York that morphed into the New Windsor Auction Gallery in Rockland County, New York. Over the years, half of the paintings the auction house listed for sale were forgeries.

The scam convinced people to buy fake works of art without seeing them. Obviously, the public will suspend their disbelief if they think they're getting a deal. In the Schuster's postings on eBay, the buyers didn't notice that the paintings were photographed under glass to keep the details fuzzy; the signatures were forged; prints masqueraded as originals; and other tricks unique to a sight unseen electronic con.

In 2000, a suit was filed by the state of New York against the Schusters to halt the scam. The following year the couple copped a plea. They agreed to refund over $100,000 to the 18 marks who had purchased over 50 fake paintings. This was not Jerry Schuster's first brush with the law. In 1980 he was fined and served time for mail fraud and using interstate transportation to defraud (selling fake art and fake Tiffany lamps).

Charles Heller

In the 1990s, Charles, working with Richard Vitrano and Jerry Schuster, flooded the market with fake William Aiken Walker (1838–

1921) paintings, which he sold on eBay, to dealers, collectors, and auction houses. Heller had a number of sources of fakes: He bought in bulk with stolen credit cards and checks. Another source was a female artist he went to high school with and an artist named Manny Marin.

In 2000, Heller copped a plea to the minor charge of withholding information on a crime and was sentenced to six months in jail, one year supervised release, and restitution.

Vincent Lopreto

Vincent Lopreto, who lives in Orange County, California, was in his forties when he was arrested in early 2008 for selling Damien Hirst forgeries on eBay. He also produced fake certificates of authentication to help convince purchasers the forgeries were bona-fide.

Authorities have been able to confirm some $300,000 in sales of the fakes but are certain the amount scammed is much higher. They have also determined that Lopreto conducted his eBay frauds under the names Whittman Alexander, Pacific Contemporary Art and Pentegram Galleries.

TELEVISION WORKS BETTER THAN EBAY

Kristine Eubanks

Fifty-one-year-old Californian Kristine Eubanks owned and operated a television show named *Fine Arts Treasures Gallery*. The show was a televised auction. Nothing wrong with that except Eubanks, along with 52-year-old Gerald Sullivan, was selling fakes of Picasso, Dali, and Chagall, among others. Eubanks manipulated the auctions for her own ends with shill bids, false appraisals, and phony certificates of authenticity.

Along the way, Eubanks ran a con that hurt unwary artists as well as collectors. Eubanks discovered a new printing system called *giclee* (pronounced zhee-CLAY.) When she realized the procedure left no telltale dots indicating the work was a copy, she put her scam into action.

First she established a printing business in Los Angeles using the new-found process. Then she began contacting artists. She would spin a tale of how they would grow rich with no risk or extra effort on their part, telling them that she would print a limited number of copies of their paintings which they would sign and number as originals. She promised the artists she would share the proceeds with them. The artists loved the concept because it would be found income entailing little work.

In the early stages of the scam, Eubanks would give the artists their share of the money. Eventually, however, the money stopped flowing to the artists, but she kept producing the copies. The unauthorized copies were sold as originals everywhere, including on her television auction show and in auctions on cruise lines.

Because the market was flooded with reproductions of their work, the artist found it almost impossible to sell their legitimate paintings. Collectors were also stung by the scam and the groups joined forces and filed a number of lawsuits.

In 2006, the authorities moved in, seizing 15 bank accounts and freezing millions of dollars. Kristine Eubanks was arrested and charged with a number of crimes, including wire fraud and conspiracy to commit mail fraud. She was already on probation for using the credit card of a dead business partner to charge almost $150,000 in goods, so she was hauled off to serve a three-year term for that crime. The government estimates over 10,000 people paid more than $20,000,000 for the fake art.

In an equally astonishing side note, Princess Cruise Line, responding to a lawsuit filed by artist Charlene Mitchell, maintained that its selling of fake works of the artist "has enhanced plaintiff's prestige and reputation and the value of her artwork." Yep, the cruise line actually said that. Officially.

REVENGE IS A PLATE BEST SERVED COLD

Ramon Cernuda

Ramon Cernuda's outspoken positions and antics have created a cottage industry of law suits in the greater Miami area, to a point where Cernuda is spending most of his time in court. Sixty-one-year-old Ramon Cernuda, the silver-haired Miami-based collector and dealer of modern Cuban art has, since the eighties, shed the traditional secrecy of most collectors and dealers and assumed a public role of crusader against fakes.

Ever since Cernuda opened his own gallery in the early 2000s, other dealers of Latin American art have resented his controversial tactics, which include picketing their galleries, screaming these people are selling fakes. What triggered Cernuda's anger was his potential purchase of a painting by Cuban artist Wilfredo Lam (1902-1982) for $200,000.

Cernuda is a smart as well as passionate collector and dealer. He sent a photograph of the painting to Lam's widow to have it authenticated, because he knew that the brilliant woman had devoted years to creating a detailed provenance for something like 1,000 of her husband's works. Cernuda learned, to his dismay, that not only was the painting a fake, the dealer had tried to force the widow to accept a bribe in exchange for lying.

The outraged Cernuda says the boom in fakes and in the prices for Cuban works is due to the rising affluence of displaced Cubans living in Miami. Mexican and South American works are also rising dramatically in value, he maintains, and therefore a tsunami of their fakes have flooded the market. Due to Ramon Cernuda's controversial tactics, several galleries that featured Cuban art were forced to close.

THERE IS NO OTHER WAY TO SAY IT: HERE ARE A FEW OF THE DUMBEST DEALERS

Jose Martinez-Canas

One of the dealers Ramon Cernuda publicly accused of selling fakes was Jose Martinez-Canas, the pioneer (and once premier) dealer in Latin American art. In 1987, Martinez-Canas opened his gallery, Elite Fine Art, in Coral Gables, Florida, located in close proximity to both the Miami airport and Ramon Cernuda. He mainly represented artists from Cuba, but also represented Panamanian, Columbian, and Chilean artists, among others. From all outward appearances, Martinez-Canas was successful: he was riding the red-hot Cuban art market of the 1990s, which was centered in Miami.

In 2003, the 67-year-old popular dealer was hit with several lawsuits alleging he was selling fake paintings by Mario Carreno (1913–1999) and other Cuban modernists. Ramon Cernuda was right. Martinez-Canas was selling fake Cuban art and forging certificates of authenticity.

Ready for this? On the fake documents, Jose Martinez-Canas used the name of a living Cuban museum curator, R.V. Diaz, who was the world's leading authority on Carreno. Needless to say, since Diaz didn't sign the (fake) certificates of authentication, when contacted he vociferously denied signing them. In late 2003, mounting legal and financial problems forced Martinez-Canas to close his gallery.

Ethem Ulge

Ethem Ulge, a native of Turkey who lived in Tampa, Florida, has to be one of the most inept eBay scammers ever. And yet, authorities figure that Ulge sold over 40 fake Picasso and Chagall paintings in 2007 alone for over $200,000. Ulge moved his residence on a regular basis to disguise his scam.

On a tip from New Jersey, a Tampa detective placed a bid of $3,500 for two paintings advertised as a Picasso and a Chagall. The policeman's bid won the auction. Believe it or not, the fake paintings arrived smelling of oil with smudges of wet paint and had tape securing the paintings to their matting. The fake certificate of authenticity was signed by an appraiser who didn't exist. Ulge was arrested in early 2008 and was charged with three felonies.

C.B. Charles and Dewey Lane Moore

In 1997, Moore placed almost 300 paintings with the C.B. Charles Galleries of Pompano Beach, Florida. The gallery planned an auction of the works and produced an expensive catalogue. They also ran full page color ads in several trade magazines trumpeting the auction. The ads stated that the collection had been "the property of a very prominent southern family, whose ancestor was a statesman, who donated the land where the US Military Academy, West Point, New York, stands today."

All of the 300 paintings were flea market fakes of such renowned artists as Picasso, Degas, Matisse, O'Keeffe and Rothko. Not all of the artist's names were spelled correctly in the sales catalogue and no information regarding provenance was given. After examining the catalogue, a number of living artists disavowed paintings attributed to them. The maligned catalogue became a huge joke in the art world, and various authorities were alerted to the scam.

Mr. Charles maintained that all of the paintings were authentic, but when the FBI showed up at the gallery to investigate the proposed auction, he cancelled the auction and returned the paintings to Moore. Dewey Moore pled guilty to mail fraud.

Mark & Boris Lass

In 1959, Russian brothers Mark Lass, 62, and Boris Lass, 65, rented a showroom in mid-town Manhattan and named it Re-Mi Gallery. The pair, who made a string of audacious claims, stocked it with almost 300 fake Picasso, Monet, van Gogh, and other masters they claimed their mother had collected back in Russia. The fakes were amateurish. Nine months later, before they could sell even one fake, the bungling brothers were indicted for grand larceny.

Jesaia Venger

Bob Venger (as he is known) should have stuck to selling stamps. In 1999, he accepted a well-traveled fake Renoir for consignment in his stamp shop in Los Angeles. Venger was told the painting and accompanying certificate of authenticity were fake. In any case, he made several false-starts which didn't result in a sale but did alert the authorities. Venger was arrested and pled guilty. He was given probation and ordered to a term of community service.

UNSCRUPULOUS FRENCH AUCTION HOUSES

Guy & Philippe Laudmer

Guy Laudmer and his son Philippe owned one of the most important auction house in France; his Drouot group was third in terms of annual sales. In his late 1960s, Guy Laudmer was a big man in the French art world. In addition to owning the auction house, he was a member of the committee in charge of authentication of the works of Fernand Leger. In 1990, Laudmer conducted what was trumpeted by the press as "The Sale of the Century," which consisted of what was labeled "The Bourdon Collection."

Lucien and Marcelle Bourdon were Paris gallery owners, collectors, and philanthropists. They were also in their nineties and anxious to fund a charity devoted to (among other things) the protection of animals. The sale, a remarkable collection of modern artists, consisted of 54 works, including paintings by Modigliani, Dubuffet, Miro, and Picasso, and attracted top collectors from all over the world.

The auction realized about $100,000,000. This bonanza, which has never been equaled before or since in France made Laudmer the country's media darling.

What the public didn't know was that Laudmer began scamming the elderly Bourdons the day after the historic sale. His fraud consisted of convincing the Bourdons to name him treasurer of their foundation and then charging exorbitant fees for his meager services. The ensuing scandal reverberated throughout France because of the individuals involved, the dollars involved, the provenance of the paintings involved, and the shady practices of French auction houses it revealed. Authorities determined that Laudmer had misappropriated millions of dollars from the foundation for his own use and transferred the funds abroad into a series of off-shore bank accounts. Almost $17,000,000 was unaccounted for.

The case was complicated, and the publicity flames were fueled by the fact that the provenance of many of the Bourdon collection was incomplete and believed to be in the possession of the Bourdons as a result of trading with the Nazis during WWII.

In 1997, Guy Laudmer was arrested and jailed. His son, Philippe, dodging the authorities on his heels, raided the company's treasury and fled France, presumably to Israel. The Laudmer case exposed certain illegal auction house practices, such as making cash advances to buyers and privately selling unsold works, both of which are illegal in France. The authorities also determined that over 10% of auction sales in France are fictitious.

Jacques Tajan & Roland Dumas

Sixty-eight-year-old Jacques Tajan owned the largest auction house in France, selling over 50,000 pieces a year.

Eighty-five-year-old Frenchman Roland Dumas, who gained notoriety as Foreign Minister in Francois Mitterrand's administration when he was charged with taking a substantial bribe, was named executor of the estate of Alberto Giacometti's widow. (Annette Giacometti died in 1993, while Alberto died in 1966.) The notorious Roland Dumas, as executor, hired his friend Jacques Tajan to inventory the estate of Giacometti's widow. For this soft assignment Tajan charged the estate over $1,000,000. Plus Dumas allocated over $2,000,000 to the notary in charge of the will. While these actions were questionable (and suspect), they were not illegal.

Moving right along, executor Roland Dumas, who was never known for his integrity, then consigned to auctioneer Jacques Tajan 14 sculptures and four paintings from the estate. The artworks were by the widow's husband, famed Swiss artist Alberto Giacometti (yes, the great sculptor was also a talented painter.) Dumas stated the items were being auctioned to pay estate expenses.

The auction produced almost $10,000,000. In his auction report to the government, however, Jacques Tajan claimed that one of the bronze statutes was unsold. A few days later he sold the piece to art dealer Joe Nahmad in a private sale. While this practice of selling unsold lots privately is common in America, it is illegal in France. Compounding his scam, auctioneer Tajan withheld about $2,000,000 (of the $10,000,000 raised at auction) for his personal use, and kicked-back about $500,000 to the executor Dumas in order to buy his silence about his withholding of the estate's funds. So we have a scam on top of a scam on top of a scam.

In 2004, Jacques Tajan and Roland Dumas were charged in the French courts with defrauding the estate of Annette Giacometti. Jacques Tajan was found guilty of breach of trust and Roland Dumas was convicted of complicity. They were each ordered to pay the Alberto and Annette Giacometti Foundation $2,000,000.

CHAPTER EIGHT
KING OF UNSCUPULOUS AUCTION HOUSES

Albert Scaglione/Park West Gallery

In the early 1990s, Albert Scaglione, now in his late 60s, owner of Park West Gallery of Southfield, Michigan, saw two trends that he felt could revolutionize how art was sold. First he saw that the cruise business was going to explode, and second, he saw that art auctions in the relaxed, happy environment of cruises could explode into a lucrative business. How prescient was Albert Scaglione?

Scaglione, through his company Park West at Sea has cornered the market and now conducts art auctions on over 60 cruise ships that sail under the flags of some of the most famed cruise lines in the world. It is reported that his fun auctions (as they are called) produce over half of his annual volume of hundreds of millions of dollars. How do the auctions produce such huge profits for Park West and the cruise lines?

The obvious key is that the bidders are an unsophisticated, mostly elderly crowd. And Scaglione really knows how to work that crowd. For example, the word print is never used, the pieces are always called works of art. Plus, the marketing is ferocious. The mechanical reproductions (there are almost no original paintings) are displayed throughout the ship 24 hours a day. Champaign is free and flows liberally before and during the auctions. A free print (called a limited-edition seriolithograph) is given away at each auction. Various raffles are held throughout the cruise. Numerous house financing plans are available to make the purchases as stress-free as possible. People even get a free (so-called) work of art if they apply for a Park West Credit Card, which is called a Collectors Card. How's this for a kicker? Everyone who attends the auction, whether they bid or not, receives a free print. Oops, work of art.

The auctioneers (almost 100 are employed) are extremely effective, always making the auctions interesting and fun. Shill and calendar bidding runs rampant in the auctions, a tactic unnoticed by the innocent attendees.

Over the years, complaints and lawsuits have plagued the operation. Artists claim that the company is selling unauthorized (fake) copies of their paintings. Disgruntled customers allege that even though the auctioneers claim the art they are auctioning is substantially below market, it turns out that Scaglione, instead of employing a disinterested third party, is appraising the works himself, a clear conflict of interest. Additionally, the so-called appraisals are based on replacement value, a useless standard as far as buyers are concerned. A certificate of authenticity, provided by an insider, accompanies every purchase. The company also routinely adds mysterious charges to their final invoices, such as Buyers Premium and Transit Fee. The invoice drastically limits Park West's liability.

Customers almost never receive the same pieces at home (six weeks later) that they inspected and purchased on the ship. For example, people who thought they were buying original Norman Rockwell prints received items with the following legend: "Norman Rockwell Authorized Estate blind-stamp gold seal from the edition of 315 Estate stamped facsimile signature examples." The Rockwell Estate denies giving authorization of any kind to the auction house. Got the picture?

CHAPTER NINE
UNSCUPULOUS COLLECTORS

If human covetousness were ever to be abolished,
art would come to an end.

— Peter Wilson

Tax avoidance was something that collectors
were always looking for.

— Robert Lacey

I believe the term "collector" is a misnomer.
It's just the desire to possess the latest, to say
"Look what I have on my walls."

— Leonard Lauder

What motivates a collector? We're not talking here about someone who buys a piece to hang over the sofa. No, we're talking about what motivates a collector. Some good things, including an aesthetic sense, an acquisitive urge, and a passion for collecting. But the real motives are usually bad: self-aggrandizement, snobbery, vanity, and/or the desire to enhance one's power, position, and personal standing. To put it another way, collecting can be summed up in three words. Lust, Power . . . and Greed.

Here's another truth. When collectors realize they've bought a fake, they keep quiet. Ego-centric collectors don't want to admit they've been suckered. Equally important, they would rather resell the fake as authentic and recoup their initial investment. As any collector will tell you, it's the last buyer who gets stuck. A major money-making scheme of collectors is to donate their artworks to museums. Indeed, some collectors admit they only collect to make a profit by selling their collections to museums.

Maurice Templesman, born in 1929, the diamond king, whose 15 minutes of fame were not reflective of his enormous wealth or substantial collection of antiquities, but rather were due to his being the lover/companion (take your pick) of Jackie Kennedy Onassis.

Templesman admits he collects artifacts solely as a business, to later resell them to museums.

How close are the collector and the museum? Over 80% of the works the Met owns have been acquired through gifts and bequests from collectors. Because of the favorable tax situation in America for collectors, you cannot separate private collectors and museums. So when you think collectors, think museums, and when you think museums, think collectors. While it's common knowledge (at least in the art world) that fakes abound in museums, the number of fakes in private collections is seldom focused upon. For example, the estimates of fakes in private collections in China are placed at 90%.

TAXES? NEVER HEARD OF 'EM

Walter Anderson

Walter Anderson, originally Mark Roth, like most major collectors, collected art to prove to the world that he was a major league player. Arrested in 2005, Anderson was charged in a 12 count indictment with evading over $200,000,000 in taxes over five years. The telecommunications entrepreneur hit the big time, but in the wrong way: his scam is considered the biggest tax fraud case in US history.

A frequent buyer of expensive paintings at Christie's auctions in New York and London, Anderson failed to pay tax on his acquisitions, setting up a large number of off-shore companies to work his scam. In 2006, the 52-year-old Walter Anderson, facing an 80-year prison term, coped a plea in exchange for only ten years in jail. What, exactly, did Anderson do?

In 1998, a year in which he earned over $126,000,000, he reported his income of just under $68,000, and paid tax of under $500. Think that's bad? From 1987 to 1993, he didn't even file an income tax return.

IF AT FIRST YOU DON'T SUCCEED . . .

John Bass

The Bass Museum of Art, which opened in an old library in Miami Beach in 1964, sported a collection donated by 74-year-old financier

John Bass and his wife Johanna. Bass was a frustrated artist who turned to Wall Street where he made his fortune. Over the years, Austrian born Bass repeatedly tried to sell his collection to dealers and at auction in New York with no success. His problem was that far too many questions had been raised about the authenticity of the collection.

In 1963, the city of Miami accepted the collection of some 100 artworks. In accordance with the donor's wishes, the city asked no questions, and no appraiser was hired to evaluate the collection for tax purposes. Controversy raged in the community, including, in 1967, a broadside leveled by Ralph Colin, then president of the Art Dealers Association of America, who cried "fakes" and questioned the oversight of the city council.

In 1971, finally responding to charges by scholars that the museum was plagued with a collection of fakes, the city began to seek disinterested evaluations, including requesting help from the International Foundation for Art Research (IFAR). It was eventually determined that there were some 100 fakes in the Bass collection. Most (62%) of the 77 so-called masterpieces were judged to be outright fakes, and a whopping 80% of the moderns were also forgeries. In 1973, the museum closed for three months to re-label and/or remove fake paintings.

MISTER NAIVETÉ?

Walter Chrysler, Jr.
Walter Chrysler, Jr. (1909–1988), the dour, heavy-set scion of the founder of the automobile company of the same name, had to be the most naïve collector of all time. How else would you describe a person whose art dealers told him to make any attribution he desired to paintings he purchased from them? Who purchased paintings "attributed to" rather than "by"? Who said, when challenged about the authenticity of his collection, "I'm satisfied with all the pictures [in my collection]. I don't make any claim for their being the greatest examples of each artist; but we can't look at masterpieces all the time. I think that would be rather dull"? Who made a deal (at highly inflated prices) with Knoedler's for several paintings the dealer had been unable to sell, giving up a Cezanne masterpiece in exchange.

Chrysler was blind-sided by the great salesmanship of dealers Harry Yotnakparian and Joseph Hartert. (The FBI seized over 800 fakes from Hartert's warehouse.) Chrysler was also blind-sided by an obstinate belief in his own eye. This is why he personally authenticated most of the works in his collection.

On the other hand, perhaps Chrysler wasn't that naïve. He took excessive tax deductions for the blatant fakes in his collection. The deductions for the fakes were disallowed by the Internal Revenue Service.

In 1971, Walter Chrysler, Jr established the Chrysler Museum in Norfolk, Virginia, his wife's home town. Like the Bass Museum in Miami, Chrysler's museum has had to overcome horrendous publicity and public comment regarding donated fakes.

THE NATIONAL GALLERY OF CANADA

In 1962, the National Gallery of Canada in Ottawa presented a show entitled "The Controversial Century: 1850–1950." The exhibition consisted of the collection of Walter Chrysler. (In the summer of 1961, Chrysler had put on the same fake-ridden exhibition a year earlier in his own museum in Provincetown, Massachusetts.)

Chrysler wrote the catalogue to the exhibition, with many of the painting's provenances a joke. For example, he wrote that one painting in the exhibit had been owned by A. Giez Delius, while listing another as having been owned by F. Delius Giese.

The bigger problem was that Charles Comfort, the director of the museum, had been warned that the collection contained a substantial number of fakes. When confronted with evidence that 60 to 70 of the 187 paintings were forgeries, Comfort made the impossible claim that he had no knowledge that any of the paintings in the exhibition were fakes. Adding fuel to the fire, Comfort muddled through, telling the press, "We expect we will have even bigger crowds. This is the best publicity we could possibly have." The general consensus in the art world was that the goateed artist turned museum director somehow personally benefited financially from the exhibition.

WHEN YOU'VE GOT THEM BY THE BALLS,
THEIR HEARTS AND MINDS WILL FOLLOW

Norton Simon

In the early 1970s, Norton Simon (1907–1993) was in his heyday as one of America's preeminent art collectors. In collecting, as in business, Simon was notorious for insisting on complicated arrangements, equivocating, and haggling. His shenanigans were all geared to beat sellers down to his price. Simon didn't start companies; he would find a business that was struggling and then proceed to take no prisoners.

Here is one of the art world's favorite stories, which best describes Simon's tactics. In 1965, Simon had a bidding arrangement with the auctioneer at a Christie's sale: If I'm sitting, I'm bidding on the Rembrandt; but, if I stand, I've ceased bidding; but, if I sit down again and raise my finger, I'm bidding again. The clever Simon bid verbally, which he was permitted to do under the agreement. But, and it's a big but, Simon conveniently neglected to tell the auctioneer he planned to bid orally.

Just as Simon figured, his verbal bidding tactic confused the auctioneer. When Simon appeared to have stopped bidding (since he hadn't raised his hand while sitting), the painting was knocked down to Marlborough. Simon jumped to his feet, screaming that he was still bidding. All hell broke loose and the press had a field day. The bidding was reopened and Simon got his prized Rembrandt and an international reputation as a major art collector. Just as he planned. (Simon and the painting appeared on the cover of the 4 June 1965 issue of *Time* magazine.)

In late 1972, Simon purchased a tenth-century bronze Nataraja (a dancing Shiva) from a New York dealer for some $1,000,000. The Indian government objected to the sale because the artifact was stolen and smuggled out of India. Simon, the corporate raider who made his fortune in the food business but was known to the public for having married actress Jennifer Jones in 1971, famously told *The New York Times,* "Hell yes it was smuggled. I spent between $15,000,000 and $16,000,000 over the last two years on Asian art, and most of it was smuggled." Two days later, probably after a meeting with his PR people, Simon denied that he admitted he had bought a stolen artwork. The Nataraja was impounded in England where it was being restored. In late 2004, after years of failed negotiations (and international headlines), the Indian government sued Simon for the return of the stature and monetary damages. In early 1975, after an intense fight, including a countersuit by Simon against the Indians, Simon folded and agreed to return the piece to India, its rightful owner.

Norton Simon, is the individual who gained control of the Pasadena (California) Museum of Modern Art in 1974. The museum trustees had embarked on a ill-conceived expansion plan, which thrust the museum into serious debt. According to James Stourton (and most observers), "The story of how Norton Simon ruthlessly took over the museum and its debt is a long and bruising one." After he gained control, Simon closed down the auditorium and the institution's community outreach programs, nullifying the museum's focus. Simon renamed the Pasadena Museum of Modern Art the Norton Simon Museum of Art, stuffed the board with his pals, and ran the museum as his personal fiefdom. Today, despite its controversial start, the Norton Simon Museum is considered a jewel in Southern California's art crown.

PASADENA MUSEUM OF MODERN ART

Opened in 1924 as the Pasadena Art Institute, the facility was operated by the little old ladies from Pasadena in tennis shoes until it received a historic cache: The Scheyer Collection of over 400 artworks by modern masters. The windfall turned the heads of the board. In 1954, reflecting their new-found ambitions, they changed the name of their institution to the Pasadena Art Museum.

Following years of arguments and strained relations, the board agreed to build a new facility, which opened in late 1969. Serious debt followed: The board tried everything in its power, including changing the facility's name to the Pasadena Museum of Modern Art, but kept coming up empty. This situation was the perfect opening for Norton Simon, who made his fortune feasting on other people's problems.

In early 1974, Simon concluded a deal that ended the board's dream, but gave him a home for his immense art collection. Simon spent millions renovating the flawed structure he bailed out. That's the good news. The bad news is that board's dream of a showplace for modern art in Pasadena was dead, and so was any real community involvement.

A footnote: Irked by Simon's plan to sell off a number of modern masterpieces he had acquired when he took over their museum, three of the former trustees sued Simon to prevent their sale. In late 1981, the court ruled in Simon's favor.

SNAPSHOTS

Clyde Beswick

Fifty-eight-year-old Clyde Beswick of California perpetrated what appears at first blush to be a highly unusual scam. What Beswick did was embezzle several million dollars from his own company to finance a modern art buying spree that lasted from 1994 to 1996. It turned out that he was only a co-owner of the advertising agency based in Pasadena, so he was stealing from his partner and himself.

In 1997, Beswick pled guilty to felony charges of grand theft (embezzlement) and filing false tax returns. Clyde Beswick was sentenced to two years in prison and ordered to pay over $1,000,000 in restitution, to be covered by the sale of art confiscated in raids ordered by the court.

David Compton, the 7th Marquess of Northampton

Sixty-two-year-old David Compton owns the so-called Sevso Treasure, which consists of solid silver plates, ewers, basins and caskets dating from 400 AD. (The Roman Empire silver takes its name from a dedication on a hunting plate weighing over 20 pounds.) Hungarians claim the pieces were looted from their country around 1980, before which there is no provenance.

The Sevso Treasure, with an estimated value of hundreds of millions of dollars, was acquired over the years by the Marquess with the intention of selling it. Compton tried twice in the last 25 years to sell the fourteen richly decorated silver objects, which contain intricate designs and detailed relief's, to no avail.

The outstanding claim by Hungary that the priceless antiquities were buried in their country 1,500 years ago when Hungary was a part of the Roman Empire, and the lack of provenance before 1980, act as a roadblock to any sale. Even worse for the Marquess, distinguished scholars like 71-year-old Lord Colin Renfrew are maintaining that it would be unethical for any British museum or commercial dealer to even display the pieces.

Undaunted, in 2006, the Marquess was trying again, obviously disregarding the international brouhaha about looting the Italians created by trying Medici, Hecht, and True in criminal court.

William Milliken Vanderbilt Kingsland

William Kingsland, who changed his name from Melvyn Kohn, was an eccentric collector who died in 2006, at the approximate age of 60, without a will or known heirs. The state of New York stepped in. It parceled out to auction houses Kingsland's eclectic art collection of some 300 pieces for them to sell. Subsequent research revealed that at least 20 of the pieces from his collection had been stolen from Harvard and other locations. All sales have been cancelled pending further investigations. At this time nobody is certain if "Billy Kingsland" (as he was known) stole the works or was an innocent buyer of stolen goods. The odds are that anyone who would claim he was a descendent of the Vanderbilt's is capable of just about anything.

There is a kicker to this ongoing saga. A man named Nakum Kohen (and his mother-in-law, Ori Lellouch) were hired by the state to move some of Kingsland's works from his apartment to a warehouse. The pair was arrested while trying to peddle two valuable drawings that they had stolen in the course of the move.

Andrew Mellon

In 1930, banker Andrew Mellon (1855–1937) paid almost $80,000,000, in today's money, for 21 masterpieces from the Hermitage Museum in Russia.

There are several interesting aspects to this deal. First of all, it was kept secret for public relations purposes. After all, the purchase was made only one year after the start of the Great Depression, which Mellon, through his policies as Secretary of the Treasury, was instrumental in causing. Second, since the United States did not recognize the Soviet government at this time, there were currency and other restrictions in place regarding dealing with Russia. Undaunted, Mellon (remember he was Secretary of the Treasury at the time) evaded these laws by completing the transaction in Berlin.

Samuel I. Newhouse, Jr.

In 2000, 82-year-old publications heavyweight "Si" Newhouse bought a Picasso named "Man With Guitar" that the Museum of Modern Art deaccessioned.

There was one insurmountable problem. Newhouse had been on the board of MOMA for 27 years and knew (or should have known) that purchasing a painting that was owned by the museum on which you sit as a board member is a major conflict of interest and against the rules. Even if a third party is used to front the deal. To escape being expelled from the board, Newhouse resigned.

Michael Ovitz

Fallen Hollywood mogul, Michael Ovitz, 62, is a notoriously cheap collector who apparently spends his waking hours figuring out how to cheat dealers out of their commissions by using the bullying tactics that made him, years ago, the number one agent in show business.

According to his one-time live-in nanny, Suzanne Hansen, Ovitz takes his passion for collecting to absurd heights. She relates that once Ovitz called home from a private yacht on which he was cruising with his wife and friends. The nanny answered the phone at the Brentwood residence. Ovitz came on the phone and said, "Suzy, we're calling you from somewhere in the Mediterranean. Is my art okay?"

The nanny couldn't believe her ears. She asked her readers: "Did he just say what I think he said?" Yes, Suzy, Michael Ovitz asked about his art before he asked about his children. Bottom line. The man is either the world's most fanatical art collector or the world's lousiest father. Or both.

James Renwick, Jr.

The architect James Renwick, Jr. (1818–1895) is famous for having designed St. Patrick's cathedral in New York City and the Smithsonian Institution building in Washington (known as The Castle). Renwick also had a collection of over 300 paintings from which he donated 90 Old Masters to the Met. The museum turned down the bequest, because the paintings were all fakes.

TWO ROSES AMONG THE THORNS

Linda Fryant & Brian Moran

Ms. Linda Fryant, and her supervisor Brian Moran, learned the hard way that money rules the art world. Fryant was an award winning investigator for the Department of Revenue of the state of Washington. She discovered that a large number of art collectors in Washington State had spent multi-millions of dollars buying art out of state, but were dodging the state's required use tax.

Her reward for discovering the source of millions of dollars for the state? A raise? A promotion? You guessed it. Linda Fryant's tax investigation was killed, she was demoted and reassigned to work out of her home, pending an investigation.

You read that right. Fryant was investigated for investigating art fraud. (Fryant was concerned about the welfare of her fellow workers and, as a union steward, was vocal about it.) Fryant was eventually restored to her position in the agency. When she reported for work, her fellow employees gave her a raucous standing ovation. Brian Moran, Fryant's supportive supervising boss, was treated just as shabbily. He was given the option to resign or take a demotion. He took the demotion.

Why were these conscientious public servants fed to the wolves? It turned out that the tax dodgers were wealthy art collectors and Department of Revenue internal documents revealed that a high degree of caution should be shown in dealing with them. A special procedure had even been established for handling what the department called high profile cases. As a spokesman for the state's Revenue Department put it, explaining why the rich get special treatment, "We're in Olympia [Washington], and it's a political town."

CHAPTER TEN
KING OF UNSCRUPULOUS COLLECTORS

Peter Brant

Anders Malmberg, a Swedish art dealer, executed one of the more creative scams of recent times. His client, Swedish heiress Kerstin Lindholm, owned a Warhol painting and silk screen work called "Red Elvis," which is five-feet-nine-inches tall and four-feet-four-inches wide, and consists of 36 identical images of Presley.

In 1998, Malmberg, through a front man, dealer Stellan Holm, convinced Lindholm to loan the piece to the Guggenheim Museum to be placed in a traveling exhibition. Peter Brant, 62, while a Guggenheim trustee, agreed to help Malmberg convince Ms. Lindholm to loan the work to the museum for the exhibition. To conceal his involvement (as Malmberg did), Brant used the same front man, Stellan Holm, to sway Ms. Lindholm.

A little more than one year later, while the artwork was still on loan to the Guggenheim, Malmberg sold the "Red Elvis" Warhol to Peter Brant for $2,900,000. Brant purchased the work, even though he knew the work was owned by Kerstin Lindholm. At the close of the exhibition in early 2000, in order to confuse the issue, Malmberg shipped the Warhol first to Denmark, and then to Brant in America.

In mid-2001, Kerstin Lindholm was browsing an art magazine and was shocked when she read that Malmberg had sold her "Red Elvis" to Peter Brant without her knowledge or permission, and without giving her any of the money from the sale of her artwork. When Brant, who was obviously an active participant in the con, wouldn't return the work, she sued Malmberg in Sweden and Brant in Connecticut (where she and Brant maintain lavish homes in tony Greenwich).

In 2003, 51-year-old Anders Malmberg was found guilty of criminal theft by a Swedish judge and sentenced to three years in prison. What happened in America?

The Least Logical Court Decision in Art World History

After a five-year court fight, the Connecticut courts disregarded Peter Brant's role in the con and said he could keep the piece because he was a buyer in the ordinary course of business and he had exercised due diligence.

Due diligence? Let's examine what Brant did to verify that Anders Malmberg was the legal owner of the piece. Brant, knowing that the artwork hadn't been stolen, had his lawyer check with the Art Loss Register, which is a service that tracks stolen artworks. Naturally, since the "Red Elvis" had been illegally appropriated, not stolen, the work wasn't listed as stolen. What else did Brant's lawyer do? For some unknown reason, he asked for and received a bill of sale from Malmberg. This about as much protection from a con man as a silk scarf is in a Swedish snowstorm. Now let's examine what Peter Brant (or his lawyer) didn't do to ascertain the true owner of the Warhol.

Brant (or his lawyer) didn't call Kerstin Lindholm, even though Brant had helped the Guggenheim obtain the "Red Elvis" from her for their traveling exhibition. A simple phone call to Lindholm or her attorney would have uncovered the fact that she was the owner of the work and had not sold it to Malmberg.

Brant (or his lawyer) also didn't make the obvious phone call to the Guggenheim to verify that Malmberg was the owner of the piece even though "Red Elvis" was on loan to the museum, and even though Brant was a star trustee of the Guggenheim. (The red-faced museum later acknowledged that the fact Kerstin Lindholm was the rightful owner of "Red Elvis" was readily available from the museum if trustee Brant or his lawyer had simply asked.)

Is there a logical explanation to the Connecticut court's bizarre ruling? No. One can only guess. Perhaps Kerstin Lindholm was outlawyered. Or perhaps the judges didn't understand the facts. Or perhaps the judges did not pay sufficient attention to the facts. Or perhaps there were secret considerations, if you know what I mean.

In 1999, the Guggenheim's downtown New York satellite held a Warhol exhibition that was not curated and was stocked with minor works that were co-owned by trustee Brant. Brant's foundation was a co-sponsor of the Warhol exhibition, hyping his own works. Brant owns the building at the corner of Prince and Broadway in which the museum was quartered. Trustee Brant charged the museum rent. (When deputy director Michael Govan was asked where the money was coming from for the museum's contemplated move to SoHo, he said the landlord [Brant], "Has been encouraging in structuring terms that would accommodate our needs.") Can't you just picture the man who talks like that negotiating a lease with Peter Brant?

Brant, is also well-known for coping a plea in 1990 for the misdemeanor of intentional failure to maintain tax records (tax evasion), for which he served almost three months in jail and paid over $500,000 to the court. (Meanwhile, two corporations [The BATO Company and Riviere du Loup Newsprint Ltd] of which he was president, pled guilty to willfully filing false tax returns, which is a felony.)

When Peter Brant got out of jail, art dealer Larry Gagosian (who is in his early 60s), threw a party for his buddy Brant. Besides partying, they must have done some serious talking because also in 1990, Brant and Gagosian, with partners Jay Gordon and Geoffrey Kent, took the infamous double delivery scam to a new level. The four co-conspirators funneled almost 60 artworks through a shell corporation they established to avoid paying about $6,000,000 in taxes. In 2003, the IRS filed a civil $26,000,000 lawsuit against Brant, Gagosian, Gordon, and Kent. The case was settled in late 2004 for $9,100,000.

Peter Brant is the same man who is famous for marrying knockout supermodel Stephanie Seymour (hey, what's the point of having money if you don't have the emoluments). He augmented the fortune he inherited from his father by selling newsprint. He is well-known in Greenwich social circles for his love of polo. Brant and his celebrity wife winter in polo-mad Wellington, Florida.

In 2007, Peter Brant's 35-year-old son, Ryan, was charged with perpetrating a scheme whereby he back-dated options. Ryan copped a plea and paid over $6,000,000 to the Securities and Exchange Commission and $1,000,000 to the State of New York to settle the matter. What's that line again?

Now I remember: the leaf never falls far from the tree.

CHAPTER ELEVEN
UNSCRUPULOUS MUSEUMS

In the United States, it is axiomatic
that the undertaker and the museum director
arrive almost simultaneously."

— John Walker III

Museum staff and scholars
constitute a large component
of the forgery culture.

— Oscar White Muscarella

[The Getty and the Met] have sailed
into a Bermuda triangle
of money, power and hypocrisy.

— Patrick McCaughey

To get a feel of museums in the big picture, consider: The Metropolitan Museum of Art in New York was founded in 1870, the National
Gallery in Washington opened in 1941, and the Getty Museum in Los
Angeles opened in 1954 as a tax dodge in Getty's Spanish Colonial house
in Pacific Palisades, California.

The American museums are new kids on the block. The British
Museum was founded in 1753, the Uffizi Gallery in Florence officially
opened to the public in 1765, the Louvre palace in Paris became the
Louvre Museum in 1793, the National Gallery in London began operations in 1824, and the Hermitage in Saint Petersburg and the V & A both
opened to the public in 1852.

The unscrupulous behavior of museums is far and away the most
shocking aspect of the complex and sordid business of the art world.
Why? In the eyes of the general public, art museums are created to
enhance the cultural and intellectual life of their visitors and the general community. Every year, the public pours millions of dollars into art
museums (through donations and tax breaks) trusting museums to
deliver on these ideals.

To put it another way, as James Cuno, director of the Art Institute of Chicago has stated, "Nothing museums do is more important than adding to our nation's cultural legacy and providing visitors access to it." Unless museums operate in an open and honest fashion, they cannot possibly fulfill their obligations to the public. What's needed? James Wood, director of the Getty, said it concisely: "The legitimacy of our museums is based first on trust." Unfortunately, history shows that museums betray the public's trust when they attend to their own agendas or act for a privileged few rather than the general public. Following are examples of what museums tell the public they do, and examples of what they really do.

Michael Steinhardt

Michel Steinhardt, 69, was a major collector of antiquities. He purchased a fourth-century gold phiale (a vessel used for pouring or drinking wine) for $1,200,000. The phiale was excavated in Sicily and smuggled into Switzerland. The agent, Robert Haber, a middleman, took delivery in Lugano, Switzerland, and flew to New York from Geneva. The reason for this two-step is that according to Italian law, since 1939 all antiquities are the property of the government and may not be privately owned or exported.

In the mid-1990s, the Italian government learned of the looting and subsequent sale of the phiale to Steinhardt. Responding to a request by the Italian government, the United States Customs Service seized the artifact. Steinhardt sued for its return, claiming, among other things, that the country of origin of the phiale was Switzerland, and its value was only $250,000. In 1997, a judge ruled that the phiale should be returned to Italy. Steinhardt appealed.

So far, this case of looting and smuggling of antiquities looks like thousands of others. But there is a distressing kicker. The American Association of Museums, was founded 100 years ago and has about 16,000 members, including over 11,000 museum professionals and trustees from 3,000 museums.

Here's what the museum's leaders and workers tell the public. The American Association of Museum's Code of Ethics says, among other things, museums must insure that "collections in its custody support its mission and public trust responsibilities; (that) collections in its custody are lawfully held . . .(and that) acquisitions . . . are conducted in a manner that respects the protection and preservation of natural and cultural resources and discourages illicit trade in such materials."

Here's what the museum's leaders and workers do. The American Association of Museums, in an amicus curiae (friends of the court) filing in the Steinhardt appeal, asked the court to hold that Italy has no right to enact legislation concerning antiquities found within its borders. Furthermore, the museums pleaded that antiquities, smuggled out of countries having such laws, should be able to be freely traded within the United States. The three judge Appeals Court ignored these outrageous positions and Steinhardt lost his appeal. The phiale has been returned to Italy. (The Met has a near twin phiale, which they purchased in 1962 from the notorious antiquities dealer Robert Hecht.)

Is the Steinhardt case an isolated example of museum hypocrisy? Not really. The Association of Art Museum Directors is an elitist group whose membership consists of persons who are directors (the officer who has the ultimate responsibility for the works of art owned or lent to a museum) of art museums in the United States, Canada and Mexico. No museum may have more than one member and the association has a ceiling of two hundred active members.

Here's what museum's top brass tell the public they do. The Association of Art Museum Director's Code of Ethics says (among other things): "The position of a museum director is one of trust. The director will act with integrity and in accordance with the highest ethical principles . . . A museum director should not knowingly acquire or allow to be recommended for acquisition any object that has been stolen, removed in contravention of treaties or international conventions to which the United States is a signatory, or illegally imported in the United States."

Here's what museum's leadership really does. You guessed. In a filing in Steinhardt's appeal, cheek to jowl with the American Association of Museums, the Association of Art Museum Directors also supported Steinhardt. As we will see, this same Association of Art Museum Directors publicly supported the Brooklyn Museum of Art in its chicanery with Charles Saachi. The organization is presently talking publicly of revising its Code of Ethics.

How big a problem is looting and smuggling of antiquities and how involved are museums? Peter Watson, the ace English investigative reporter and writer says there is a looting network of eight levels, stretching from the tombarolo (tomb raider) to the museum curator (who, he says, have been known to take a 10-20% cut of what the museum pays for the illicit artifacts). Peter Blome, director of the Antiques Museum in Basel, Switzerland has said, "I presume that I only know 10% of the provenances of about 6,000 of our objects. . . . If a collection is offered to me, then I don't ask after the provenance, as I know it won't come to anything." Paolo Ferri, an Italian prosecutor, estimates that over 100,000 tombs have been looted in Italy alone, with artifacts stolen worth well over $500,000,000.

In early 2008, armed with subpoenas, American authorities raided four museums in Southern California, including the Los Angeles County Museum of Art and the Mingei International Museum in San Diego. The spectacular operation was the highlight of a five-year undercover investigation into the smuggling of looted antiquities from protected archeological sites in China, Burma (Myanmar), Thailand, and even from Native American locations.

Here's how the scam worked. Jonathan Markell, co-owner, with his wife Cari, of the Asian Art Gallery in Los Angeles, regularly purchased illicit antiquities from looters and smugglers like 79-year-old Bob Olson. Markell, 62, would sell the artifacts to clients, along with forged, inflated appraisals. He would then arrange for his clients to donate the works to museums he specified. The cooperating museums would then provide tax write-off documentation to the donors at the highly inflated value.

The art world was shocked, shocked to learn that, in order to obtain the valuable antiquities, the museums were complicit in the scam: One highly ranked staff member stated that she was ordered to offer token resistance to accepting antiquities without proper documentation. Here's a classic: The attorney for the Mingei Museum blames the murky laws of other countries and the lack of knowledgeable experts as the reasons museums cheat.

The scam reached beyond Southern California. Barry MacLean, a

Chicago businessman and prominent Asian art collector, who is a high profile member of the board of the Art Institute of Chicago and owner of a private museum, was also charged with violating the National Stolen Property Act.

There have been numerous attempts at reining in the illicit traffic in art and antiquities including the UNESCO Cultural Property Convention of 1970, though it excludes works purchased before that year. It took 13 years for the United States to get around to ratifying it. Senator (at the time) Daniel Patrick Moynihan introduced a bill for the benefit of his collector friends that eased the restrictions. It passed.

In America, there are three museum trends that are disturbing. The first is the trend to charge to enter their hallowed halls (in England, happily, the publicly supported museums are free.) Art museums are not-for-profit entities that own art and artifacts, but in reality, they are merely custodians of the objects for the public and are mostly sustained by public funds. If you think of museums as libraries, you will roil at the practice of museums charging admission. After all, both museums and libraries are custodians of knowledge for the general public, and who in his right mind would support charging people to enter a library. Besides, admissions are a miniscule 5% on any museum's revenue sheet, a number that can be covered in numerous other ways, including a jump in dollars from community conscience donors.

Philippe de Montebello, the haughty, long time director of the Met once pontificated that people pay huge amounts to attend rock concerts and sporting events. "What is it about art that it shouldn't be paid for?" he sniffed. For openers, if de Montebello came down from his ivory tower long enough, he would learn that those scruffy sport teams and rock bands are for-profit activities, while the Met is a not-for-profit, public entity that not only sits on public land and receives public money, it pays no taxes due to its non-profit status. To be sure, the Met has a Pay-What-You-Wish-But-You-Must-Pay-Something policy. The problem is that the Met deleted that sign from its tickets desks when it changed its suggested admission from $15 to $20 in 2006, and neglected to announce the change to the public until the fact was exposed by the press. The Met also changed the wording at its ticket kiosks from suggested to recommended, a much stronger marketing word. While the dollar prices are plenty large, the word recommended is so small, most people standing in line cannot see it.

In this regard, there is one crucial point the Met always neglects to mention. The only reason the Met has a suggested donation policy is because New York City dictated that policy as one of its conditions to granting the museum over 10% of its annual budget, about $25,000,000 each and every year.

In a parallel concern, museums are operating more and more like their corporate counterparts, rejecting aesthetic concerns for marketing concerns. Museums are soliciting donations from dealers and in return are agreeing to exhibit their artist's work. In other words, private, for-profit art dealers are determining what is displayed in museums. How bad can this trend get?

The Bruce Museum of Arts and Science in Greenwich, Connecticut, allowed its controversial director, Peter Sutton, to exhibit paintings on its walls from a dozen art dealers. The paintings being displayed in the museum were for sale. The Hirshorn Museum in Washington, DC, announced a charge for access to its educational programs. The public outcry at the brazen attempt to charge for what is the museum's primary mission, caused the charge to be dropped. The museum denied that the bad press and adverse public reaction had anything to do with cancellation of the ill-conceived charge.

In addition to charging admission, today's materialistic museum culture (as opposed to their core education and preservation missions) is pervasive. Here are a few examples of museums helping private individuals and companies sell their products, and embarrassing themselves in the process: the San Francisco Museum of Modern Art show on the American Sneaker, entitled "Design Afoot: Athletic Shoes, 1995–2000"; the motorcycle exhibition, sponsored and paid for by BMW, and the two Armani exhibitions sponsored and paid for by Giorgio Armani, at the Guggenheim; the *Star Wars* touring exhibition sponsored and paid for by George Lucas; the Met's Tommy Hilfiger exhibition sponsored and paid for by Tommy Hilfiger; the Los Angeles County Museum of Art Eames furniture show, sponsored and paid for by Eames; the Corcoran Gallery of Art's exhibition of Judith Leiber handbags, sponsored and paid for by the handbag company; the New

York Museum of Modern Art's PIXAR exhibition, sponsored and paid for by PIXAR; and the Kansas City Nelson Atkins Museum of Art exhibition on Disney Theme Parks.

The practice of deaccessioning is one of most controversial actions museums can take. It often indicates that museums are treating their collections like investments, instead of acting as guardians of classic works for the public who really own the art. Deaccessioning is only supposed to occur when a museum suspects a piece is a fake or has shaky provenance, is redundant and/or of poor quality, or if a museum wants to trade-up. That's the theory. Why? The public expects museums to display art based on its aesthetic, not its financial value.

Selling off paintings and other pieces is contentious for numerous reasons. For one thing, the sales are a slap in the face of the original donors. If the donations are so questionable, museums should not accept them in the first place. Moreover, tastes change, and paintings that are not hot today can be important and worth multi-millions in the future. (There is an overlooked angle to this practice of selling-off: When a museum sells its artworks to dealers, it receives wholesale prices. But when the museum buys from dealers, it pays retail.)

The Museum of Modern Art in New York (called MOMA) is the king of deaccessioning. Labeled by critics the K-Mart of art sales with basically no accountability to the public, no other museum in the world is more active in selling off premier works from its permanent collection, and the scandals that follow have been legion. (In 2004, Eugene Thaw, an honorary trustee of MOMA and co-editor of Jackson Pollack's catalogue raisonné predicted that the museum's sale of a key Pollack masterpiece "will come back to haunt them.")

In the mid-1950s, the Minneapolis Institute of Art conducted what journalist Lee Rosenbaum (who carries the handle The Culture Girl) called, "One of the most infamous art selling sprees in American Museum history." Led by then director, Richard Davies, between 1955 and 1958, the museum sold off some 4,500 artworks, including Hudson River School paintings.

About 50 years ago the Art Institute of Chicago sold a group of Impressionist paintings to acquire a Tintoretto to upgrade its collection. The Tinoretto turned out to be a fake (workshop) Tintoretto and the

Impressionist paintings went through the roof in value.

Over the years, the Fitzwilliam Museum in Cambridge, the Exeter City Museum, the Leeds City Art Gallery and Museum, the Royal Cornwall Museum in Truro, and others in England not only sold off priceless paintings, they did it for pennies, without public notice.

In May, 1972, the Met secretly and privately sold off works by van Gogh ("The Olive Pickers") and Rousseau ("The Tropics," also known as "Monkeys in the Jungle") to Frank Lloyd, owner of the Marlborough Galleries. One month later, the Met secretly deaccessioned at least 50 paintings of the Adelaide Milton de Groot collection which she had bequeathed the museum. The gift had the proviso that the museum not sell any of the artworks but should keep what it wished and give the rest to one or more important museums it selected. (Outside counsel agreed with the museum brass that this was a non-binding provision.) The Met and its lawyers operate on the premise that since a provision of a bequest is not legally binding they can trash the wishes of the donor and substitute the will of the current museum administration.

Part and parcel of the de Groot fiasco, the Met made another highly disadvantageous deal (to the museum) with Frank Lloyd. The museum traded him a Picasso, a Bonnard, a Modigliani, a Renoir, and two paintings by Gris from the de Groot collection; in return, the Met received a David Smith and a Diebenkorn. This later deal was made without the knowledge or approval of the board of trustees, which later rubber-stamped the inequitable exchange.

When the public learned of the deals, the outcry over the shenanigans was so severe (did Lloyd have dirt on the museum's leadership, was a bribe passed under the table, or what?) the New York State Attorney General was forced to step in and investigate.

The Attorney General's intervention resulted in the Met adopting stringent new procedures for deaccessioning artworks, including the requirement that the museum promptly inform the Attorney General when it intends to sell art over $5,000 (which keeps rising due to inflation); sales must be at auction if over that set price (except to other museums); give public notice prior to sale of any work over $25,000 which had been on exhibition within the last ten years; receive permission from the donor (or heirs) to deviate from a non-binding provision; and binding restrictions can only be removed with court consent and notice to the Attorney General.

The Met deaccessioned about 11,000 rare ancient coins to help defray the purchase of the looted Euphronios krater (a rare two handled bowl used for mixing water and wine).

In 1996, art historian John Wilmerding helped the Shelburne Museum in Vermont sell off classic Impressionist works (which had been donated by his grandmother) to pay bills, which is a major breach of museum ethics. In 1982, the Los Angeles County Museum of Art sold almost 600 works at auction. In 2005 it announced it was selling off prime pieces by Giacometti, Modigliani and Max Ernst, works that had been proudly displayed by the museum in previous years. In 2007, the Albright-Knox Art Gallery in Buffalo conducted a massive (over 200 items) controversial deaccessioning of some of its most valuable and beloved historical artifacts. Critics lamented that the deaccessioning had the effect of selling off a piece of the city's patrimony, and maintained that the museum was selling its past to pay for an uncertain future. Their lawsuit to stop the sale was dismissed.

In 1984, the Museum of Fine Arts in Boston secretly traded two Renoirs, a Monet (and threw in $600,000) for a minor Pollack drip painting. A curator resigned over the ill-conceived move.

From the mid-1940s to 1972, the British Museum deaccessioned 30 Benin Bronzes, claiming at the time that the artifacts were duplicates. In recent times, the museum admitted that the pieces were merely similar and not duplicates, and expressed regrets for the mistake in judgment. In 1996, the Guggenheim Museum in New York was engulfed in a major deaccessioning scandal.

There are two additional deceitful actions of which museums are guilty and that have been going on forever, so they can hardly be called trends. First, museum's displaying and promoting artworks owned by trustees, donors, and sponsors is particularly troubling. This cunning maneuver validates the authenticity of the exhibited works and increases the value of the insider's holdings. While not illegal, the move borders on the immoral. Second, the museum's stonewalling of inquiries about their governance and/or about fakes found in their collections is equally troubling. What this stonewalling does is raise doubts in the minds of the public about the integrity and stability of the museum. Museums can ill afford these doubts.

Mark Jones, when he was the director of the V & A in London said it best. "If a museum contains things which are inauthentic, then what it is saying becomes a lie." Tragically, most of America's most prestigious museums display a pervasive lack of integrity.

IF YOU WISH TO DROWN, DON'T TORTURE YOURSELF WITH SHALLOW WATER

The Getty

The case of the J. Paul Getty Museum and Trust (called the Getty) in Los Angeles, and its flaunting of almost every ethic known to man, is, in many ways, the most depressing example of unscrupulous museum behavior. The Getty is the richest museum in the world. That's world, with a capital W. And the Getty Trust, which owns the museum, a research institute, a conservation institute and a grant program, is the third richest nonprofit organization in the World. Again, that's world, with a capital W.

One would think that its riches would make the Getty the most honest, honorable and admired museum in the world. To put it another way, shouldn't the Getty's unimaginable wealth make it want to be the standard by which museums all over the world are judged? Shouldn't they aspire to be the beacon piercing the dark secrets of the unscrupulous world of art?

Of course they should. But no such luck. The Getty has gone its own way and consistently maintained a code of take-no-prisoners silence: Its arrogance and hubris are hurting every other museum in the world instead of helping them. ARROGANCE: A feeling . . . of superiority manifested in an overbearing manner. HUBRIS: Exaggerated pride or self-confidence often resulting in retribution.

J. Paul Getty (1892–1976), made his fortune in oil. He established a trust, which he left shares of Getty Oil worth $700,000,000 at the time, which today gives the Getty Trust a $5,000,000,000 endowment and assets of over $9,000,000,000.

Starting in 1954 with a mediocre collection (Getty was a notorious cheapskate), the Getty trust eventually made three basic decisions in an attempt to move into the big time. The most dramatic was to build a world-class museum on a hilltop in the Brentwood section of Los Angeles (completed in 1997 at a cost of $1,000,000,000), the second was to refurbish the original Getty Villa in Pacific Palisades (which opened in 1974, closed in 1997, and reopened in 2006 as an antiquities museum), and the third was to stock both museums with the best art and antiquities money could buy, regardless of legalities. And therein lie the seeds of the Getty's self-destructive behavior.

The board of trustees is the governing body of the Getty trust: Trustees are elected for four-year terms and may serve no more than three terms. Over the years, in addition to its policy of stonewalling every question, the board has made a series of disastrous decisions, decisions that will resonate throughout the art world for years to come. The board's greatest blunder was the 1997 hiring of Barry Munitz, 55, as Chairman and CEO of the Getty trust, to replace the retiring Harold Williams. (Munitz began serving in January 1998.) The second biggest blunder occurred in 1982, when Marion True was hired. Third, for eight years the board basically gave no oversight to Munitz and True, both of whom played the board like a violin. The board even allowed John Biggs to be chairman of the trust's audit committee without insuring that he audit Munitz, an audit that was demanded by his position. Fourth, in 2004, the board elected Biggs as chairman of the board. The result was that Biggs' private and public actions and pronouncements in unequivocal support of Munitz encouraged Munitz in his flagrant rape of the Getty.

Harold Williams, chairman of the Getty trust and CEO for 18 years, from 1981 to 1998; John Walsh, Getty museum director for 17 years, from 1983 to 2000; Deborah Gibbons, museum director from 2001 to 2004; the members of the board of trustees of the Getty trust; and the people they hired must all share the blame for the tsunami of tragedies that have engulfed the Getty.

The unraveling began back in 1973, when J. Paul Getty himself hired Jiri Frel away from the Met and made him curator of antiquities. Frel was given the assignment of acquiring the best classical works of art available, either through purchase or donation. Don't sweat the details (wink, wink), the boss must have told him. Whatever Getty said, Frel was allowed to operate like a loose cannon. Getty, who died in 1976, would have been thrilled with what his prodigy accomplished.

In time-honored art dealer (and in some cases curator) fashion, Frel was triple dipping and definitely not sweating the details. He was buying fake antiquities; he was buying looted antiquities (mostly Italian), which he helped smuggle into the country; and he convinced collectors to buy certain pieces and then gave them highly inflated evaluations for their personal tax purposes. Between 1973 and 1984, Frel conspired with over 100 donors. In each instance, Frel made sure he was adequately rewarded.

In 1982, Harvard graduate Marion True, was hired as assistant to Juri Frel. Arthur Houghton, 42 at the time, also a Harvard graduate, was appointed associate curator of antiquities. In 1984, after more than ten years of frenetic unregulated and unrepentant illegal activity, the board had enough of Frel's antics. The high living, bon vivant Frel was demoted (but kept on) and Houghton was appointed acting curator-in-charge of antiquities.

Arthur Houghton tried to change the mentality of the Getty. He even tried to get his superiors to investigate Krel. All to no avail. 1986 was a pivotal year at the Getty. Frel resigned under fire and fled to Europe, where he died in 2006 at the age of 82. Totally frustrated, Arthur Houghton also resigned in 1986, only four years after being appointed. He left because of what he called the Getty's "cultural avarice" and "self-enforced ignorance of fact" by knowingly buying from known criminals. Houghton also warned the museum that continuing on that course of action would lead to "catastrophic consequences." The man's instincts were as good as his morals.

As Houghton's assistant Marion True gained confidence and authority. In 1986, she was appointed head of the antiquities department to replace Arthur Houghton. Perhaps the leadership was swayed by the fact that the 38-year-old Marion True was a lithe, blue-eyed, fair-haired beauty. (True is now 60 years old.) Or maybe they were taken with her persuasive powers, charm, elegant manners, and erudition. Who knows. Maybe it was her classic and proper wardrobe. Whatever.

What they didn't take into account was the fact that True was trained by two notorious proponents of artifact looting and smuggling, Cornilius Vermeule of the MFA and Dietrich von Bothmer of the Met. With True's appointment, the Getty's leadership signaled that they either knew and didn't care (or didn't want to know) that in her four years as an assistant, True was more and more responsible for the cultural avarice that would lead to catastrophic consequences. In 1987, one year after True's appointment to the top job, the Italian government warned the Getty that its principal dealers were selling them antiquities looted from Italy, a crime in their country. (Bruce McNall, Ali and Hisham Aboutaam, Fritz and Harry Burki, and Frieda Tchacos fronted over the years for these four dealers.)

Giacomo Medici

Giacomo Medici, born in 1938, grew up in Rome where his parents ran a small shop that sold tourist items. An impatient and intuitive young man, Medici realized that he could make a lot more money if he cut a few corners. Young Medici went to the source. He began a life long career meeting, making friends with, and dealing with tomb raiders.

In 1963, 25-year-old Medici served a three month jail term for smuggling Etruscan vases. With the eyes of the Italian police now on him, in the early 1970s Medici realized that Switzerland, unlike Italy, had lax laws regarding origin and movement of artifacts, so he moved his operation to the Geneva Freeport, which is a duty free zone.

Medici, a six-foot-tall, virile, swaggering, self-confident man worked both sides of the street with gusto. Besides selling, he continued to nurture the source of the antiquities to insure a constant flow of works, supplying a network of tombaroli (tomb-robbers) tools; shovels at first, later backhoes, and eventually, believe it or not, radar. He also paid certain individuals regular wages to dig up precious items his organization could sell. Because of his hard work at the bottom level of the illicit trade, Medici was able to purchase almost all of the antiquities dug up by the tombaroli.

Since Medici figured out that jail time was not high on his list of fun things to do, he decided that he should stay in the shadows (as much as possible) and let others be out front and take whatever risks there were in dealing with looted and smuggled artifacts. Consequently, Medici developed an efficient organization to sell the works he acquired. As an example of how well his plan worked, no fewer than 42 major acquisitions by the Getty Museum in Los Angeles came from Giacomo Medici, but his name never appeared as seller on even one. (The Italians learned of this from Medici's records, not from the Getty.) Another example. Medici moved thousands of items through Sotheby's and other auction houses through fronts: From 1983 to 1994 alone he used the auction house a whopping 110 times, and supplied almost 100 looted works to almost a dozen museums.

One of his favorite tactics was to have his people buy his own pieces back at the auction (a practice that is illegal), thereby establishing price and provenance for collectors. Sotheby's pretended it didn't know that it was helping the smugglers launder looted artifacts. Medici and his cohorts were also expert at producing documents that faked ownership history.

In 1995, the Swiss government granted permission and the Italian Carabinieri raided Giacomo Medici's warehouse in Geneva. Medici had the offices of his three companies in the Geneva Freeport, a sprawling complex of low buildings that scream secrecy and security. Goods stored in the Freeport are not subject to custom's regulations.

In the raid, the Italian Carabinieri (military police) uncovered almost 4,000 photographs of looted antiquities, 35,000 documents, and some 4,000 looted artifacts in various stages of restoration, many of them covered with dirt and even wrapped in Italian newspapers to confirm their origin to buyers. Many of the photos confiscated from Medici's offices were identical to photos True had in her files at the Getty. Not only that, a whopping 42 of the Getty's most treasured masterpieces turned up in the photographs. In 2000, after Italy had spent years studying the contents of the Medici warehouse, the Swiss finally turned over its contents to the Italians. This was a major victory for the Italians in general, and for Roberto Conforti, head of the Carabinieri Art Squad and prosecutor Paolo Ferri, in particular.

Giacomo Medici was brought to trial. In 2005, in a 659 page judgment written by Judge Guglielmo Muntoni, he was convicted of neglecting to report archeological discoveries, illegal export, receiving contraband, and conspiracy. He was sentenced to ten years and is appealing the sentence. In 1968, Medici started working with a man named Robert Hecht, who later became his partner.

Robert Hecht

Robert Hecht, born in Baltimore in 1919, is the heir to the fortune of the Washington, DC, department store chain of 80 stores (founded by his great-grandfather, now history) that carried his family's name. The aristocratic Hecht, who wears wire-rimmed glasses as a badge of honor, is a brilliant man who speaks several languages fluently and has always lorded his money and talent over lesser mortals. Called an incurable gambler and chronic alcoholic by Marion True, Hecht has been called a nasty old man by everyone else in the field.

In the late 1940s, Hecht obtained a scholarship to study classics and architecture at the American Academy in Rome. Like his future partner Giacomo Medici, Hecht began his life of crime at an early age. When his scholarship ended in 1949, Hecht was already dealing in looted artifacts. Hecht stayed in Italy for the la dolce vita years, learning, in the trenches, how to survive and prosper in the shady world of antiquities. Hecht decided to leave Italy following the uproar by the Italians over his 1972 sale of the Euphronios krater to the Met for the then unheard price of $1,000,000. He moved to Paris and relied on numerous agents and partners to represent him and Medici.

During this period, Hecht perfected his fragment scam. Through an associate, he would donate a fragment of a priceless ancient vase or cup to a museum (the Getty was the biggest sucker for this scam). The works were almost always broken to facilitate the smuggling. In any case, one by one, the other fragments would then be sold to the museum by other dealers working for him. Example: one *phiale* [libation bowl] at the Getty was compiled from no less than 25 fragments purchased over a period of 15 years from five different dealers. The point of the exercise, of course, is that late fragments always sell for a great deal more than early ones. (Fritz Burki, Hecht's most faithful aide and sometime straw man, was a restorer who would piece together pottery shards when that move was necessary.)

In 2001, the police raided the Paris residence of Robert Hecht. They

seized thousands of incriminating photographs and documents, including Hecht's incendiary unpublished tell-all memoir which meticulously covered some 50 years of Hecht's life.
The manuscript detailed many of his deals with True and other
major museums. (Hecht was referring to this memoir when he
threatened to destroy his rivals, or anyone who crossed him, in
a book to be published after his death. This threat not only
made people afraid, it made them careful when dealing with
Robert Hecht.)

The historic raids confirmed for the Italians that Medici was
one of the primary sources of looted antiquities, and that Hecht
was the main man smuggling them out of Italy and fronting
their sales to museums and collectors for Medici. Additional
raids by the Italians on Medici's home north of Rome and of
Fritz Burki's warehouses confirmed that the looting and smuggling of artifacts was not only a huge business, it was also a
highly organized business.

Robin Symes

Robin Symes, now almost 70 (although he has always
guarded his age), was a mildly successful dealer in ancient art in
London when he met Christo Michaelides in the 1960s.
Lightning struck, and by 1970 both men left their respective
families and the newly formed couple set up housekeeping.

In a way, Michaelides and Symes were the classic odd couple. Symes was the soft spoken reserved formal Englishman we
all know from books and movies (he even had a close-cropped
grey beard), while the younger, sensuously attractive Michaelides was outgoing and fun-loving. Then there was the matter of
money. Michaelides was the scion of a Greek shipping family
and therefore extremely wealthy: He supplied Symes with a
lifestyle Symes dreamt about in his youth. With Michaelides's
financial backing, Symes was able to belong to, and operate in,
the rarified world of the super rich and powerful, which, as
everyone knows, is where art collectors reside.

Robin Symes nurtured and exploited Michaelides' backing

shamelessly. He also became a master at forging provenances which helped him sell antiquities to the world's wealthiest collectors and major museums for top prices. Working with Medici and Hecht (Symes had the same address as Medici at the Geneva Freeport), Robin Symes became one of the top antiquities dealers in the world. A legend in his own time.

In 1999, the jet setting life of Robin Symes came to an abrupt end. Under extremely suspicious circumstances, at a dinner party given by two of his wealthy clients, Leon Levy and Shelby White, Symes' life-long partner Christo Michaelides slipped and fell (or, most likely, was pushed) down some cellar steps and fractured his head on a portable heater. The beautiful, happy young man died the next day.

The grief stricken family had naturally assumed their son Christo was Symes' 50–50 (financial) partner. Symes, on the other hand, making the mistake of a lifetime told the family that he owned 100% of the firm. Seven years and numerous lawsuits later, Robin Symes ended up disgraced, in bankruptcy, and in jail, sentenced to two years for contempt of court. Lying, cheating, and stealing worked well for Symes in the lurid world of antiquities but didn't cut the mustard with the determined Greeks or the English judicial system.

When his dream life and empire unraveled, investigators determined that Symes had a multitude of off-shore companies, bank accounts, and 33 warehouses, crammed with some 17,000 objects, estimated to be worth a fortune. Italy intends to file charges against Robin Symes so his troubles are not over.

Gianfranco Becchina

Gianfranco Becchina was born about 1940 in a small town in Sicily. He originally ran his enterprise out of Basel, Switzerland, but after the Carabinieri raided Giacomo Medici's warehouse in Geneva he determined Switzerland was no longer the safe haven it had been, so he moved back to Sicily.

Becchina is the opposite of Giacomo Medici, which is perhaps the reason they were always bitter enemies in the business. Becchina is by nature calm and reserved as opposed to the braggadocio Medici. Physically, the two men don't compare either: Becchina is short and slight (like Berenson) while Medici is tall and on the heavy side (like Duveen).

Medici obtained his artifacts from tombaroli who dug around Rome and north, while Becchina bought his goods from tombaroli in the south of Italy and Sicily. Also, while Medici sold his looted and smuggled antiquities anywhere and everywhere in the world, Becchina concentrated his sales mostly to Japan, the Getty, and Sotheby's in London. In 2002, the Carabinieri raided Gianfranco Becchina's four warehouses in Switzerland and found some 5,000 objects and thousands of incriminating documents and photographs.

The most significant difference that defines the two men (Medici and Becchina) was best stated by Paolo Ferri, the Italian prosecutor. According to crack investigative reporter Peter Watson, Ferri says that while Becchina admits nothing, "Unlike Medici, he has never tried to convince me he is innocent."

Not only did the Getty stonewall Italy about the nefarious dealers, after being appointed head of Antiquities, True continued where Frel left off. She ignored the Italian's persistent warnings and bought from those same criminal dealers (and their intermediaries) for the next 20 years. True was not only a curator, she was also named head of the long term project to turn the original Getty villa in Pacific Palisades, California into a stand-alone museum of antiquities, a museum that desperately needed better artifacts if it was to become world-class. In addition to her willingness to flaunt legalities, this appointment helped keep Marion True in the collect-regardless-of-the-legalities trap. Marion True and Juri Frel were different in every possible way. Frel was eccentric (to give him the best of it), while True was cunning.

True regularly sent out public pronouncements that she and the Getty were paragons of virtue regarding antiquities, while, at the same time, she was in the forefront of acquiring looted and smuggled artifacts. To mask her private buying with a do-good public persona, True, among other things, organized scholarly conferences where she said all the right things; began a dialogue with the Italians about returning a number of disputed (but inconsequential) works; and pushed through museum policy that seemed to say the Getty would no longer acquire looted antiquities.

Marion True, with her calculated, brilliant moves, fooled not only the art world, but also the Italians. Or so she thought. Italian prosecutor, Paolo Ferri, said that they learned Marion True had a double nature. She was not Dr. Jekyll and Mr. Hyde, he said, but very similar.

A statement made by John Walsh, director of the Getty from 1983 to 2000, shows how active True was in the illicit trade, and how little the museum cared that it was an accessory to the crime of looting and smuggling of antiquities. "Collecting was at its most productive between the mid-eighties and mid-nineties [not coincidently Marion True's reign.] It was about ten years of absolutely tremendous acquisitions."

This remark is from the man, internal Getty documents disclosed, who blithely stated in 1987 that he knew and approved that the museum was buying looted and smuggled antiquities from unscrupulous dealers. In 1994, Walsh wrote, "The only considerations for the collector [and museums] are, Do I like it? Can I afford it? Can I live with it?" Walsh conveniently skipped the most critical question: Will buying the historical artifact from smugglers destroy its ability to tell us about the culture of the people who lived in the area where the antiquity was ripped from the soil?

Harold Williams, as head of the trust, once stated publicly that it had been common practice for decades for reputable museums and collectors to acquire artifacts with no documented ownership history, particularly when possible countries of origin were doing nothing to protect their sites or enforce their laws. In other words, the Getty's crimes are justified if Italy doesn't protect its patrimony according to the Getty's standards. No wonder the Getty was known in the trade as the Museum of the Tombaroli.

In 1995 True learned about the spectacular and historic raid on the Swiss warehouse of one of her key sources, Dominico Medici. In an extremely shrewd move, True quickly pushed through the board of trustees (and then announced) a new policy: The Getty would only purchase antiquities if they were documented as existing before 1995 (the year of the raid.) At the same time the art world was praising her leadership role in fighting the looting and smuggling of antiquities, the double dealing True was spearheading the Getty's purchase of the Lawrence and Barbara Fleischman 300+ piece basically undocumented collection of Greek, Roman, and Etruscan artifacts. In 1991, True began her relationship with the Fleischmans.

Barbara & Lawrence Fleischman

Over the years, Barbara and Lawrence Fleischman (1925–1997), in more-or-less friendly competition with Leon Levy and Shelby White, built a substantial and impressive antiquities collection. It has been characterized by the *cognoscenti* as the world's finest private collection of ancient art. Over 90% of the Fleischman collection had no documentation. The Fleischman's voracious appetite for antiquities was fed by the same network of dealers and auction houses who sold their smuggled pieces to Levy/White; Medici, Hecht, and Symes. They also dealt with the Aboutaams.

It was believed, in the cloistered art world, that the Fleischmans (New York residents) were going to donate their treasure chest of artifacts to the Met. When the Met co-opted Levy/White, however, the Fleischmans took it personally and defected to the Getty. They became close friends of Marion True, antiquities curator. (Based on the seized Polaroid photographs from the 1995 raid on Medici's warehouses, the Italians positively identified 14 pieces the Getty acquired from the Fleischman collection as having been looted from their country.)

Moving aggressively, in 1992 True made a major acquisition from the Fleischmans, acquiring nine works for $5,500,000. The highlight of the transaction was a rare Syriskos cup. The Fleischmans had acquired the Syriskos cup from Robin Symes in 1988. In the same year Fritz Burki, a restorer and front man for Medici and Symes, sold a fragment of the same cup to True. If you are following this, you have figured out that the cup the Fleischmans bought from Symes was reconstituted from fragments, and the Getty paid for it twice: Once (to Burki) for the fragment, and a second time (to the Fleischmans) for the artifact. (While Giacomo Medici's name does not appear on these transactions, the Italian's raids on his warehouse in Geneva produced photographs of the cup before and after restoration, which confirmed Medici's ownership of the Syriskos cup and his relationship with Symes.)

In 1995, True purchased a vacation home in Greece, on the island of Paros, with financing arranged by one of Robin Symes's friends and his companion Christo Michaelides. True did not officially notify the Getty of the financing, which was a breech of its code of ethics.

In 1996, True closed on the Fleischman's multi-million dollar, 300+ piece collection of Roman, Greek, and Etruscan antiquities. The Getty paid the Fleischmans $20,000,000 cash, and valued their donation of the other pieces at $40,000,000. Three days after the blockbuster deal was struck, the Fleischman's gave True $400,000 to refinance her Greek home. The house was not put up as collateral for the money, which the parties creatively labeled an unsecured loan. True also neglected to report this conflict of interest to her employer. (In 2000, at True's urging, Barbara Fleischman was appointed trustee of the Getty Trust.)

In 1999, Italian authorities presented evidence to the Getty that their 2,300-year-old masterpiece Asteas krater had been looted and smuggled out of Italy. True had purchased the work from Giovanni Becchina. In its typical arrogant approach, the Getty stonewalled Italy about the matter. Also in 1999, in a fairly clever attempt to change the subject, True orchestrated the return of three looted artifacts. Included was a red-figured terracotta fifth-century *kylix* [drinking cup]. This particular piece was included because several other fragments from the same artwork were found in Medici's possession and pointed straight at the Getty. While the tactic was effective with her contemporaries in the museum world and raised her considerable (albeit false) reputation as guardian of the patrimony of foreign countries even higher, the Italians were not fooled.

In 2001, in reaction to the Italian investigation, Getty's lawyers sifted through the museum's files and interviewed staff. They concluded that Getty officials knew as early as 1985 that three of their principle suppliers (Medici, Hecht, and Symes) were selling them looted artifacts but the museum ignored the situation and through Marion True continued to buy from the trio anyway.

In addition, the attorneys concluded that the museum had purchased 82 antiquities from dealers under investigation by the Italians, including 54 of the 104-works the museum classified as masterpieces. Getty's lawyers also uncovered letters from Medici and Hecht to Marion

True, wherein the dealers made no effort to hide the fact they were selling looted and smuggled artifacts. Called "troublesome" by Getty's lawyers, they advised the museum to withhold them from the Italians. The internal investigation also uncovered the fact that in 1987 Harold Williams (CEO of the Getty trust) and John Walsh (museum director) discussed the Getty's on-going purchasing of looted antiquities and condoned the practice.

In 2002, with reams of hard evidence in hand, Italy requested negotiations with the Getty on 40 disputed artifacts. This conciliatory request was stonewalled by the Getty. But then, later in 2002, the Getty finally went too far and the noose snapped shut. The shocked Italians discovered that the Getty, following the advice of Richard Martin, their New York criminal lawyer (why did they hire a criminal lawyer?) withheld innumerable incriminating documents from them, even though attorney Martin himself repeatedly reassured the Italians that he had given them all of the Getty's documents that related to the Marion True affair.

When the Italians learned of the subterfuge and subsequently viewed the secret documents (which had been obtained by the *Los Angles Times*), they were stunned. (They had naively believed attorney Richard Martin when he assured them that the Getty had turned over all relevant documents that related to Marion True.) What really rankled the Italians was that based on attorney Richard Martin's lies they had ceased pursuing their legal options to obtain documents from the Getty.

Further complicating matters for the Getty, a 2005 internal review by the Getty's lawyers found that a whopping 350 antiquities had been purchased from dealers identified as being suspected (or convicted) of dealing in looted artifacts, most of whom were under investigation by the Italians. Since the Italians were once again not informed of the results of this internal review, the Italians were outraged when the fact came to light a year later when the *Los Angeles Times* broke the story.

Fed up with the arrogance, hubris and bad faith of the Getty and its lawyers (as well as the double talk of True) the Italians notified the Getty that Marion True was under investigation for the crime of conspiring to buy looted art. In a last ditch conciliatory effort, Italy graciously offered masterpieces to the Getty on special loan terms if they would agree to stop doing business with suspected dealers. Deborah Gribbon, director of the museum, probably on orders from above, flatly refused the offer.

Sure enough, in 2003, Marion True, Robert Hecht and Giacomo Medici were charged by Italy with the crime of conspiracy to traffic in stolen goods. The charges stunned the art world because never before had an American museum official been criminally charged with involvement in the looting and smuggling of artifacts from a foreign country. The case involved about 40 artifacts, including the statute of Aphrodite, as well as many of the pieces that were included in the Fleischman purchase and donation. In 2004, the United States Attorney's office filed a forfeiture complaint against the Getty on behalf of the Italian government.

In 2005, after a speeded-up trial which a defendant in Italy can request (so that if he is found guilty, his sentence is cut by one-third), Giacomo Medici was found guilty of the crimes of neglecting to report archeological discoveries, illegal export, receiving contraband, and conspiracy. Medici was sentenced to ten years (instead of what would have been 15 years) in prison. He is presently free on bail while his two mandatory appeals wind their way through Italy's legal system.

Also in July, 2005, the True/Hecht criminal trial began in Rome. In a classic example of the art world's incestuous snobbery and denial (and a tribute to Marion True's hard work at cover-up), in November 2005, on the eve of the True/Hecht trial in Rome, a vice-president for professional responsibilities of the Archaeological Institute of America, Malcolm Bell III, wrote an OP-ED column for the *New York Times*, which they printed.

Speaking of the Getty's policy which states that the museum will not purchase or accept as gift any antiquity whose existence is not documented before 1995, Bell wrote, "The Getty policy is arguably the strongest of any major museum, and as far as we know it has not been violated." (Italics by the author, who suggests the highly admired professor of art history at the University of Virginia do his own homework before requiring it from his students.) (If pushed, Bell will undoubtedly justify the True purchase of the Fleischman collection by saying that part of the Fleischman collection had been published about one year before the purchase, in 1994 and 1995, when it had been exhibited at the Getty and the Cleveland Museum of Art. The art world laughed at this lame, self-serving, excuse when it was previously advanced by True, as it was common knowledge that close to 100% of the Fleischman collection had no known provenance.)

In November, 2005, the Italian prosecutor began to present his evidence in the True/Hecht case that was closely followed by extremely nervous museum trustees, directors, and curators around the world. In October 2005, Barry Muniz, CEO of the Getty trust, a full three years after he possessed the information, confronted Marion True about the Fleischman money. At that time Munitz was under heavy fire for financial improprieties and other possible crimes. (Munitz's timing was calculated to divert attention from his legal and ethical troubles.)

True resigned, stating she wanted to concentrate on the defense of her charges in Italy. Everyone in the art world knew she was forced out by Munitz and why. Simultaneously (the day True resigned her post), in a not-so-subtle attempt to build good will, the Getty announced it would return three ancient masterpieces to Italy, including the famed 2,300-year-old Asteas krater (a vase for mixing wine and water) and a bronze Etruscan candelabrum. The Getty's flagrant attempt to bribe Italy failed abysmally. (Bribe is an appropriate word to use in this context because criminal attorney Richard Martin had been recommending the tactic to the Getty for some time.)

About 1993, True informed Greece that the Getty intended to purchase several priceless vases, a marble torso of a young woman, and a 2,500-year-old solid gold funerary crown, asking if they knew anything about their origin. The Greek government responded that the funerary wreath and the marble torso were undoubtedly looted and smuggled illegally out of Greece. They also asked the Getty for documentation of one of the other artifacts, a tombstone (which they later confirmed was also looted). Displaying the same hubris and arrogance the Getty displayed in all previous confrontations, the museum stonewalled Greece's request for information about the provenance of the tombstone. But much more important, a few short months after the warnings and concerns were expressed by the Greeks, the Getty followed True's recommendation and purchased the antiquities for $4,400,000.

In 1997, Greece demanded the return of the three artifacts, which are ranked among the masterpieces of the Getty's collection. The Getty stonewalled the request. In October of 2005, Greece renewed the demand it made nine years earlier for the return of the looted artifacts. A month later, tired of being stonewalled by the Getty and with significant help from the Italians, the Greeks stated, "It is always our principle to make every possible effort of goodwill negotiation. In this particular case our goodwill negotiations have not been fruitful, as our written communications to museum officials have repeatedly remained unanswered." Greece prepared its lawsuit to retrieve the works, and ennobled by the Italians, the Greeks began to turn up the heat.

In 2006, in a series of raids on the small island of Schinoussa, the Greek police uncovered some 300 illegal artifacts owned by one of the Getty's prime antiquity suppliers, Robin Symes. In addition, the officials seized more than 60 items in raids on two villas on the island of Paros. Meanwhile, the Greek police also raided True's villa on the isle of Paros several times. They confiscated a number of items and announced that it planned to press charges against True for illegal possession of 29 artifacts. In their raids the Greeks also confiscated several handfuls of photographs of artifacts sold by Symes to the Getty.

Also in 2006, Greece filed criminal charges against persons unknown for looting, smuggling and receiving stolen goods in connection with the ancient golden wreath owned by the Getty. This tactic allows a Greek magistrate to open an official wide-ranging investigation to determine if anyone should be brought to trial. The determination was made to charge Marion True with the crime of conspiring to acquire for the Getty the gold wreath which was plundered from Greece and illegally removed from the country. The criminal charge was dismissed on a technicality; the statute of limitations had expired. The civil trial against True for illegally possessing antiquities continues. Fearing a broader criminal prosecution, in late 2006 the Getty agreed to return the marble bust and the ancient gold wreath to Greece. Needless to say, Greece's culture minister, George Voulgarakis, is ecstatic that he followed Italy's lead.

The matter of fakes during True's tenure burst onto the world's headlines at least twice. In 1988, only one year after the Italian's warning, True purchased from Robin Symes a fifth-century BC limestone and marble statute of a Greek goddess of love (probably Aphrodite). The Aphrodite, which True stated would be "the single greatest piece of ancient art in our collection," had no accompanying provenance, merely the dealer's claim the artwork had been in a Swiss collection since 1939.

In late 1987, prior to the acquisition, Luis Monreal, director of the Getty Conservation Institute, raised objections to the potential purchase because there was clear evidence (dirt in the folds of the gown and new breaks in the torso for easier smuggling) that the statute had been recently plundered. Monreal implored director Walsh to run a test on the dirt which would most likely indicate the location from where the statue was looted. The test was never run. In spite of this and a number of other warnings, the remarkably preserved huge statue was purchased from the notorious Robin Symes for $18,000,000, a record for an antiquity.

In 2006, under pressure from Italy, the Getty hired their own investigation into the origin of the statute. They determined that the statue had come from Sicily, and that the story the Getty had been sticking to for 18 years regarding the work's provenance was one big, fat lie.

The other time was in 1983. Federico Zeri (1921–1998), art critic, collector, connoisseur, one of the world's leading and outspoken authors, and an authority on classical and Renaissance art, insisted a kouros was a fake. The Greek kouros is a marble statue of a naked young man. The Getty was contemplating its purchase from the notorious Gianfranco Becchina for some $10,000,000. (Zeri was the only art historian on the Getty board at the time. He resigned from the board when he could not persuade his fellow board members that the kouros was a fake.)

Even though it was early in her career at the Getty, True was a rabid supporter of the authenticity of the kouros. Prior to purchasing the piece, True quarterbacked a year of scientific tests, including core sampling, X-Ray diffraction, and electron spectrometry. True then pushed her boss Frel to purchase the sculpture. Zeri and the other experts were subsequently, unequivocally, proven right. What clinched the matter was the proof Giacomo Medici sent to the museum.

What the wily dealer did, in order to discredit his archrival Becchina who had sold the artifact to the Getty, was have a second fake kouros created (made by the same forger) with the same unique features as that of the statute the Getty bought. Game, set, and match. Not so fast. The never-surrender-no-matter-what-the-odds Getty displays the statue and labels it, "Greek, circa 530 B.C. or a modern forgery."

Nicholas Turner, an Englishman, is acknowledged to be the most distinguished curator of drawings in the world. His credentials are impeccable. He was in charge of Italian and French drawings at the British Museum for 20 years and worked for the Queen as well.

In 1994, lured by lofty promises, Turner joined the Getty: He was a real catch for the museum. In turn, Turner ecstatically joined the world's richest museum, where he was assured he would have carte blanche in all aspects of his position as curator of drawings. Trouble plagued the marriage from the start: Turner suspected that at least six of the Getty's most prized drawings were fakes, probably created by the notorious forger Eric Hebborn.

After careful and thorough study, which confirmed his suspicions, Turner went to his superiors, director John Walsh and Walsh's deputy, Deborah Gribbon. They gave Turner approval to take his case to the board of trustees but revoked it shortly thereafter, leaving Turner in limbo. A flurry of lawsuits followed, culminating in a large settlement for Turner and an agreement by the Getty to publish a book he had written, a book that would include a discussion of the fake drawings. In return Turner agreed to resign. Faster than you can say bad faith, the Getty reneged on its publication agreement. The Getty has consistently denied that the six drawings are fakes, stonewalling all questions about them. The museum even attempted to gag Turner, its own expert, via the courts. They lost.

The Getty's continued hubris and arrogance were putting a choke-hold on the institution. But it was the appointment of Barry Munitz as CEO of the Getty trust (which owns the museum) that was the trigger of the series of problems and charges that even the third richest nonprofit institution in the world finds difficult and challenging. Beginning his term in office in January, 1998, the smooth talking, colorful dressing, mustached, Brooklyn born, Munitz was not only right at home in the Getty's culture of the public be damned, he took it into the rarefied stratosphere of major league greed, politics, and, yes, hubris and arrogance. Munitz is a character with a history of questionable ethics; a perfect fit in the art world.

In 1988, he was CEO of United Savings Association of Texas, a collapsed Savings and Loan, that was sued by regulators for cooking the books (among other things), and cost taxpayers $1,600,000,000. In 1991, Munitz left the company, MAXXAM, under a cloud (including a prohibition from working at a federally insured bank or similar business for three years) to become head of the Cal State University System. In 2005, Munitz was quoted as saying, "Part of my task seven years ago [when I was hired] was to instill some sense of economic reality to the institution." Economic reality? When he was hired the staff, and many others, wondered how the Getty could possibly be run by someone who wouldn't even be allowed to work in a bank. The answer is it can't.

In his eight-year tenure as head of the Getty trust, by his actions Munitz made it clear that he conceived the Getty in terms of how the institution could augment his personal social, financial, and power status, not as a nonprofit organization committed to serving the public.

Here are the highlights: Munitz turned the Getty upside down, drastically reducing the budget for buying art; Munitz stocked the board of trustees with personal friends and then showered them with perks and gifts; Munitz treated the Getty like it was his personal kitty bank, spending the nonprofit's money lavishly on travel and personal items for his wife and himself, including using his museum staff to perform ridiculous personal errands; Munitz, while laying off staff and making cutbacks, lobbied the board for raises, which he received; Munitz authorized the purchase of illegal antiquities and stonewalled any enquiries about them; Munitz authorized withholding incriminating documents from litigants, including the government of Italy; Munitz arranged for his real estate developer friend Eli Broad to acquire a parcel of land owned by the Getty for $700,000 dollars under the appraised price, and instructed his staff to distance him from the transaction; and Munitz put pressure on the Courtauld Institute in London in a deal that has outraged the art establishment in England because the agreement was in direct contravention of the bequest of the Courtauld's major donor, Count Antoine Seilern. The Getty bought the right to tear-up the Count's will.

THE COURTAULD

The Courtauld Institute, founded in 1932, is now a free-standing college of the University of London. It houses a world-class collection of paintings in its smallish public galleries in the majestic Somerset House, but it is in the throes of a national scandal caused by Barry Munitz and the Courtauld brass.

Count Antoine Seilern (an Austrian collector who fled the Nazis to live in London) donated his impressive collection of hundreds of drawings and old-master paintings to the Courtauld. The gift is acknowledged to be one of the most significant donations ever received by the Courtauld, or any other museum in the world. Included in the extraordinary collection of some 32 Old Master paintings and 350 drawings, including a Rembrandt, are eye-popping classics by Rubens and van Dyke.

The Count explicitly stipulated in his will that works executed before 1600 could not leave the Courtauld, and those dating after 1600 could only travel within London. (The Count was understandably worried about transporting priceless paintings.) The Courtauld unreservedly accepted the conditions in the Count's 1978 will, and today the magnificent works in Count Seilern's bequest are the foundation of the Courtauld's permanent collection. (The Count was publicity shy, so he requested the collection be known as the Princess Gate Collection, after the address of his residence.)

But in 2001, Munitz waived 8,000,000 pounds (about US $10,000,000 at the time) at the Institute; words, promises, and integrity went out the window and followed the money. For $10,000,000 the Courtauld agreed to tear up the will of their greatest benefactor and lend the Getty some of Count Seilern's fragile and priceless paintings. Insulting the intelligence of both the English and American public,

Barry Munitz and Eric Fernie, the men who made the deal, vehemently denied that they had engaged in the illegal collusion.

In England, the most esteemed art historians and scholars registered their outrage at the proposed trashing of the Count's will, the subsequent pathetic cover-up, and indirectly, the hubris of the Americans, acting through the Getty with its unlimited funds.

In 2003, the *London Independent* quoted several (of the many) broadsides lobbed by eminent British art historians, rendered in classic English understatement. Sir Dennis Mahon, prominent art historian and trustee of the National Gallery, wasn't fooled by the cover-up. The Courtauld, he said, was accepting "cash for paintings. There has to be a connection between the two things." "I knew the Count," he added, "and he had very strong views about the wisdom of transporting pictures. To request to change his will in order to get hold of some cash is quite wrong, and I believe that is what has happened."

Michael Hirst (personal friend of the Count and former professor of art history at the Courtauld for 36 years) said, "I feel that the changes violate the wishes of Count Seilern only 25 years after his death." "The proposed amendments on loans," he added, "would be unacceptable to most conservators, given that many of his paintings and works on paper are well over 400 years old."

After the Courtauld pocketed the money, the Institute realized it could not finesse the terms of the will, so (still colluding) they had the Getty make a formal request to borrow certain works from Count Seilern's collection. After receiving the Getty's trumped-up request, the Courtauld then applied to England's Charity Commission (the official body that governs all nonprofits in the UK) for a variance of the Count's will.

In 2006, The Charity Commission folded (Why? Your guess is as good as mine) and changed Count Seilern's bequest to allow pictures on panel executed after 1600 to be loaned to exhibitions within the UK or abroad (to the Getty). The commission also dropped the provision that no picture may be loaned for exhibition more than once every five years. Regarding drawings, prints and manuscripts, the Commissioners dropped the Count's stated desire that the fragile masterpieces could only be loaned once in every five years, and then in London only.

The Unscrupulous

Here's what some consider the worse part of the sordid story. There is strong evidence that as soon as it received the Getty's money, the Courtauld began secretly (and illegally) shipping lower profile items from the Count's collection to the Getty in flagrant violation of the law. (Apparently the Courtauld was saying that if the Getty, the world's richest museum, can get away with questionable, nay illegal activities, why shouldn't we play the same game?) It gets even worse.

Shortly after making the deal with Munitz at the Getty, Eric Fernie, director of the Courtauld, announced that he had been hired as a Senior Research Fellow at the Getty Research Institute. Coincidence? Please!

Finally, the matter of the Getty's not-too-subtle bribery is so serious, relatives of the Count have gone on record stating that if there are alterations to the Count's bequest they will undoubtedly demand that the priceless masterpieces be forfeited by the Cortauld and turned over to them. Only time will tell if that occurs: It would be poetic justice for the self righteous and arrogant Courtauld, which seems to have retained the ethics of its nefarious ex-director, Anthony Blunt.

Munitz knew, but kept secret for three years, that Marion True had breeched the ethics of the Getty by not reporting the fact the Fleischman's had financed her house in Greece. When the heat got too hot on Munitz, he threw True to the wolves to divert attention from his questionable activities.

Munitz, to court favor with trustee Barbara Fleischman, approved payment of $64,000 of her personal legal fees. He did this despite warnings from the Getty's attorneys that paying the legal fees was inappropriate, and might even jeopardize the trust's tax status. Munitz later (in 2006) orchestrated the removal of Barbara Fleischman from the board to deflect attention from his nefarious activities.

Munitz hired young Jill Murphy as his chief of staff and had the museum personnel report to her, even though she had zero experience in the world of art (which, you will remember, is the Getty's raison d'etre). Munitz (and Murphy) created a chaotic and emotional atmosphere at the Getty, which led to the resignation of most of the key staff within a short period, including the director (Deborah Gribbon), the acting director (William Griswold), the associate director of administration and public affairs (Barbara Whitney), and the vice-president for communications and corporate relations (Pamela Johnson).

Munitz made a $300,000 deal with outgoing board Chairman David Gardner to write a coffee table book. The deal was made in return for Gardner's swaying the board of trustees to give Munitz a lucrative five-year extension to his contract instead of granting him the one-year term the board was ready to do. Munitz had several illicit relationships with young women, and used Getty's funds to finance his affairs. Munitz personally made grants of Getty funds to friends without proper authorization. He even made grants to organizations if they agreed to give him an award.

Munitz, in an attempt to receive preferential treatment in the state of California investigation, met with California Attorney General Bill Lockyer over lunch during the time Lockyer's office (which regulates nonprofits doing business in California) was investigating Munitz and the Getty. Lockyer only admitted to the indiscretion after the press exposed the meeting. As we will see, the tactic worked.

Finally, Munitz's arrogance and hubris toward the Italians forced them to sue Marion True (and therefore, in essence, the Getty) for the crime of criminal conspiracy in the first action of its kind in history, an action that affects every museum trustee, officer, curator, and benefactor, as well as every art dealer and auction house in the world.

What's the result of this culture of greed and deceit? The California Attorney General investigated all of the Getty's financial practices (particularly those relating to Munitz and his wife), including documents relating to the Italian charges, grants, gifts to trustees, and the real estate transaction with Eli Broad. The agency demanded eight years of records, and the entire action indicated the Getty's tax-exempt status was put at risk.

The United States Senate Finance Committee investigated Munitz's spending of trust dollars for his personal benefit. Federal laws governing non-profit spending say they must use their resources for the public good. Because they don't pay taxes, the Internal Revenue Service (IRS) considers excessive pay, travel, and perks by non-profit organization's officers and employees to be self-dealing and illegal. Because of his abuses, the committee is considering the first major overhaul of laws regulating non-profit organizations in 30 years. The committee is also concerned about the board's lack of supervision of Munitz's pay, perks and travel.

The Council on Foundations, the premier industry group of the nation's nonprofits, reviewed Munitz's spending. The Council suspended the Getty from its membership while it conducted its investigation because the trust failed to turn over all of the data sought in the probe. This is the first time the penalty of suspension has been imposed on a member.

In reaction to all of this, instead of working to improve the situation, Munitz hired Sitrick & Company, the public relations firm corporations retain when they have serious image problems. The first six months they were on the job the board paid the Sitrick firm a whopping $250,000 to put a favorable spin on Munitz's (and their) actions. In further reaction, Munitz appointed a special committee of his friends and business associates on the board of trustees to examine his spending and their own actions. Soon thereafter Munitz appointed four of his cronies to the board.

In late 2005, without consulting with the board, Munitz gave his controversial chief of staff Jill Murphy a severance package of $250,000 when she agreed to leave, even though he had previously promised the board he would seek their approval for any monetary decision he contemplated making concerning Murphy.

In 2005, Senator Charles Grassley (R. Iowa), then chairman of the Senate Finance Committee and one of America's experts on nonprofit institutions, rebuked the board saying, "I'm concerned that the Getty board has been spending more time watching old episodes of 'Lifestyles of the Rich and Famous' than doing its job of protecting Getty's assets for charitable purposes."

In February, 2006, Barry Munitz resigned (read fired). As part of the deal, Munitz was required to repay the trust $250,000 and forego a severance package worth some $2,000,000. Don't cry for Barry Munitz. In addition to the stash he accumulated while employed at the Getty, later in 2006 he was given a deal (which he arranged before he originally left) at Cal State to teach one class in English Lit. at double the maximum salary for a professor, at a time when the University system was enduring deep budget cuts and rising tuition fees.

The Getty was not only rotten at the top, the blatant hypocrisy and actions of Chairman John Biggs telegraphed that the Getty was also rotten at the core. Year in and year out, chairman of the board, John Biggs, consistently and unequivocally, supported his friend Munitz's spending and reporting habits. Publicly. "There is an engaged and accountable governance structure in place." And, "The board believes Dr. Munitz has done a remarkable job leading the Getty." Commenting on the book deal Munitz gave to Gardner, Biggs said at the time, "I think it's the most honorable relationship that I can imagine." He also said that, in his opinion, the money paid to Gardner was "peanuts." (Gardner was paid $178,000 for basically no work.) After Munitz left, and under pressure, Biggs cancelled the book project in March, 2006. In June, 2006, Gardner declared emphatically that he was not returning any of the money. In August, 2006, after an internal investigation by the Getty determined that the book deal violated laws prohibiting excess compensation and self-dealing, Gardner returned $99,000, and kept the rest of the money ($79,000). Gardner claimed he had put in 19 months of work, even though he had not conducted one interview or written one word. Forcing Gardner to return approximately half of the money was generally seen as an attempt by the Getty to appease the State and Federal regulators: The Getty announced that it was going to file amended returns with the IRS, which will note the repayment and which will say that it believed by repaying the money any potential for self-dealing has been corrected.

How close were Biggs and Munitz? During his entire four-year term as head of the audit committee, Biggs never once reviewed Munitz's expense reports, a task that was required by virtue of his position as audit chair. In 2004, shortly after assuming the role as chairman of the trust, Biggs negotiated a highly controversial separation payment worth $3,000,000 for Deborah Gribbon. The agreement had two problems that Biggs was able to dodge.

One, he and vice-chair Lewis Bernard negotiated the deal in secret, without informing the other board members. Two, the highly irregular, huge sum (nearly seven times Gribbon's annual compensation) was agreed to in order to silence Gribbon. The Getty obtained severe nondisparagement and non-disclosure clauses from Gribbon, who had threatened (through her attorney) to expose Munitz. The parties also agreed to have Gribbon claim philosophical differences with Munitz to hide her concerns about his lack of artistic vision and frequent absences. (For example, in 2002 alone, Munitz was out of his office almost 40% of the time and spent some $250,000 on travel.)

In response to questions about Munitz's use of Getty resources for his personal benefit (and to counter a memo from the Getty's general counsel which stated that many of Munitz's spending practices violated various laws), Biggs wrote the editors of the *L.A. Times* that any implication that Munitz was making decisions that benefit him at the expense of the Getty were "untrue." Biggs wrote that conclusion without ever having seen or reviewed Munitz's expense reports. And yet, what did Chairman Biggs, who steadfastly maintained over the years that Munitz's expenses were 100% proper, say publicly about Munitz's monster separation payment of $2,250,000 to the museum? Biggs said the $2,250,000 was an estimate of what the trust felt Munitz owed because of perks, expenses and other costs that should not have been charged to the trust.

John Biggs, feeling the heat coming from all directions, including the press, attorneys, and other board members, finally announced his resignation from the Getty board in July, 2006 before his term was up and a few weeks before the California Attorney General's planned release of the results of its investigation.

Even though it's impossible to measure in dollars the damage Barry Munitz inflicted on the Getty trust and museum for creating a disconnected Orwellian administration, let's at least put the figures on the table and see how close Biggs' estimate is. Paid so far:

Well over $1,000,000 to defend Marion True;

Over $2,000,000 paid to the New York law firm of Heller Erman White & McAuliffe to advise on how best to respond to allegations regarding the acquisition of looted antiquities;

Over $700,000 to Michael Sitrick for public relations advice;

Over $4,000,000 paid to the Los Angeles law firm Munger Tolles & Olson to be a fact finder and conduct an internal management review. (Ronald Olson, a name partner, has a number of serious conflicts of interest. Olson's firm represents KB Homes, which was founded by Broad, who was involved in the contentious real estate deal with Munitz and whose board included three current or recent Getty trustees. Plus, Ron Olson's firm represents Edison Electric, a large energy firm of which John Bryson is CEO. John is the husband of Getty trust chairman Louise Bryson.)

These figures do not include any dollar estimate of staff, administration, or board of trustees time and effort in regard to the Muniz fiasco.

When the Getty Villa reopened in January, 2006 after more than a $250,000,000 eight-year renovation, in its latest slap in the face of the rightful owners, the museum placed 1,200 of its prized artifacts on prominent view, which included 33 objects claimed by the Italians and the Greeks, and featured the disputed 2,500-year-old statute of the goddess of love Aphrodite.

Is a new era dawning at the Getty? Maybe. In August 2006, the Getty trust elected Louise Bryson chairman of the board. A trustee since 1998, here's what she said at the time of her election. "Essential changes in leadership and in board controls and processes have been made, but we as a board should have dug into these issues deeper and acted sooner. I speak for the entire board in committing that we will not allow that to happen again." In addition, the board of the Getty Trust is undergoing a radical realignment, with resignations and other changes occurring with unprecedented regularity, including the resignation of the duplicitous Chairman John Biggs. So, the board seems to be on track.

There are indications that the new director of the Getty, a quiet, 50-year-old Australian named Michael Brand, born in 1958, previously the director of the Virginia Museum of Fine Arts, is a precious find. For one thing, Brand has his priorities straight. He has worked full time to resolve the Italian and Greek claims, which he stated were his prime challenges as well as his top priorities. Indeed, shortly after taking office Brand convinced the board to agree to the return of two of the artifacts Greece had claimed for a decade, a large grave marker and a small marble relief. Furthermore, under Brand's leadership, the Getty has expanded its website to include much more information about its finances and operations. Also, the Council on Foundations has restored the Getty trust to full membership, citing newfound cooperation in its inquiry.

The Greek authorities say Brand's placating style was pivotal in their negotiations. "For the first time in ten years we had a Getty director coming to us with a proposal to work things out." The Getty has also strengthened (at least in theory) its rules for buying or accepting antiquities.

In 2006, Brand started negotiating with the Italians but an impasse developed. What caused the stalemate? Brand stopped conferring with the Italians and the museum's attorney Ronald Olson began to handle the negotiations. This was definitely counterproductive from the Italian point of view because they felt that Olson was conducting the negotiations from the point of view of what surrendering a looted object will mean to the Getty collection, rather than from the point of view that the Getty should do what is moral and right.

Miffed, the Italians, through their Culture Minister, Francesco Rutelli, threatened an unprecedented cultural embargo on the Getty, which would have prevented the museum from borrowing artwork or conducting artistic research, cultural studies or excavations in Italy. Considering the fact that (according to a UNESCO study) Italy has more art than the rest of the world combined, this is a serious threat.

In late 2006, the Getty trust announced its third president: Sixty-five-year-old James Wood came out of retirement to lead the beleaguered institution. Wood had previously been director of the Art Institute of Chicago and built the museum into a powerhouse, free of scandal. (The appointment of Wood bodes well for the future because Wood is the first veteran art professional named president and he has impeccable integrity.)

Wood, shortly after his appointment, in a brilliant move, assigned Michael Brand to take over the negotiations from attorney Ron Olson. (From the Italians point of view, Olson was obstructing a settlement rather than working toward one.) Putting Brand in charge worked. In mid-2007, the Getty agreed to return 40 of the finest pieces in their antiquities collection, including the seven-foot stone sculpture of Aphrodite. The fate of a statute of the fourth-century BC bronze of a young boy, which had been holding up the settlement, was put on hold pending a judicial ruling regarding it.

Why did the Getty finally settle this matter? The aforementioned cultural embargo by the Italians against the Getty was to go into effect within a few days of when the settlement was reached. In a diplomatic thank you for the settlement, Italy graciously agreed to drop the civil part of Marion True's trial. (The criminal trial continues with considerably less enthusiasm.)

While the agreement takes its toll on the Getty's collection, which used to be one of the best in America, Italy has agreed to make long-term loans to the museum to help fill the gap. Indeed, the Italians, in a shocking, unprecedented move, loaned the Getty several Bernini masterpieces that never would have crossed the Atlantic prior to the settlement. (The spectacular Bernini/Baroque exhibition ran from August to October, 2008.)

On the other hand, there is some disturbing news. The Getty refuses to release a report of the findings of an internal investigation it conducted. Whether Michael Brand, Ron Olson, the board, or someone else is blocking the needed sunshine, the secrecy decision sends shivers through everyone interested in the world of art.

Another question. Is Brand being swallowed-up in the Getty's culture of arrogance, hubris, and double-talk? Reflecting on the stalemate with Italy over the return of plundered and smuggled artifacts, Brand said, "There are many objects that have perfectly good provenance." When asked by the reporter for a for instance, tellingly, Michael Brand declined to elaborate.

More disturbing news. In mid-2007, Karol Wight, the newly appointed curator of antiquities and former assistant to Marion True said, "In order to do my job, I can't boycott any dealer, so to speak." Has Karol Wight been living in a cave?

Late in 2006, after a 14 month investigation, Bill Locklear, the California Attorney General, determined that Munitz and the board violated their legal duties but declined to take criminal or civil action against either because Munitz has returned the money he scammed. That's like a prosecutor saying he will not charge a kidnapper because he returned the kidnapped child to his parents. This result is not surprising when you remember that Locklear is Munitz's close, personal friend, who reluctantly admitted that he met privately with Munitz while the inquiry was underway. In a pathetic attempt to look serious, Locklear appointed a monitor to oversee the Getty trust until 2008.

Let's give past director John Walsh, who is more sanguine than most people about the situation at the Getty, the last word. Walsh recently said that the Getty once had, "A certain intellectual and moral position which was, ironically, brought about by its financial position. But the Getty is losing the high ground." Unfortunately, many people fear the Getty has already lost the high ground and may be melting down faster than it was built up.

The Met

The Metropolitan Museum of Art in New York, founded in 1870, may trail the Getty in the size of its endowment, but due to its head start and location, it is America's most important art museum. The Met, like the Getty, however, is hardly a paragon of virtue. It is also known for its hubris and arrogance.

The administrations of Thomas Hoving, who served as director for ten years (from 1967 to 1977) and Philippe de Montebello, who succeeded Hoving and reigned as director for over 30 years, paint the disappointing picture.

Hoving, 78, is normally described as flamboyant, provocative, and dynamic. Add arrogant and deplorable to the list. Hoving was oblivious to the feelings and rights of other countries, purchasing antiquities that he knew were plundered illegally from the countries of origin, and then laughing about it. The most extreme example of this cavalier attitude was his purchase of the Euphronios krater, which he dubbed the hot pot.

Ha, ha.

Over the years, the Met has always publicly denied buying and exhibiting fakes. This attitude goes back to the nineteenth century when it received dozens of fakes from J.P. Morgan and Cornelius Vanderbilt (the mogul's grandson) and continued to display them even after the works were exposed as fakes.

Then there's the case of the Egyptian bronze cat, acquired by the museum in 1958. The sculpture was so popular, it was given a prominent display in the museum, and the Met put it on a poster sold in the bookstore. But the experts cried fake. Finally, some 30 years later, in the mid-1980s, de Montebello, the relatively new director, in an attempt give the impression he could be reasonable, admitted that the cat was a modern fake and the work was put into storage.

Tall and thin, the pompous and condescending Philippe Lannes de Montebello was born in Paris in 1936. His parents brought him to America when he was 14 years old. De Montebello joined the Met as a curatorial assistant in 1974 and, after a stint in Houston, was made director in 1977, replacing Hoving. Working the board diligently from the start of his tenure, the egocentric de Montebello eventually overcame the chaos and instability he created at the Met in his early years and co-opted the board, rendering it superfluous and turning it into a virtual rubber stamp.

In a July 29, 2007 article in *The New York Times,* reporter Charles McGrath not only confirms this, he trumpets, "He [de Montebello] now runs the Met the way the Sun King ran Versailles." Can you believe McGrath is bragging about this?

The Met has a strict gag order instigated by de Montebello. That is, no staff member is to talk to the press and all press inquiries must be referred to the appropriate department (HIM). The significance of de Montebello's draconian measure is best understood when one considers the Met is a public not-for-profit institution. The museum receives over $25,000,000 a year from New York City (which represents over 10% of its budget), pays no taxes, and is located on Central Park (public) land.

De Montebello once said, "Every effort should be made to insure the absolute integrity of what we do." In 1984, it was revealed that 45 artworks the Met had been displaying were fakes. The pieces of European jewelry, including the famous fake Cellini Rospigliosi Cup, were claimed to date from the Renaissance, but were produced some 300 years later by a German goldsmith named Reinhold Vasters. Did de Montebello apologize to the public? Get serious. Here's what he said: "Most likely every major repository of Renaissance jewelry, metalwork and mounted crystals will find that a disturbing proportion of their holdings date from the 19th and not the 16th or 17th Century." Can you believe it? De Montebello is saying don't blame us for displaying fakes, everyone does it. The Met quietly placed all of the 45 fakes into storage.

British artist John Craxton, along with numerous other experts, charges that the Met's highly-touted Cycladic Harp Player, prominently displayed and labeled from 2,700 BC, is a fake. Craxton met the elderly man who sculpted the piece from a photograph in the 1940s. He learned that the forgery was commissioned by a dealer in Athens. In the face of this, the Met continues to insist the work is genuine.

The museum is smarting over the fact that their least favorite curator, Oscar White Muscarella, has also charged that the Cycladic Harp Player is a fake, and they are embarrassed that the work has been on the cover of a brochure advertising the Met. (This kind of bad luck [placing a fake on a brochure cover] has struck many museums, including the Getty and the Louvre. For example, the Louvre used a fake Assyrian royal marble head to promote the museum in the Paris metro.)

In 2001, after only six months on display, the museum removed from prominent display an archaic fifth-century Greek head it had on loan. It learned that the piece's authenticity was about to be challenged in a *New York Times* article. The Met stonewalled all requests for information about the fake and the brass at the Times killed the fake head portion of the story. Peter Landesman, the author of the lengthy article (which dealt mostly with forgeries at the Getty), is convinced the Greek head is a fake.

In the late 1960s the museum acquired hundreds of artifacts, including gold and silver sphinxes, jewelry and wall paintings called the "Lydian Hoard" because the treasure dated from the sixth-century BC from the reign of Croesus, the last Lydian king. Knowing that the looters were caught red-handed in Turkey, the Met decided not to display the priceless pieces so the Turkish authorities wouldn't know where they were. The museum even gave the treasure a fake name to help the deception. Finally, in 1984, almost 20 years after acquiring the artifacts, de Montebello bowed to pressure from donors whose money had financed the acquisition to the tune of almost $2,000,000, and put 50 of the 350 pieces on display. Big mistake.

Ozgen Acar, journalist and cheerleader for the protection of Turkish patrimony, saw the announcement and informed the Turkish government. As soon as they learned that their priceless artifacts were at the Met, the government of Turkey began an immediate investigation. The Met stonewalled the investigation, forcing Turkey to sue. The Met's defense that Turkey waited too long to sue (claiming a statute of limitations had expired) was rejected by the court.

Finally bowing to the irrefutable eyewitness evidence of the looters themselves, the Met admitted the artifacts did indeed come from Turkey so the museum then tried another tact. How about a compromise, they suggested. Why don't we share the goodies? Turkey, which now had the Met by the throat, refused. In 1993, after almost ten years of bobbing and weaving and 30 years after the Met acquired the looted artifacts, the embarrassing facts of their attempted cover-up were about to become public. That did it. The museum returned the "Lydian Hoard" to the government of Turkey, its rightful owner. This result represented another hard-fought victory for the art specialty branch (Larry Kaye, Howard Spiegler, and Harry Rand) of the law firm Herrick, Feinstein.

At the beginning of the 1980s, Cornelius Vermeule of the Museum of Fine Arts in Boston (the MFA) purchased half of a bronze original statute of Hercules dating from 330 BC and attributed to the Greek master Lysippos of Sicyon. The other half of the work was owned by voracious collectors Leon Levy and Shelby White. In 1990, the work was loaned to the Met, who displayed it.

When questioned by reporters about the charges of looting, the MFA referred the interrogator to the owners of the artifacts, Levy/White. Levy/White, even though they owned the artifact, referred questions to the Met. Philipp de Montebello deflected the accusations saying the charges mean nothing until someone comes along with absolute proof of them.

Leon Levy & Shelby White

Leon Levy (1926–2003) and Shelby White began buying antiquities in the mid-1970s and proceeded to build one of the world's largest private collections of ancient artifacts. Unfortunately, most of the couple's impressive works were smuggled out of Italy, and other countries.

In an effort to avoid purchasing fakes, Levy and White used the

Met's labs and employees to authenticate the pieces they were contemplating purchasing. This museum service, which reeks of conflict of interest, assists smugglers because the stamp of authenticity from one of the world's greatest museums enhances the value of the work as well as helping distance the dealer from the crime.

While Levy/White did their due diligence in spades regarding fakes, they had no interest in authenticating the source of the antiquities: They were dealing in an illicit enterprise and they knew it. Sometimes they bought at auction, but they also purchased their booty from the usual suspects, nefarious dealers Italian Giacomo Medici, Englishman Robin Symes, and American Robert Hecht.

It has been estimated by leading experts in the field that well over 90% of the items in the Levy/White collection have no known provenance, a fact underscored by two respected Englishmen (Christopher Chippindale and David Gill) who made a careful study of Levy/White pieces when they were on display at the Met. To help increase the value of their antiquities, pieces owned by the couple have been on display at the Met for years.

Everything was going their way; Shelby White was appointed to the board of trustees of the Met, a coveted position New York society envies, and in 2001, she was appointed to President Clinton's Cultural Property Advisory Committee. (Nancy Wilkie, president of the Archeological Institute of America, said that appointment was "Like putting a fox in charge of the chicken coop.")

Leon Levy, who died in 2003, carved out his fortune on Wall Street as the founder of the Oppenheimer Funds. In his lifetime, Levy was a leading philanthropist in the field of archeology, parceling out his money so that it acted as a sort of balance to his illicit antiquity collecting. Since his death, his widow Shelby White has continued her husband's philanthropic activities through the Leon Levy Foundation. (Many consider the Levy/White gifts to be avoided because of the couple's dubious collecting tactics and the damage that has caused to the field of archeology. Several prominent universities, including Bryn Mawr and the University of Cincinnati, refuse to accept funds from organizations connected to Levy/White).

In 1997, when Italy began to flex its legal muscle, Levy/White established a program at Harvard to support research on terminated and unpublished field sites in several countries. But Italy was on a roll. They asked Shelby White to return more than 20 pieces for which they have proof were illegally ripped from its soil and then smuggled out of their country. In direct response to Italy's veiled threats, and undoubtedly fearing Marion True's fate, Shelby White made a bold move.

To deflect attention, and to win the hearts and minds of the archeology community, she orchestrated a $200,000,000 donation to New York University from the Levy Foundation. When various academics rebelled at the maneuver, White established the Phillip J. King Professorship at Harvard. Not coincidentally, King, a distinguished scholar, and the director of the Shelby White-Leon Levy program for Archeological Publications at Harvard, has been a vocal supporter of Shelby White.

Consider: To dispute charges that Shelby White's monetary grants were dangerous (because the nature of her collecting undermines the premise of archeology, which is to protect the world's patrimony and to study artifacts in their original context) King went so far as to proclaim publicly that their actions were okay because Levy/White always bought from public auction. King knows, or should know, that this is patently false. More important, King also knows, or should know, that buying at auction would make no difference as far as provenance is concerned.

There is no question that by accepting Levy/White money, the scholars and universities are tacitly approving their practice of buying looted antiquities. As they say, money talks, and even distinguished scholars and universities listen.

Meanwhile, de Montebello, director of the Met, is up to his old tricks, working both sides of the street. He is distancing himself from the Shelby White/Italy dispute ("The Levy/White collection presents very little concern to me because it is not mine"), and at the same time he is fighting Italy's demand to review all of the documents concerning works on loan to the museum from private collections. That is, the Levy/White papers. In early 2008, after 18 months of intense negotiations, Shelby White transferred title to ten (out of the 20 requested) prized antiquities to Italy. In mid-2008, she returned two artifacts to Greece.

The Unscrupulous

In the now storied 1995 raid on Medici's warehouse in Geneva the Italian government positively identified some 30 objects in the Met's collection that were illegally looted from their country. Included in their charges is a 15 piece set of third century silver, for which the Met paid almost $3,000,000 in the early 1980s. The evidence from the raid established that the priceless 1,700-year-old cutlery set had been stolen by tomb robbers in Morgantina, Sicily three years earlier.

A Sicilian middleman swore under oath that the priceless artifacts went from tomb robbers to a Swiss dealer (Medici) and then to Paris (Hecht). The Met dismissed the middleman's claim out-of-hand, and in spite of Hecht's handwritten memoirs with substantiating pictures, the Met repeatedly called the Italian government's evidence inconclusive.

The Met then switched gears. It claimed that the silver came from Turkey and was acquired legally in Switzerland.

In 1993, the Italian government asked Malcolm Bell to investigate the origin of the Morgantina Silver. De Montebello refused to allow Bell to view the pieces. A full six years later, in 1999, with heat coming from all sides, the director capitulated and allowed Bell access to the treasure. He confirmed what the Italians had known for years. The silver was plundered out of a tomb in Sicily and smuggled out of Italy, and then sold to the Met for almost $3,000,000.

The priceless Morgantina silver pieces are only one example of the objects the Italian government insisted must be returned to them. Others include the sixth-century BC Euphronios krater, which is considered one of the Met's most prized antiquities. Looted in 1971 in Cerveteri, which is north of Rome, the tombaroli who dug-up the priceless masterpiece sold it to Medici, who sold it to Hecht, who sold it to the Met in 1972. The krater depicts the death of Sarpedon, son of Zeus, (as related in Homer's Iliad), was painted about 2,500 years ago by Euphronios, a potter and painter from Athens. The Euphronios krater is not only considered the jewel of the Met's antiquity collection, it is one of the signature works of the entire museum. Scholars and experts agree that there is really nothing quite equal to it. (The krater is so consequential to Italy that Hecht was barred from the country for his involvement in the transaction with the Met.)

For his entire tenure, de Montebello countered Italy's demands for return of its precious artifacts by demanding incontrovertible evidence that objects were looted from Italy. Suddenly, however, de Montebello became worried about the real possibility of jail time. Why?

First, there were the detailed and extensive photographs, records, and even memoirs from the Medici and Hecht raids (hard evidence) tracing the history of thousands of objects. Second, there was Medici's 2004 conviction and ten-year jail sentence for conspiring to deal in stolen artifacts. Third, there was the True/Hecht high profile criminal trial for the same crimes, which began in earnest in November of 2005.

In this highly charged atmosphere, de Montebello and the Met's board could see that Italy was deadly serious about retrieving its plundered treasures. Consequently, and not coincidently, de Montebello went to Rome to talk things over. Italy wasn't buying the sudden sweet talk. In a not-so-veiled threat, Francesco Rutelli, the Italian Minister of Culture, told de Montebello, "We don't want to arrive at the point we got to with the Getty. . . . Had the Getty listened to us then, we probably would not have arrived at the point we are now in Rome [holding a criminal trial of True and Hecht.]"

In December, 2005, the Italians went for the Met's jugular, issuing a subpoena for the contested items through the United States Justice Department. The subpoena did it. Overwhelmed by the Italians evidence, tenacity, and actions, in a stunning reversal of 30 years of defiance, denial, and demanding incontrovertible evidence, the Met surrendered and agreed to return the Euphronios krater, the Morgantina Silver and nineteen other pieces to Italy, their rightful owner.

Obviously, de Montebello was not interested in doing hard time in an Italian jail. At the time, de Montebello sheepishly stated, "I am not a lawyer, and the wording 'incontrovertible' that I used, it has been brought to my attention that even in a murder case it is not used."

Sadly, de Montebello quickly returned to his arrogant and contentious posture by trivializing the entire matter. De Montebello stated in an interview with The New York Times that, "[I returned the priceless artifacts to Italy because] you want to get irritants, you want to get vexing issues, behind you." Which once again proves the adage that when it's not your house that is looted, it's nothing more than a trivial irritant. Which reminds me of one of Mel Brooks' most famous lines. To paraphrase, If you have an open-heart operation, that's minor surgery, if I have a sliver removed from my thumb, that's major surgery.

In late 2007, Italy held a joyous ceremony heralding the return of the Euphronios krater. It was displayed with 68 other recovered artifacts in an exhibition entitled "Nostoi: Returned Masterpieces" at the Presidential Palace, known as The Quirinale. According to journalist Elisabetta Povoledo, the vase received a hero's welcome, and Rocco Buttiglione, the former cultural minister who initiated the talks with the Met, said "This is a success story. The Italians have won."

In exchange for the artifacts, Italy has agreed to lend the Met objects of equivalent beauty and artistic or historical significance. De Montebello claims that this idea of a trade deal, receiving the loan of antiquities from Italy in return for returning works plundered from their country, was his idea. The reality is that years earlier, in 2003 the Italians proposed the idea to Deborah Gribbon, when she was the director of the Getty. At that time, the only thing the Italians requested in return for loans was that the Getty pledge to stop dealing with suspect dealers like Medici, Hecht, and Symes. Gribbon rejected the offer. De Montebello has also made the preposterous claim that the Met and other museums had little part in driving the illicit trade in antiquities.

Listen to the internationally respected Lord Colin Renfrew, the retired director of the McDonald Institute for Archaeological Research at Cambridge University in England, "The final solution to looting is to stop buying, handling or displaying looted material." Lord Renfrew then took a direct shot at the Met and de Montebello. "Museums like the Metropolitan which have no proper ethical policy are indirectly funding the looters."

Among his other regrettable traits, De Montebello is a hypocrite. Once he crowed, "I specifically resist the blockbuster mania." Yet, in 2001, he scheduled, "Jacqueline Kennedy Onassis: The White House Years." It doesn't get more blockbusterish (is that a word?) than that. De Montebello once turned down a Chanel show because Karl Langerfeld wanted too much control. He received major points from all sides for this display of integrity. Hold on. In 2001, de Montebello did mount a Chanel exhibition at the Met. But this time, he used two of his own curators, which he claimed would now give the show legitimacy and would prevent a corporate sponsor from affecting curatorial policy. It turned out that Karl Langerfeld had more control over the exhibition then he had demanded previously. In fact, the curators made no secret of their anxiety to please him. Langerfeld personally picked the show's designer (a friend) and Lagerfeld's work was featured almost as prominently as Chanel's. Most say more so.

To quote one of de Montebello's curators, "There couldn't have been a show without Karl's intervention." The curator also admitted the Met received "extravagant support from Chanel, Inc." (When quizzed some two years later about the insidious control the private for-profit sector has on museum exhibitions, the Met's spinmeister Harold Holzer said, "We've racked our brains and examined our records and there are no examples we can find where a gallery sponsored an exhibition.") To spinning that's spinning.

The case of Oscar White Muscarella, the Met's Ancient Near East Art expert since 1964, tells us more than we may want to know about the way the Met (its board and leadership) thinks. Muscarella, 77, is one of the world's acknowledged experts on antiquities. His educational credentials are impeccable, he is a world-renowned scholar, and has written numerous academic books and articles. He has also worked in the trenches, having excavated all over the world.

Three times, in 1971, 1972, and 1974, Hoving fired Muscarella, charging him with all sorts of fictitious improprieties and infractions of museum rules. What Muscarella was doing was demanding equal pay for women who worked at the museum, lobbying the institution to pay its curators a living wage, and things of that sort.

What rankled Hoving most of all, however, was that Muscarella opposed Hoving's acquisition of the now famous Euphronios krater in 1972 and said so publicly. Muscarella not only opposed the purchase, he maintained the priceless treasure had been looted from Italy and smuggled out of the country. (Incidentally, today experts agree that Hoving was duped by notorious dealer Robert Hecht into paying a reported $1,000,000 for the artifact, more than eight times the bowl's worth, thereby triggering an explosion of prices for antiquities which, in turn, triggered wholesale looting and smuggling of various country's patrimony.)

The Unscrupulous

The Met's purchase of the Euphronios krater triggered a second unfortunate situation. In the 20 years after the museum bought the treasure, a flurry of five vases supposedly painted by Euphronios appeared on the market. Since no such vase surfaced for over a hundred years prior to the Met's purchase, it is safe to assume the five were fakes.

Here are more reasons for Hoving's vendetta. Muscarella maintains that collecting antiquities is a rape, and the people who do it are destroying the documentation of our human past. He also said that antiquity collectors and museums are actively engaged in erasing this planet's history, because objects should stay in the ground until the site can be excavated scientifically and every object in the find can be documented. That's how we know about our ancient history. The repeated firings were the direct result of his logic and passion. But the Met didn't count on one thing. Oscar Muscarella is a man of strong principles. He appealed his firings and fought the mighty Met for a full seven years. And won.

The Met, however, had the last word. After their losses in court they assigned Muscarella to a lesser position and gave him what he calls a Mickey Mouse title. He has not had a raise since 1978 or a cost of living increase since 2000. Pathetically, de Montebello not only perpetuated Hoving's unconscionable treatment of Muscarella, he isolated him. How isolated is Muscarella, one of the Met's most knowledgeable and esteemed employees? De Montebello's public voice, Harold Holzer, the Met's communications director who carries his boss's attitude wherever he goes, says to whoever will listen, "I don't think I've ever spoken to Oscar Muscarella."

Here are more Muscarella pronouncements, which have shed light on the Met and which drive the institution to distraction. He states that there is a forgery culture in the antiquities world because of the heavy overlap between plundered antiquities and forged artifacts, and that most of the antiquities in museums like the Met are plundered or fakes. Museum staffs, he maintains, know what pieces are fake but keep quiet out of embarrassment, scholarly rivalry, and/or the desire not to offend wealthy donors.

Listen to these statistics Muscarella has gathered in his lifetime as an expert in the world of antiquities: Of the pieces sent to Oxford's ther-

227

mo luminescence laboratory to determine the age of objects, a full 40% are fakes, and 25,000 forgeries of artifacts enter the market every year. More startling numbers. More than 1,000 fake artifacts are in the collections of the world's leading museums, including 16 in the British Museum, 37 in the Louvre, 21 at the Ashmolean, and, get this, 45 at the Met.

Speaking of fakes, in 1973 the Met reattributed 300 paintings, a full 15% of the museum's European collection. Although not all of the artworks were downgrades, a good number of high-profile paintings were, including paintings by Francisco Goya (1746–1828), Diego Velasquez (1599–1660), Hubert van Eyck (c. 1366–c. 1426), and Jean Ingres (1780–1867).

Dietrich Von Bothmer, born in 1988, is the antithesis of Muscarella. The ethics of this curator with the piercing eyes, blond hair, turned down mouth, and square jaw, are highly questionable. Bothmer, who was the longtime curator of the Met's Greek and Roman departments (now retired and curator emeritus), is the individual who quarterbacked the purchase of most of the looted antiquities. Consider: in 1985, when he spotted a looted artifact in a Sotheby's catalogue, he notified Felicity Nicholson of the auction house, not the authorities.

Here's another interesting maneuver. Bothmer donated over 100 fragments of antiquities to the Getty museum, in direct conflict with his position at the Met. Most important, although he is an archeologist, Bothmer has always had a cavalier attitude toward looting and smuggling, having been involved in both activities while at the Met.

He once asserted that the history of an object he purchased for the Met "is not important to archeology." His attitude is best illustrated by his now famous quote regarding the Euphronios krater: "Why can't people look at it simply as archeologists do, as an art object." Needless to say, archeologists were flabbergasted and outraged over this remark. How could an archeologist, in essence deny a basic tenet of the profession that location and other circumstances of discovery are critical to understanding the past?

In February 1973, half a dozen scholars from Hunter College dispatched a powerful letter to Bothmer, in which they said (among other things), "Your statement made in defense of the acquisition of the vase [the Euphronios krater] betray a lack of understanding of that discipline [curator of a major museum] and, in our opinion, cast doubts on your professional qualifications." In a more significant rebuke, this time by the entire membership of the Archeological Institute of America, Bothmer, who was on the official slate of six scholars selected to serve on the board of trustees, lost after a seventh nomination was made from the floor.

Marion True told the Italian prosecutor Ferri that Bothmer once showed her a photograph of the necropolis at Cerverteri, Italy, pointed to a spot on the photo and said this is the place the Euphronios krater was found. (Between 1949 and 1973, 400 of the 550 tombs in Cerveteri were looted.) When one considers that both Juri Frel and Marion True both worked for Bothmer at the Met before moving on to the Getty, it becomes much easier to understand their attitude and illicit activities.

Bothmer also figures in the infamous case of the three fake Etruscan warriors. Between 1915 and 1918, the Met purchased an ancient ceramic statues of a Warrior, a Colossal Head and a Big Warrior, all believed to be some 2,300 years old. The Met was so proud of itself, the three Etruscan warriors were given a gallery devoted almost entirely to what it considered its prize catches. To the unwary public, the warriors became one of the museum's most beloved exhibitions.

In 1959, a scholar was offered the opportunity to see the three artworks. He declined, saying don't bother, I know who made them. The scholar's name was Harold Parsons, and he was confident the pieces were fakes. Parson's repeated public charges the works were fakes triggered action by the Met. In 1960, the Met ran chemical tests on the works to appease the persistent scholar. In 1961, Parsons was proven right beyond any doubt when Alfredo Fioravanti, now a Roman repairman of antiques and jewelry and one of the creators of the fakes (along with members of the Riccardi family), confessed.

The Met continued to live in its cocoon of denial, but James Rorimer, the director at the time devised a plan. He dispatched Bothmer to Rome to confront Fioravanti. Both Rorimer and Bothmer were confident the artworks were authentic and felt that they could prove Fioravanti was bragging and lying when he confessed to producing the fakes.

In Rome, Bothmer, as planned, gleefully produced a plaster cast of one of the warrior's hands from which the thumb was missing. Fioravanti, who was bright as hell, smelled a rat as soon as the meeting was arranged, so he was prepared. Fioravanti smiled at von Bothmer and produced a thumb that he'd kept as a memento of his brilliant fakes for almost 50 years. The thumb matched the hand perfectly. Bothmer sulked back to New York and one month later, the Met, for one of the first times in its history, announced to the world that the esteemed museum on Fifth Avenue had been displaying fakes.

In 1972, the curator of ancient art at the Cleveland Museum of Art told a reporter that 95% of antiquities in the United States were illegally smuggled in. In a typical display of his (and the Met's) arrogance, Bothmer called the scholar's statement "odd" and "crude."

In 2005, the Met placed with Sotheby's a large steel sculpture by Eduardo Chillida (born in Spain in 1924) for auction in London. Nothing unusual here; museums deaccession all the time. As long as the selling is conducted in the light of day for the right reason, there's no problem. But in the Chillida case, the Met had a major problem. A seven-foot one.

The seven-foot-long sculpture was donated to the Met in 1986 by Frank Ribelin, a Texas collector, and the Met's own deaccessing policy states the museum must get the permission of the donor (or his/her estate) to sell the gift within 25 years of its donation. The Met was clearly in violation of its own rules. The Met's long-time curator Gary Tinterow certainly knew about the clause but didn't notify the donor, Mister Ribelin, of the impending sale. Indeed, he (and his boss de Montebello) tried to finesse the collector by selling the piece in faraway London.

The tactic would have worked except one of Ribelin's friends saw the sculpture advertised in Sotheby's London catalogue and called him. Ironically, underscoring the importance of the work the catalogue stated the sculpture is, "Unquestionably the most important work by Chillida to ever appear at auction." Frank Rebelin resented the insult to him and the artist and informed the Met of his displeasure. When confronted with Ribelin's not unreasonable, heated objections, Gary Tinterow adamantly stated the Met would go through with the sale even though he acknowledged the illegality of the sale. (Yes, Tinterow's arrogance mirrors that of his boss de Montebello, which undoubtedly explains his lengthy employment at the Met.) The Met's general counsel overruled Tinterow and, based on Rebelin's objections, withdrew the sculpture from Sotheby's. An appalled Rebelin said, "I feel like we caught them speeding." Doing ninety in a school zone, during school hours.

While conflicts of interest abound in the art world, particularly in museums (displaying trustee's collections to enhance the value of their pieces, for example), the case of Arthur Ochs Sulzberger, Sr. is particularly troubling. Sultzberger, while publisher of *The New York Times,* was a member of the board of the Met for over 30 years (from 1968 to 1999), and chairman of the board of the Met for 11 of those years. He also headed the Met's acquisition committee for years. (Sultzberger's father, Arthur Hays Sultzberger, was a Met trustee from 1945 to 1964.)

If you were a reporter for *The New York Times* (America's most influential paper) writing about art, and learned that the Met was illegally buying plundered artifacts, or had acquired paintings of questionable provenance, what would you write if the man you work for was directly involved in the impropriety? I'll tell you what you would do. You'd do what most *Times* writers caught in that situation have done over the years. You'd equivocate.

In a classic example of equivocation, or worse, on February 6, 2006, a few days after the Met agreed to return the Euphronios krater and the Morgantina Silver, the *Times* published an editorial which stated, "The Metropolitan Museum has rightly agreed to return the krater and several other antiquities to Italy, not as a matter of principle, but because the Italian government has demonstrated to the museum's satisfaction the likelihood that they were stolen." I suggest that the editorial board of the Times examine the facts which incontrovertibly reveal that de Montebello knew for decades that the items he agreed to return were looted and only agreed to their return when faced with jail time in Italy.

There is a ray of hope. Sulzberger Senior's son, Arthur Ochs Sulzberger, Jr., who is the present publisher of the Times and sits on the Met's board, has said that he rejects all invitations to sit on various boards to avoid any impression of conflict of interests.

It's a start, but *The New York Times* remains guilty of an overly cozy relationship with the Met that borders on being unscrupulous. Example. In 2004, the Met made its most expensive acquisition since its founding, paying (through Christie's) $45,000,000 for what de Montebello believed was a rare thirteenth-century masterpiece by Duccio di Buoninsegna. At the time of the acquisition, de Montebello claimed the small (8-inch by 11- inch) painting was "The single most important purchase during my 28 years as director."

The painting was purchased on de Montebello's gut feeling, since the work has no provenance prior to the early 1900s, leaving a paper trail gap of over 600 years. (De Montebello was going for a grand slam, undoubtedly reflecting the truism that there are three ways a director of a museum can acquire immortality [so to speak.] Major building additions, blockbuster exhibitions, and the acquisition of master-pieces.) Not so fast.

James Beck (1930–2007), the distinguished author, professor of art history at Columbia University, Renaissance scholar, and founder of the not-for-profit ArtWatch International in 1992, said it's a fake, and not even a good one at that. In his opinion, the money was thrown down the toilet. To back up his claim, Beck cited a major anachronism in the work, plus numerous other perplexing aspects, all of which add up to a definite difference in technique between Duccio and the forger, who he believes was working in the late 1800s. The Met has countered that the painting was carefully examined prior to being purchased (which is patently untrue) and is a signature work of Duccio dating from 1300. Two things are interesting about the debate.

First, De Montebello is nowhere in sight. The Met's banner, includ-ing writing letters to the editor and turning down Beck's offer to debate the issue in front of the painting, for example, is being carried by cura-tor Keith Christiansen. Secondly, in a fascinating illustration of the The *New York Times*' consistent loving treatment of the Met, reporter Robin Pogrebin wrote an article published in July, 2006 in the *Times,* in which she reviewed the heated debate about the painting.

Pogrebin wrote that she had held a telephone interview with noted Italian Renaissance scholar Luciano Bellosi, "who chuckled when told of Professor Beck's remarks." She then quoted the internationally renowned Bellosi as saying, "I assure you I have never doubted that it was a masterpiece by Duccio." Ready for the punch line? Some time later it was revealed (not in the *Times* but by Lee Rosenbaum) that professor Bellosi had never seen the disputed painting the Met had purchased, only a tattered black and white photograph of it. Since the Bellosi observations and quotes are the linchpin of the article, a number of questions spring to mind.

Did the *Times* reporter neglect to ask Bellosi if he had ever seen the disputed painting? Or, did the *Times* reporter ask Bellosi if he had seen the disputed painting and fail to report his negative answer, an answer that would have undermined the Met/*NY Times* position?

Last example. In 2007, Michael Kimmelman, writing a puff piece about the opening of the new antiquity galleries at the Met, wrote, "Archeologists who now argue that antiquities are better served in the dirt where they came from than disbursed among public museums like the Met imply that they prefer the past remain dead and buried." Nothing could be further from the truth. In fact, the opposite is true. *The Times'* highly knowledgeable art critic Kimmelman either has a major gap in his art education, or he was just writing what he thought his bosses wanted to hear.

Shortly after receiving $3,300,000 under his retention agreement, the 72-year-old Philippe de Montebello announced his resignation as director of the Met. Beginning in January, 2009, he will teach The History of Collecting at the NYU Institute of Fine Art and advise the university on other matters. In late 2008, Thomas Campbell, a curator in the Met's department of European sculpture and decorative arts, was named director.

The Smithsonian

The Smithsonian Institute (founded in 1846) owns the National Gallery in Washington, DC, and the American public owns the Smithsonian: A full 70% of the institutions billion dollar annual budget is supplied by taxpayers. This means that the public shells out over $700,000,000 each year to help support the Smithsonian, which has 6,300 employees (including 500 scientists), 6,500 volunteers, 19 museums, nine research centers and the National Zoo under its umbrella.

That in itself is not the problem. After all, that's a small price to pay for culture in America. The problem has been Lawrence Small.

Sixty-eight-year-old tall, bespectacled Lawrence Small worked at Citicorp for almost 30 years, was the head of Fannie Mae for about ten, and was appointed Secretary (that's what they call the head man) of the Smithsonian in 2000. Small, like his counterpart at the Getty, Barry Munitz, had a checkered past when he was appointed to the top post. In 2004, a scandal boiled over from the years Small was at Fannie Mae. A government report found that Small pressured his subordinates to ignore generally accepted accounting rules (read he ordered them to cook the books) to boost paper profits so his personal compensation would rise proportionately.

Small not only created an imperialistic culture, which caused a governance crisis, he treated the Smithsonian like his personal piggy bank. For example, Small spent $160,000 to redecorate his office after he took over. To add insult to injury, he received a staggering $2,000,000 in housing and office expenses during his six-year tenure. Over $1,000,000 was paid to Small for the use of his $3,500,000 mansion on the theory that his residence would be available for official functions. After a flurry of events in the first years of his tenure, Small had very few events there for most of the subsequent years. For the last two years of his tenure Small never used his house for entertaining, but he still collected the expense money. The inspector general determined that $90,000 were unauthorized expenses of Small, which include the usual scammer's charter jet travel, chauffeured cars, top hotels, lavish meals and so on. The $2,000,000 in house and office expense payments were on top of his salary of almost $1,000,000 a year (which Small essentially doubled from the beginning to the end of his six-year tenure.)

Like Munitz at the Getty, Small was filling his pockets and spending recklessly (think $14,000 for a jet charter and $700+ for hotel stays for his family) while publicly urging employees to operate more frugally by, for example, turning off decorative or accent lighting and using desk lighting instead of general lighting. There is something else Small learned from Munitz: co-opt the board of trustees so they will turn a blind-eye to your corporate approach of governance, lavish perks, questionable expenditures, unsupportable deals, and indiscretions. Which is exactly what happened at the Getty and the Smithsonian.

The board of trustees of the Smithsonian is called the Board of Regents, which is responsible for its administration. The board consists of 17 members, with the US Supreme Court's Chief Justice as Chancellor, the Vice-President of the United States, three Senators, three Congressmen, and nine other political appointees.

With a board of that nature, is it any wonder that: Small was able to keep the board in the dark about problems, such as the backlog of a $2,500,000,000 (yes, that's with a "B") backlog of critical maintenance as revealed by the General Accounting Office; Small was not only able to hide problems, he was able to limit and polish negative information about the operation that was revealed by internal and external audits; Small was able to edit and downplay all criticism of his personal leadership; Small was able to cover-up illegal expenses in an unethical way.

Small made a 30-year deal with the television network Showtime which restricted access of others to the Smithsonian's archives and scientists. This violates the public status of the Smithsonian, but, hey, who was checking?

Small consistently promised big donors control over how their funds would be used. For example, in what became a highly controversial situation, Small promised donor Catherine Reynolds she could basically select which prominent Americans would appear in her schlock exhibition called "Spirit of America" and "Hall of Achievers' in exchange for her $38,000,000 donation. After a public outcry, Reynolds withdrew the majority of her grant.

In 2001, again without consulting with the board, Small moved to close the Smithsonian's highly regarded Conservation and Research Center, a 3,200 acre field station devoted to preserving endangered species. Small was forced to back off when the scientific community (and public) screamed bloody murder.

What else? Did somebody ask if were there conflicts of interest? Small and his deputy, Sheila Burke, both sat on the board of directors of the Chubb Group which sells over $500,000 worth of insurance to the Smithsonian every year. As a reward for their blatant conflicts of interest, the pair was highly compensated annually by Chubb. Small received almost $170,000 a year in cash and stock options, and Burke grabbed almost $200,000 a year from the insurance company. Since 2000, this comes to a total of almost $5,000,000 for Small and almost $3,000,000 for Burke.

And then there is the small matter of what most people call going to work. Small took nearly ten weeks of vacation a year. In his seven-year role as head of the institution, he was absent from his job 400 work days, and collected some $6,000,000 for serving on various outside boards (which took Small away from his job at the Smithsonian). While employed by the Smithsonian, Burke took off a full 25% of her required work days and collected an eye-popping $10,000,000 from outside sources. Burke, born in 1951, after leaving the Smithsonian, now pretends that she never worked there.

What was art's role during Lawrence Small's corporate approach? Art, in America's signature art museum, was relegated to near obscurity. An external committee report regarding the National Gallery said, "The museum's chief weakness is the later 20th Century and contemporary collection, which has evidently been formed much more by opportunism than by strategy."

Again, as in the Munitz tenure at the Getty, during Small's seven-year tenure at the Smithsonian, numerous top people fled the hostile environment he created, including four museum directors. Benefactors Andrew Mellon and his son Paul (1907–1999) would turn in their graves.

In 2006, the Smithsonian's inspector general resigned in protest after Small tried to squelch an internal audit of the business ventures division (called the SBV). The SBV was formed to centralize sales outlets (gift shops, cafes and other for-profit units) in the various museums. Small hired Gary Beer to head the effort.

Beer, 48, arrived at the Smithsonian with a reputation as a high-flying ex-Washington lobbyist and lavish expense account spending Hollywood wannabe (he was a minor executive at Robert Redford's Sundance Institute). Beer had no outside employment when he was hired to run the Smithsonian business unit. Perfect.

Beer's budget projected a profit of over $50,000,000 a year, but year in and year out the salaries of the SBV went up as the profits declined from about $28,000,000 the first year to about $24,000,000 in 2006. In 2006, Beer's salary was over $500,000 per year while the top ten executives in his unit made a total of almost $3,000,000. When released, the audit found numerous accounting errors and questioned the accuracy of its financial statements. The report also criticized the business unit's performance, and investigated Beer's financial transactions and expenses.

Lawrence Small resigned (read was forced out) in early 2007 when an internal audit revealed controversial compensation, including charging the institution $90,000 in unauthorized expenses. Like Muniz, Small left without receiving a severance package.

In early 2007, shortly after Small's departure, Senator Grassley sent a seven-page letter questioning Beer's performance as head of the business unit. The Senator also questioned Beer's intimate relationship with a direct subordinate whom he had promoted and lavished bonuses on. The female employee, Jeanny Kim, 40, received five promotions and four raises in six years, moving from executive assistant to vice-president and general manager of media services, earning more than $140,000 in 2006 (one of the highest paid employees in the SBV).

In August 2007, based on an inspector general's report, Gary Beer was discharged forthwith, even though he had previously requested to stay to the end of his contract. Beer was also required to reimburse the Smithsonian $30,000 of unsupported expenses. How seriously flawed was Beer's leadership of SBV? Representative Vernon Ehlers of Michigan suggested several solutions, including disbanding Smithsonian Business Ventures altogether. Anything to prevent it from being something "autonomous that can run wild, as this one has done."

Also in August 2007, James Hobbins, who had been a highly likeable employee with the Smithsonian for 40 years, suffered what is known as collateral damage. This important employee resigned under a cloud created by Lawrence Small. Hobbins was Small's executive assistant whom Small co-opted with unauthorized bonuses, six months after being named secretary. Over the years, Small gave Hobbins a series of higher then average raises. Poor Hobbins. In his mid-sixties, he confessed that, out of misplaced loyalty to Small, he destroyed transcripts from a key Board of Regents meeting in January, 2007, when the board discussed Small's exorbitant and illegal expenses, compensation, and housing allowance.

Hopefully the Small/Beer go-go era of corporate-style compensation, out-of-control expense account spending, and questionable deals has come to an end. Even with Small, Burke, and Beer gone, however, there remains a critical problem at the Smithsonian.

The problem is Roger Sant. Roger Sant, 79, chairman of the executive committee of the Smithsonian's Board of Regents (in a horrifying mirror image of John Biggs at the Getty), publicly defended Lawrence Small's every action. Sant ignored the aforementioned Inspector General's report, and when that failed, he tried to quash it. Sant justified Small's lavish spending and excessive salary by claiming that Small had raised absolutely monstrous amounts of money for the Smithsonian. Sant was either lying or was completely uninformed.

The truth of the matter is that Small raised less money than his predecessor but was taking credit for the successes of his predecessor. In mid-2007, however, immediately after the Smithsonian's new Committee on Governance issued its scathing 55-page report that charged (among other things) the Board of Regents failed to provide oversight that might have prevented Small's extravagant spending, Sant ran for cover.

"We continue," he now crowed to the world, "to express real regret and accept responsibility for the lack of strong oversight for the former secretary and for the Smithsonian in general." And, "We realize in many areas we should have applied much more due diligence, but I can't say strongly enough that we are doing everything we know how not to let this happen again." For the Smithsonian to eventually put its house in order, more than the administrators need to go. The fact of the matter is that arrogant, double-talking regents like Roger Sant undermine the public's trust as much or more than money and time-stealing people like Small, Burke, and Beer. Is it any wonder critics are calling the Smithsonian endangered.

Fortunately for American taxpayers, Senator Charles Grassley, who earlier openly rebuked the corporate atmosphere at the Smithsonian and the Getty, is on the case. "The former secretary [Small] discounted the educational mission, took credit for fund raising successes that others had achieved, overstated fund raising gains, was AWOL much of the time, [and] when questioned on his expenses, he reacted with arrogance and a sense of entitlement." "There clearly needs to be," Grassley added, "a big broom to sweep out the problems at the Smithsonian and the 'anything goes' culture. The authorized expenses are over-the-top by any measure. The manipulation of the audit might be even worse."

Minor changes have been made to curb abuses, such as adding a fourth board meeting each year, but real hope appears to be on its way. In early 2008, a distinguished scholar, G. Wayne Clough, 66, was appointed Secretary of the Smithsonian. Clough, ex-president of the Georgia Institute of Technology, appears to be an inspired choice. Thankfully, he's not a politician.

MORE LEADERSHIP TREACHERY

The Brooklyn Museum of Art

In 1999, the Brooklyn Museum of Art opened an exhibition entitled, "SENSATION: Young British Artists from the Saatchi Collection." The contents of the exhibition caused a furor, but that's immaterial to this discussion. Here is what's material: The exhibit's largest donor was also its Number One financial backer. When confronted with the fact that Charles Saachi had pledged $160,000 to the museum over three years, the director Arnold Lehman, 64, tried (in vain) to conceal the fact. Lehman also tried to conceal the fact that he solicited donations of $10,000, and over, from the dealers who represented artists whose works were on display.

In addition, Lehman made a secret deal with Christies, giving the auction house the right to handle future articles the museum would put up for sale in exchange for $50,000. Lehman also made a deal with rock star David Bowie to the tune of $75,000, giving him the rights to record and use the audio tour anyway he chose and to use the art featured in the exhibition on his website.

Until the facts were exposed by *The New York Times,* Lehman consistently, and vigorously, maintained that commercial considerations never entered any discussions with donors to the exhibition. From the museum staff's point of view, Lehman's worse sin was giving Saatchi control over what went into the exhibition. Ceding artistic control not only neutralized the staff, Lehman essentially said to the world that in today's materialistic museum culture, curators are unnecessary and expendable. This is the mess the Association of American Museum Directors supported in a widely circulated news release.

In 2006, further evidence of Lehman's disdain for his board of trustees and curators was splashed across the headlines and brought dissent and resignations to the museum. Lehman, without telling the board, did away with the traditional departments, such as European art, Egyptian art, and so on. In their place, he created two teams, one for collections, and one, no surprise here, for exhibitions. (Clearly, Lehman was de-emphasizing the museum's collection and focusing upon unrelated exhibitions, such as *Star Wars* in 2002, which was basically a display of costumes and drawings of the movie series.) This draconian measure led to the resignation of three veteran curators, one who had served 37 years, and two board members, one who had served over 20 years.

In 2008, the museum announced that its collection of over 30 pieces of Coptic Art (Egyptian sculptures made by Christians) dating from the fourth to the sixth centuries was riddled with fakes. Specifically, over half of the works are obvious fakes and the others have problems, such as being re-touched and/or re-carved.

Gary Vikan, one of the most down-to-earth museum directors active today, almost immediately (in the late 1970s) raised doubts about the authenticity of the works. Vikan, a 1967 graduate of Carleton College, is a Byzantine specialist. He is also an author, teacher, and scholar. He was appointed assistant director of curatorial affairs of the Walters Art Museum in Baltimore in 1985 and has served as its director since 1994.

Vikan has had many successes at the Walters, but the decision most popular with the public is free admission since 2006, which has resulted in a serious spike in attendance. Here is what he said to help explain the Brooklyn Museum stonewalling the fake Coptic Art and claiming it to be authentic for fifty years. "Whether it's because we've paid for it or someone with a fancy degree said it was genuine, once we make a decision, everything that happens after that . . . is to vindicate the decision."

Walters Art Museum

Henry Walters (1848–1931) of Baltimore, Maryland, inherited a railroad empire and an impressive art collection from his father, William Walters, who died in 1894. Henry was an excellent businessman who also had a good eye expanded both: He built a railroad empire and added substantially to his father's art collection. Walters is a collector who was not unscrupulous, but rather was hoodwinked, at least that's what all of the experts in the art world once thought. What triggered their snickering was the bold move Henry Walters made in 1902. Walters purchased the Don Marcello Mazzarenti collection from the notorious Godfrey von Kopp, for what would today be about $30,000,000.

The collection, which the Italian priest Mazzarenti accumulated over a 50-year period and housed in Palazzo Accoramboni in Rome, consisted of a large number of fakes. In fact, at the time, the collection, which consisted of over 1,500 artworks, was called rubbish and worthless by condescending experts. While it is true that there were a large number of fakes in the Mazzarenti collection, this rush to judgment proved to be dead wrong. Works by Giovanni Battista Tiepolo (1696–1770), Pontormo (c. 1494– c. 1557), Bernardo Strozzi (c. 1581–c. 1644), El Greco (c. 1541–c. 1614), and Giulio Romano (to name just a few of the paintings), and numerous artifacts of historical significance shined through the haze. Upon his death in 1931, Henry Walters donated his artworks, which had grown to 22,000 pieces, to the City of Baltimore, where they are today housed in the culturally important Wallace Art Museum.

WHEN YOU'VE GOT A COMPLICATED SOLUTION TO A PROBLEM, YOU'VE STILL GOT A PROBLEM

The Guggenheim

The Guggenheim Museum was founded in New York in 1937. Thomas Krens and a compliant board of trustees have taken a museum that was a respected member of the cultural life of the community and turned it into a pathetic shell.

Born in Brooklyn in 1946, Krens was hired as director in 1988 and retired as director in 2005 when he was fired-up to Chairman of the Guggenheim Foundation, which owns the museums. Krens has been vilified by the press and the art world. He is usually described as cold, distracted and rarely on hand. Jerry Saltz in *New York Magazine* called Krens "reckless, destructive, myopic, and misguided."

Under Krens' watch, the avant-garde structure on Fifth Avenue designed by Frank Lloyd Wright has ceased to be a museum as such. It has basically become a growth, market-driven commercial enterprise with a Wall Street mentality. Krens publicly crows, "The Guggenheim is a business." In the process, like most business entities, when problems arise, chaos reigns. Exhibitions have been cancelled, dedicated staff has been laid off, and the museum's endowment has been raided for operating costs and debt payments. The Guggenheim reflects Krens' approach to his job as director: He has thought about the museum without thinking about art. To say it another way, no one in the museum world has been as willing as Krens to reject museum's traditional concerns.

Consider: On his watch, the Guggenheim's research library, research program, and in-house scholarship have all been compromised. Further, the majority of the curators are ad-hoc so there is no on-going study or care of the permanent collection, such as it is. (The Guggenheim owns only 15,000 objects worldwide, compared, for example, to the Met's 2,000,000+ artworks.)

In 1994, the Guggenheim cancelled its major fall exhibition due to lack of funds. Nothing wrong with that except the works were scheduled to be sent to the Walker Art Center in Minneapolis so that exhibition also had to be cancelled. Director (at the time) Kathy Halbreich was, understandably, not happy. "If you don't respect your partners, some day you won't have any." In 1996, the museum was forced to put a note in its exhibition catalogue that a Rothko painting in the show was displayed upside down. Was it just a mistake, lack of a qualified curator, or lack of an art culture? In 1999, Krens solicited and received a secret $15,000,000 (over three years) from Giorgio Armani in exchange for exhibition of his frocks. When confronted, Krens denied there was a deal, and then, after finally admitting the secret agreement existed, refused to confirm the amount of money involved. In 2002, still scrambling, Krens made a deal with artist Norman Rockwell's estate: The Guggenheim would mount a display of Rockwell paintings if they would provide the necessary funds.

But it was Krens' vision was to brand the Guggenheim, which would have the effect of producing money for the franchise holder, not unlike McDonalds, which has been at the root of the museum's problems. Numerous Krens planned satellite museums have been cancelled due to financial problems, including one in Guadalajara, one in Taiwan, one in Rio de Janeiro, one in Saltsburg, one in Hong Kong, one in Tokyo, and two in Las Vegas. In late 2002, the Frank Ghery designed museum tower planned for downtown New York City was scuttled, after spending $1,000,000 on the model alone.

SoHo Guggenheim, which was opened in 1992, has been plagued by problems and has been shuttered. The museum's digital and online ventures also folded. (The wildly successful Bilboa satellite in Spain, and the Berlin satellite were in business at publication time but neither are museums in the true sense of the word. Not even close. They are merely commercial galleries.)

Incidentally, in 2001 when Krens announced the opening of the satellite in Vegas at the Venetian Hotel and Casino (called the Guggenheim Hermitage Museum), Krens (exposing his putrid innate nature) boasted that it was going to bring in millions for the Guggenheim, the Hermitage, and the Venetian, because we're bringing art to Las Vegas "where the heathens are." The Guggenheim Hermitage Museum in the Venetian Casino closed in early 2008. Christopher Hawthorne, heralding the closing of the second Las Vegas Guggenheim, wrote in May, 2008, in the *LA Times,* "During his controversial reign, Krens turned the Guggenheim into the art world equivalent of a colonial power, seizing opportunities for expansion around the globe. And as with any failed colonial enterprise, the hand wringing and the post mortems are going on back in the home country, which is to say in New York and in the museum world."

In 2007, French billionaire Francois Pinault (who owns numerous high-end brands, including Christie's) beat out the Guggenheim in its bid to turn an unused ancient customs building in Venice, Italy (named the Punta della Dogana) into a contemporary art center. How, you may ask, can an individual collector (no matter how rich) win out over a museum, indeed, a New York museum with branches all over the world? The Guggenheim's bid lacked one essential element. It failed to list the works destined for the permanent collection, which was one of the basic elements of the contest. Was this blunder negligence? Or was the omission a symptom of the deeper problem that art is immaterial to Krens? Pinault, by the way, met all of the terms, including the listing of over 140 works that will be part of the new museum's permanent collection over a 30-year period.

If well-known philanthropist Peter Lewis, 76, one of the largest donor to the arts in modern times, hadn't financially bailed out the foundation that owns and controls the Guggenheim Museum, the entire Guggenheim museum network would not exist today. Lewis, chairman and principal stockholder of the Progressive Insurance Company of Cleveland, Ohio, joined the board in 1993, and was elected chairman in 1998. Over the years, Lewis donated $40,000,000 to the endowment and $15,000,000 toward the repair of the flagship Fifth Avenue building.

In 2001, Krens started to raid the endowment (established by Lewis) to cover operating deficits. This triggered Lewis' investigation into the books, which, in spite of his brilliant business mind, he was unable to understand. "There was a mess about how the finances had been managed at the museum," Lewis said, "which had first used yesterday's reserves and then used tomorrow's optimism." In 2003, the reporting format was finally revised according to his wishes.

Over the years, Lewis begged the other members of the board to donate to the museum. Not at his level, which was out of reach for most of the board, but at least at a reasonable level. With few exceptions, however, the frustrated philanthropic marvel, who donated three times as much as any previous donor to the Guggenheim, got nowhere.

Finally, in 2005, the tipping point came. Lewis had enough of Krens' unrealistic, quixotic expansion plans and manic management style and resigned in disgust as chairman of the foundation (and therefore the museum). "I concluded that Tom was not manageable. He's got one idea [expansion] and he's obsessed with it." David D'Arcy confirmed Peter Lewis' frustration in a *Wall Street Journal* article in 2005, "At the core of his [Lewis'] despair was Mr. Krens." Also in 2005, Lisa Dennison was named director of Guggenheim's Manhattan Museum. She left less than two years later (in the summer of 2007). Attempts to fill the post were unsuccessful; no qualified candidate wanted to work under Thomas Krens.

Finally, in early 2008, the arrogant 61-year-old Krens was pushed out the door of the Guggenheim. Naturally, the firing was sugar-coated. Jennifer Stockman, board president, put it this way. "This [his leaving] is something that Tom and the board decided together." Also, in early 2008, the financial officer was fired after 11 years on the job under Krens (who gave no oversight), for embezzling $800,000.

In late 2008, Richard Armstrong, 59, was appointed head of the Guggenheim. Armstrong comes from the Carnegie Museum of Art in Pittsburgh and has years of curatorial experience. Thankfully, Armstrong is the antithesis of Krens. His appointment signals a long overdue major change of direction for the museum.

Here's a final Thomas Krens item that pinpoints how he romanced the board and public over the years. In a 2007 puff piece in the *London Times*, the "six foot, five inch tall, tanned, white-haired Krens" was described by writer Joanna Pitman as a "sharp business brain," who also "sometimes curates major exhibitions."

Pittman, in the face of overwhelming evidence to the contrary, also wrote that Peter Lewis was kicked out as president when he challenged Krens, and that "Krens rejects reports that he has dipped into the endowment in the past for running costs." The interview with Krens was conducted in Bilboa over a long lunch, so one can only conclude that Krens poured Ms. Pitman a substantial amount of strong Spanish wine to accompanying his fairy tales. The fairy tales worked for Tom Krens for 20 years.

UNFORTUNATELY, IN MUSEUMS AS IN PEOPLE, AGE DOESN'T NECESSARILY TRANSLATE INTO HONORABLE

The British Museum

The British Museum, founded in 1753, has some 13,000,000 objects in its collection but displays only 75,000 at any one time. This means that some 12,925,000 artworks are in storage at any given time. While the number is staggering, storing artworks is not unusual; most museums own many more works than they are able to display. What's disturbing about the British Museum situation is that over the years, for unknown reasons, it has consistently dismissed the charge that its storerooms are overflowing with unseen treasures.

In the late 1930s, Sir John Soames was the director of the British Museum in London. In order to receive a large donation from Joseph Duveen for a new gallery to house the Parthenon Sculptures (known as the Elgin Marbles), Soames sold out.

Thomas Bruce (1766–1841) was the seventh earl of Elgin. He was appointed ambassador to the Ottoman Empire by King George III. Lord Elgin had a real love of art, and so from the start it was his intention to steal as many artifacts from Greece as could possibly be hauled out of that country. To that end, in 1799, while in Italy on his way to his assignment in Constantinople, Elgin hired the Italian artist Giovanni Lusieri (court painter to the king of Naples) to hire and supervise the team of artists and workers he (Elgin) was in the process of hiring to do his dirty work in Athens. Elgin had every possible sculpture and frieze pulled down from the Parthenon, including a giant frieze over 160 yards long, 17 carved figures, and 15 metopes. To put it another way, between 1801 and 1804, Elgin stole over half of the surviving sculptures from one of the world's most famous and important monuments. (Tragically, in the process of denuding the Parthenon, there were several spectacular accidents due to failure of the ropes and pulleys that shattered irreplaceable historic treasures.)

After raping the Parthenon and leaving it almost entirely stripped, Elgin traveled throughout the area and seized any antiquity he could find, in and outside of Athens and beyond. His dream was to possess every valuable antiquity in Greece. In all, Elgin shipped over 100 cases of marble sculptures from Greece to England.

Various Greeks and traveling Englishmen objected to Elgin's pillage. The most prominent figure to scream bloody murder was the famous romantic poet Lord Byron (1788–1824), who wrote a devastating indictment of Elgin's actions. Richard Payne Knight was another severe critic. Eventually, the English press and general population joined in condemning Elgin for his plundering the Parthenon marbles from Greece.

Elgin defended himself, saying he was merely trying to improve the British arts. He also maintained that he wanted to rescue the marbles from the Turks and travelers who pocketed every loose stone. Elgin also claimed that he had official written approvals from the Turkish authorities regarding his excavations, but was unable to produce any evidence of this when questioned in England. This claim was advanced for several hundred years by scholars but has been proven to be bunk. Heavy bribery was Elgin's primary tool, although his position as ambassador gave him a certain amount of immunity.

At first, Elgin displayed his booty in a small, private museum in central London (for which, surprise, surprise, he charged a fee). Finally, in 1816, after innumerable attempts, the bankrupt Lord Elgin was able to sell the Parthenon Marbles to the British government. The treasures were hung in the Elgin Saloon of the British Museum in 1832.

Back to Joe Duveen and his donation, which created the Duveen Gallery in 1939. Duveen felt the most famous antiquities in the world looked dirty and needed to look whiter, disregarding the fact that the Pendelikon (also spelled Pendelicon) marble originally used acquires a mellow honey color when exposed to the air. Brightening artworks to increase their salability was a Duveen trademark. In this instance, however, pure ego drove Duveen's demand.

In any case, at Duveen's insistence, director Soames agreed to unprecedented heavy-handed cleaning. Over a period of over 15 months, workers used copper chisels, wire brushes and abrasives to satisfy Duveen's demands that the precious relics must look more clean. The problem was that when the workers pounded away at what they were told was dirt, they were removing an ancient, honey-colored patina. The aggressive over-cleaning also damaged the priceless artifacts, destroying details like the original chisel marks that were an integral part of the marbles. In addition, there was an excessive loss of original material and alteration and distortion of the original forms. When the Elgin Marbles were finally displayed (with their now infamous cleaning) the public was outraged, and the scandal dominated the press for years, only quieting down when Duveen died in 1939. For the next 60 years the British Museum vehemently denied the charges that the marbles had been injured by reckless cleaning.

Over those decades, the museum engaged in one of the art world's most blatant cover-ups. They destroyed files, they hid reports, and they repeatedly outright lied to the world at large. Then, in 1996, strictly due to the law's demands, the British Museum allowed art historian William St. Clair to see the damning file. St. Clair published his book *Lord Elgin and the Marbles* in 1998, in which he categorically stated that the sculpture had been damaged by the cleaning.

At first, the British Museum even rejected his complaints, claiming they were exaggerated. Exposed, after much hemming and hawing the British Museum officially owned-up to their heavy-handed cleaning and to the damage the cleaning inflicted on the marbles. Greece called the over-cleaning and cover-up shameful and outrageous. They forcefully pointed out that this over-cleaning proved that the British claim that would be better custodians of the marbles than Greece was utter nonsense. (Since 1839 the Greek government, in the art world's most famous controversy, has demanded the return of the Elgin Marbles from Britain, to no avail.) There's more. Chris Smith, Britain's Culture Secretary at the time the scandal became public said, "The [the Elgin Marbles] have been kept in very good condition." Even that can be topped.

When the secret cleaning and 60-year cover-up were revealed, in classic, embarrassing museum public relations babble, the museum spokesman said, "We were embarrassed at the time, in the late thirties, because we knew it should not have happened, but when it became clear, the trustees made it public immediately." In museum spin, a 60-year cover-up is immediately.

At least the British Museum trustees finally admitted that the cover-up of the damage inflicted by the cleaning was truly a scandal. Over the years, polls in the UK have consistently shown that the English population favors returning the plundered Elgin Marbles to Greece. In 1996, a whopping 90% said so. One wonders how long the British Museum can ignore the wishes of its citizens. At the beginning of the twenty-first-century, this question became even more cogent.

After three decades of preparation, overcoming more than 100 lawsuits, and ten years of construction, Greece finally finished a museum (named the New Acropolis Museum) at the base of the Acropolis. The museum has a full view of the Parthenon, and in 2007, the government began the year long process of moving some 4,500 antiquities into the building. Designed by Swiss/American architect Bernard Tschumi, the 226,000 square-foot, $200,000,000 museum will (among other things) cleverly emphasize the loss of the Elgin Marbles to England.

In the museum's top-floor galleries, which mimic the layout of the Parthenon, the original friezes will be mounted in an unbroken sequence, so the viewer can follow the classic narrative. In the places the panels have been lost to antiquity, they will be left blank. Here's where the brilliance comes in. The panels that were looted by Lord Elgin will be reproduced in plaster. It will be clear that the plaster casts are copies because the plaster casts will be lighter than the originals (which have the honey colored patina). It gets better.

The imitations will be placed exactly where the original sculptures and frieze particles would have been had they not been plundered. As Greek Culture Minister, Michalis Liapis, has stated this new museum (co-sponsored by the European Commission), effectively undercuts England's arguments that Greece cannot properly house its treasures.

The importance of the museum cannot be overstated. Journalist Nicolai Ouroussoff, writing in *The New York Times* in late 2007, summed up Greece's position perfectly. "In dismantling the ruins of one of the glories of Western civilization, Lord Elgin robbed them of their meaning. The profound connection of the marbles to the civilization that produced them is lost," he wrote. After this powerful set-up, Ouroussoff nails his point home. "Mr. Tschumi's [the architect] great accomplishment is to express this truth in architectural form. Without pomp or histrionics, his building makes the argument for the marbles' return."

In 1818, the British Museum acquired a portrait bust of Julius Caesar, which it believed was a Roman original. In the ensuing decades, the museum and art historians promoted the forgery as the authentic likeness of Caesar in history books and all other areas, until it was exposed as a nineteenth-century fake in 1936. For almost 120 years the museum displayed a fake, but stubbornly refused to admit it had been duped.

In a similar vein, in 1871 the museum acquired a life-sized terracotta burial casket, supposedly Etruscan from the sixth century B.C.

The museum maintained it was genuine for sixty years after it was judged a fake, and finally removed it from display in 1935. Unfortunately, like the fake bust of Caesar, during this period the piece was touted as an authentic Etruscan artifact in school books and other areas. In 1897, the museum acquired a crystal skull that they believed was from the Aztec era. In 2005, over 100 years later, they finally admitted they had been duped and had been displaying a fake.

London's National Gallery

The National Gallery in London (founded in 1824) has works by Michelangelo, Raphael, Velazquez, and Leonardo (among others) under fire. Most connoisseurs around the world believe that certain of these paintings are misattributed at best, fakes at worse. The museum has stonewalled all of the scholar's charges. For example, in 1980, based on Ludwig Borchard's authentication (which he made in 1930), the museum purchased what it thought was a painting by Rubens called "Samson and Delilah." The acquisition raised a storm of protest from experts who challenged the work's authenticity, but the museum relied on Borchard's opinion. After all, Borchard was an authority on Rubens. As in the cases of Bernard Berenson and Abraham Bredius, Borchard's reputation was so strong, the museum would not even consider the possibility that he could have been mistaken or that he sold his signature.

They were wrong. Thirty years earlier, in 1950, Borchard advised a college not to buy the painting because it wasn't by Rubens. In 1954, however, Borchard wrote a certificate of authenticity for a London dealer affirming the painting was by Rubens. In recent years, Ludwig Borchard has been exposed to be as corrupt as Berenson (although he was a minor leaguer compared to B.B.) routinely selling signed certificates of authentication

While the matter of conserving masterpieces through cleaning has been controversial for over 2,300 years (Pliny the Elder complained about it), the National Gallery has been guilty of over cleaning and therefore ruining paintings more than any other institution. The museum's woes regarding over zealous restoring began in 1844 when scholars and the public complained, and the museum ignored their concerns. Over the years the museum has been under fire for misattributing paintings. For example in 1939, then director Kenneth Clark relabeled a group of paintings which had been labeled "anonymous artists in the Venetian School," to "Giorgione." Clark apparently made his move in an attempt to hype attendance. The public and staff were outraged. But the last word went to the outraged staff. The staff locked Clark out of the library. Ah yes, there will always be an England.

The Royal Academy

The Royal Academy in London is one of the oldest, and most unusual, arts organizations in the world. The RA (as it is called) was founded in 1769 as a home for accomplished artists working in Britain. In 1780, the Academy moved from its location in Pall Mall to Burlington House, its spectacular present home in Piccadilly. Eighty academicians (14 sculptors, 12 architects, eight printmakers, and 46 painters), who are known as RA's, run a staff of 200. From among their number, three of the artists are paid, and 20, with two-year rotating terms, sit on a governing council. The president is elected annually from among their group by the 80 academicians, so by necessity, is an artist. A secretary, on the other hand, is appointed to run the organization, and is historically a person with administrative skills.

You read that right. The president and secretary share the power at the top. Any high-school business student will tell you that a structure such as this cannot possibly work. Not only is the ultimate responsibility ambiguously divided, the power is divided between an artistic-orientated individual and an administrative type, a classic clash of standards, ideals and goals.

What has the ancient governance structure of the Royal Academy wrought? Bloodletting, mostly. Shortly after being pointed to the position of secretary, Ms. Lawton Fitt, an American (the first) who joined the RA in 2002, cancelled a major exhibition ("Citizens and Kings: Portraiture in the Age of Goya and David" scheduled for September 2005) organized by Norman Rosenthal, the long time, highly successful, exhibitions secretary. Fitt, who many claim cancelled the show to punish Rosenthal and show him (and the Academy) who was in charge, cited financial concerns. Rosenthal, and the academicians, howled bloody murder, and the lines between artistic expression and money were drawn. In the squabble that was tearing the RA apart, Fitt called for Rosenthal's resignation.

In December, 2004, however, after only two years in the job, Ms. Lawton Fitt (not Rosenthal) resigned in, well, a fit. In the course of this power struggle, the Academy refused to make museum officials available for interviews. Meanwhile, in October 2004, president, Sir Philip King, an architect, resigned, citing ill health. King denied that he had received a letter, signed by over thirty fellow academicians, detailing his managerial shortcomings and calling for his removal. In the middle of this imbroglio, in July, 2004, Brendan Neiland, the head of the Royal Academy's art school and one of the three paid academicians, resigned when confronted with evidence that he was embezzling money from the Academy. Less than one year later, in May 2005, in a move that shocked the art world and the nation as well, the outspoken Neiland was expelled from the Academy, with 39 fellow academicians voting in favor of the expulsion, the first artist to be stripped of his membership in over 200 years. It seems clear that professor Neiland's blatant and unusual expulsion was a result of his highly publicized incendiary statements to the press. He called for artists (especially painters) to have more influence in Britain's art market. Professor Neiland not only charged that curators wield too much power, he directly attacked collector Charles Saatchi and Tate director Sir Nicholas Serota, charging (among other things) that the two rich and powerful men "run art, and they should not. They decide who and what should be shown. They merely follow fashion."

In 2006, Charles Saumarez Smith was appointed chief executive of the Royal Academy. This is the same Smith who was unceremoniously dropped by the National Gallery after losing a power struggle with Peter Scott, chairman of the gallery's board of trustees.

The Tate

The Tate Museum in London, founded in 1897 and now called Tate Britain, in utter disregard for its own Code of Ethics, and those of the UK Charity Commission, purchased a 13 canvas installation called "The Upper Room" from trustee Chris Ofili. This is illegal because by law in England, trustees cannot receive monetary benefit from the charity on whose board they sit without express permission from the UK Charity Commission. In 2006, following a nine month investigation, the UK Charity Commission ruled that the Tate was guilty of breaking charity laws. (As a matter of fact, in the last nine years the museum purchased $1,500,000 worth of paintings of artists sitting on the board of trustees of the museum.) In response to the withering, landmark ruling, Sir Nicholas Serota, the stern director of both Tate galleries, and the doyen of British modern art, allowed that in the future, procedures regarding conflicts of interest would be tightened and made more public.

The Charity Commission also indicated that it will investigate further many more of the museum's purchases of paintings by artist/trustees, going all the way back to 1960. Adding insult to injury, in 2004, the Tate solicited (and received) a 75,000 pound grant from the National Art Collection Fund to help meet the 600,000 pound purchase price of the Ofili work. This was called a "technical error" by director Serota, now in his 50s, because the museum had already committed to purchasing the work. This is significant because the Fund does not pay money to institutions that have already made a commitment to purchase a work of art.

What did the National Art Collection Fund do? It waived its rules for the organization that had waived its rules and allowed the 75,000 pound grant to stay. Ready for the kicker? When the National Art Collection Fund agreed to allow the grant to remain in place, the Chairman of the fund was David Verey, the very same David Verey who was the Tate's Chairman and a trustee when the grant was approved.

Breaking the law is nothing new for the Tate. Over the last 50 years, the vaunted museum of modern art has committed the crime of failure to seek permission before it illegally purchased paintings by artist/trustees at least 17 previous times. In 2006, the Tate again broke its own rules against showcasing a private collection when it made three rooms available to the Swiss bank, UBS, to hang 150 photographs from the bank's private collection. This exhibition will be followed by the display of over 100 drawings and paintings from the bank's private collection. The cash-for-access scheme has caused an uproar in England.

Inexplicably, in 2004, the Tate acquired a bushel of some 1,200 pieces of controversial Francis Bacon material after turning most of the same items down in 1992. The works were donated by Barry Joule, the controversial figure who was Bacon's chauffer and handyman. Joule came forward with the stash a full six years after Bacon died and supposedly gave him the items. The Bacon estate, and most experts, maintain that the trove of photographic images and sketches on paper are fakes. For example, in 2000, the Irish Museum of Modern Art in Dublin (and the Barbican Gallery in London in 2001), both displayed a portion of the disputed works, labeling them "attributed to Francis Bacon." As we all know, the words "attributed to" are death to any artwork. So why did the Tate accept the items? Something is up.

The MFA

The Boston Museum of Fine Arts (called the MFA) was founded in 1870. Like the other major American museums, it has had a history of scandals and unconscionable behavior. Cornelius Vermeule III, born in Scotland in 1925, was made curator of classical art at the MFA in 1957. He served in that position almost 40 years, until 1996. Vermeule, with no real supervision, purchased most of the looted antiquities. For example, in 1998, an examination of the MFA's records showed that 61 of the 71 antiquities acquired by Vermeule between 1985 and 1987 had no history of prior ownership. Primarily through Vermeule, the MFA acquired over 115 artifacts and 1,200 ancient coins from disgraced antiquities dealer Robert Hecht (and intermediaries) which had no credible provenance.

How close were curator Vermeule and dealer Hecht? In 1988, Hecht held an exhibition of artifacts at his Atlantic Antiquities Gallery in New York and Vermeule wrote a glowing introduction for the catalogue (read sales piece). Hecht is the dealer who was ordered out of Italy in the 1970s, banned from Turkey in the 1980s, and is on trial in Italy for the crime of dealing in stolen antiquities and criminal conspiracy.

The MFA has over 30 artifacts that Italy claims have been looted. In 1995, when the MFA was shown Polaroid's from the now famous raid on the Geneva warehouse, deputy director, Katherine Getchell, said airily, "There's absolutely nothing we've seen or heard that proves anything to us." Think that's arrogant? Ms. Getchell also stated the MFA would continue dealing with Hecht.

The Unscrupulous

Segue to 2005. When approached by the *Boston Globe* about the evidence the Italians unearthed (no pun) in preparation for the Hecht/True trial, Getchell, stated she would not discuss the matter because the MFA had not been contacted by Italy. Nor would the museum contact Italy. "I really don't think it's the right way to approach it," she trumpeted. "We can't start going to every government in the world."

They must be very busy at the MFA. Less than two weeks prior to the beginning of the Hecht/True trial in Rome, however, Katherine Getchell went into hiding and spokesperson Dawn Griffin surfaced. Griffin announced that, indeed, the MFA was going to contact the Italian government. The museum decided that taking matters into their own hands was the thing to do, "Because of conflicting press coverage."

What really triggered the MFA to change its decades-old policy of stonewalling? Paolo Ferri, the Italian prosecutor, announced that he was going to turn his attention to the world's other museums, particularly the Boston Museum of Fine Arts, as soon as the Hecht/True trial was over. The MFA policy change occurred within days of the announcement. Like their counterparts at the Met in New York, obviously no one in Boston is interested in doing hard time in an Italian jail. In August 2006, the MFA and Italy (represented by Maurizio Fiorilli) announced a deal, calling it a cultural partnership. Thirteen looted archeological treasures are being returned to Italy (including a marble statute of the empress Sabina which dates from 136 AD) Italy will loan comparable works to the MFA.

Over the years the MFA has had other scandals and unconscionable behavior. In 1914, the museum first displayed a six-inch high delicate ivory and gold statue of a goddess holding a snake in each hand, their tongues hissing. The MFA featured, what they called one of the most famous pieces of ancient art in the world, in an honored location in the museum, and labeled it "Late Minoan, 1600-1800 B.C." Scholars became suspicious when over a dozen goddesses surfaced around the world. (The most notorious was the "Fitzwilliam Goddess," which the Fitzwilliam Museum in Cambridge, England purchased in 1926 as one of the earliest examples of Minoan sculpture.)

A cottage industry of Minoan fakes had grown up shortly after 1903 when Sir Arthur Evans, a wealthy English anthropologist, discovered artifacts on the island of Crete that were the remains of statuettes depicting female snake handlers (and other antiquities), which he called Minoan.

Year in and year out the experts insisted to the MFA, the Fitzwilliam, and other collectors that the goddesses had suspicious provenance, and, when compared with authentic Minoan artifacts, they also had stylistic discrepancies and lack of fine details. When the museums and collectors allowed the experts to technically test the goddesses, the results displayed anachronisms that proved they were fakes. After some eight decades of denial, the MFA (and the Fitzwilliam in the late 1990s) admitted they had been displaying Minoan fakes for approximately 80 years.

What triggered the sudden burst of honesty? A book! Kenneth Lapatin, a young anthropological genius, published a book called *Mysteries of the Snake Goddess* in the early 2000s (when he was a rising professor at Boston University) that laid the museums low. Like the never-say-die Getty and its fake Kouros, the MFA now labels its fake Snake Goddess "Late Minoan, 1600-1800 B.C. or early 20th Century."

In 1969, director Perry Rathbone surreptitiously acquired a smuggled Raphael portrait for some $1,00,000. Rathbone bragged to the world about its latest acquisition, stating that it had acquired a lost masterpiece by Raphael, just in time for its centenary celebration. Italy wanted the small (8-inch by 10-inch) painting back. The MFA (and Rathbone) stonewalled the request. Worse, Rathbone stuck to his original story that the Raphael had been legally imported into the United States. Rathbone's story was shattered, however, when an Italian investigation discovered that one of the MFA's curators, Hanns Swarzenski, carried the small painting in his suitcase through customs and didn't declare it to either country. This action violated both Italian and American law, and in 1971 the US Customs entered the MFA and seized the painting. THEN the museum agreed to return the work to Italy. In December of 1971, Rathbone resigned because of his leadership role in the scandal. The irony of this case is that the Raphael is not a Raphael, it is a fake.

In 1998, the MFA, through its director Malcolm Rogers, rejected out of hand claims by Mali for terracotta sculptures, and by Guatemala for Mayan vases. This is the man who rented 21 Monet masterworks from the permanent collection of the MFA to the for-profit Pace-Wildenstein gallery in the Bellagio Hotel and Casino in Las Vegas for $1,000,000. The reaction to Rogers' deal to put money in the promoter's pockets, a deal which at best can be called dicey, has been brutal. Brushing aside Rogers' claims that the MFA is merely trying to broaden its audience, Professor Selma Holo, head of the University of Southern California museum studies program and authority on museum issues said, "I will not buy that this is about non-elitism. This is about desperation and about making money, and nothing else." Christopher Knight, art critic of the *Los Angeles Times,* said it best when he wrote that the MFA and Rogers should be ashamed of themselves for selling out to private commercial interests.

Query. Why doesn't the MFA focus on taking its magnificent collection to the neighborhoods of Boston instead of to the desert thousands of miles away? In 2005, Rogers led the MFA further away from its role as a cultural institution and into that of an entertainment venue. Rogers, who has proven happy and willing to cater to celebrity culture (he mounted an exhibition of Ralph Lauren's cars), mounted an exhibition entitled "Things I love: The Many Collections of William I. Koch." Defending the show, which garnered scathing reviews both for content and for selling out, Rogers said that the critics are unduly concerned about "minor ethical questions."

Minor ethical questions? Koch, born in 1940, paid the museum to exhibit his things. He also paid for publication of the catalogue, which included an interview with Koch, photos of his wine cellar, and descriptions of the art in the show, written by MFA's curators. Rogers also said, "One of the things I wanted to do was to unveil the personality of a man of great passions, to help people understand the psyche of a collector." As one wag hilariously observed, apparently museum directors now have a new responsibility, that of ego-enabler.

Notorious lawyer-wielding Koch, who parked two of his boats on the front lawn of the museum and included empty wine bottles in the show, threatened to sue the *Boston Globe* over a scorching article by OP-ED columnist Alex Beam. Referring to the "Things I Love" exhibit Beam wrote, "He [Koch] also loves money, sex, litigation and any combination thereof." This is the same William Koch (a 68-year-old Palm Beach collector) who purchased, in 1984/1985, more than 1,600 ancient coins. Known as the "Elmali Treasure," the collection dating from 467 BC is called "The Hoard of the Century." Turkey, represented by high-powered lawyers Larry Kaye, Howard Spiegler, and Harry Rand, insti-gated a lawsuit to recover the treasure, which it charged was plundered. After a contentious ten-year battle, Koch folded and returned the coins.

This is the same Malcolm Rogers, in order to solidify his position as director, abruptly fired 18 people in 1999. Many of the terminated staff had national reputations, invaluable expertise, and years of sterling service to the MFA. Later in the year, one of the survivors, Theodore Stebbins, noted curator for 22 years, abruptly resigned, unable to work with Rogers. Rogers' talent drain of the MFA is known around bean town as "The Boston Massacre."

The Saint Louis Art Museum

Founded in 1879, the Saint Louis Art Museum is the oldest art museum west of the Mississippi river. Egypt, through Zahi Hawass, chief of Egypt's Supreme Council of Antiquities, ennobled by the Italians, is pursuing museums all over the world for return of its plun-dered treasures. Egypt has been after the Saint Louis Museum to return a 3,200-year-old burial mask it acquired in 1998 from Ali Aboutaam, the notorious antiquities dealer. Egypt's position is compelling:

The mask was excavated from a pyramid in Saqqara, Egypt in 1952 and has documentation from 1959 that the wood and plaster piece was stolen from the Egyptian Museum. (The burial mask has glass eyes for Ka Nefer Nefer, the woman whose head it covered.) Brent Benjamin, direc-tor of the Saint Louis Museum, is stonewalling the request in classic, albeit archaic, fashion. He demands valid evidence, a variation of de Mon-tebello's incontrovertible evidence. We all know how that turned out.

In 1953, director Perry Rathbone, publicly bragged that his (bril-liant) purchase of a four foot Etruscean Diana revealed an unprecedent-ed link with antiquity. The statute was tested in 1968 by two scientific laboratories and revealed to be approximately 40 years old. Like the Getty's kouros, it has been determined that the fake was sculpted by master forger Alceo Dossena.

The Detroit Institute of Art

The Detroit Institute of Art (one of the largest in America) was founded in 1888 as the private Detroit Museum of Art. In 1919, the museum was given to the city of Detroit. In 1927, a new building (now called the Detroit Institute of Art, or the DIA) was opened. A German scholar named Wilhelm Valentiner was hired as the first director and served in that capacity for some 20 years. Valentiner, edited the publication *Art in America* from 1913 to 1931, and was the first director of the Getty museum (1954). Like his college, Ludwig Burchard, all of his life Valentiner made false attributions, which he sold to art dealers and commercial galleries. In addition, Valentiner had a cottage industry: He kept discovering Rembrandts, attributing more than 1,000 paintings to the Dutch master. Not a bad business. Most of Wilhelm Valentiner's Rembrandt attributions have not held up and have been downgraded to school of Rembrandt, or worse.

As America's auto industry tanked, so did the Detroit museum. Beginning in the mid-1980s, to avoid closing down, the museum cut staff, cut hours, and hosted no major exhibitions for 14 years. Fortunately, by 2000, after a management restructuring (that basically moved the publicly-owned museum back to the private sector), and a subsequent infusion of cash from the new trustees, the museum not only avoided closing, it sprang back to life with a blockbuster van Gogh exhibition.

ALAS, YOUTH DOESN'T NECESSARILY TRANSLATE INTO HONORABLE, EITHER

The Kimbell

Founded in 1973, the richly-endowed Kimbell Museum in Fort Worth, Texas, proves the point that (to paraphrase badly) money corrupts and monstrous sums of money corrupt absolutely. For example, in 1998, within days of the departure of museum director Ted Pillsbury, a special committee of the non-profit foundation that runs the Kimbell surreptitiously voted trustees Kay and Ben Fortson, president and vice-president, $1,500,000. When the scam was exposed by the press, the couple returned the money, apparently to avoid prosecution.

The interesting aspect of the story is that Kay and Ben Fortson, the recipients of the windfall, are relatives of the original Kimbell museum donor, and they had been performing typical trustee volunteer duties. Not only that, the special committee that awarded the money consisted of the Fortson's children, other relatives, and dear, close, personal friends. In a replay of the Biggs/Munitz fiasco at the Getty and the Sant/Small fiasco at the Smithsonian, the Kimbell treasurer, Brenda Cline, supported the payoff, saying that the museum was compensating the Fortson's for the years they worked as volunteers in 1996, 1997 and 1998. She actually said that.

The Kimbell, which used to rank as one of America's premier art museums, has slipped in several other ways. Troubles were simmering, but burst into the public eye with the hiring of the wrong director, Timothy Potts. Hired in 1998 to replace Pillsbury, Potts is an Australian archeologist. Among other sins, he double talks the press about his income from the museum and his acquisitions, and works at avoiding their scrutiny altogether. Examples. In 2001, he purchased a Sumerian statute from the notorious Ali and Hisham Aboutaam brothers for almost $3,000,000 and then returned the fake seven months later. At about the same time, Potts agreed to pay the same dealers $4,000,000 for an ancient torso, except this time he changed his mind prior to delivery and the matter ended up in an acrimonious lawsuit. Timothy Potts, who is clearly out of his league running a museum as important as the Kimbell, is an archeologist and should know better. In mid-2007, Potts suddenly (and mysteriously) left the Kimbell and joined the Fitzwilliam Museum in Cambridge, England.

MOMA

The Museum of Modern Art (called MOMA) in New York was founded in 1929.

In 1974, MOMA shamelessly sued Kate Rothko (the artist's young daughter) in the midst of the emotional Rothko trial, demanding possession of two paintings by her father which she had promised to the museum. Young Kate Rothko was astounded by MOMA's lack of compassion for her position; she had repeatedly told the museum that once her legal problems were over and she had clear title to the paintings, she would complete the gift. Forty-two Warhol drawings vanished from the museum after a 1988 retrospective. The works were never found and the insurance company paid $1,100,000 to the Warhol Foundation for the Visual Arts. (Speaking of Warhols, in 1989, the authenticity of 19 Warhol Superman collages owned by MOMA was questioned. People who knew the artist well testified the works were definitely fakes.) Ronald Lauder has been a trustee of MOMA since 1976, and has held the titles of president and chairman of the board.

Ronald Lauder

Ronald Lauder and his brother Leonard spend parts of the winter in Palm Beach, Florida, in side-by-side mansions on the ocean. They are both billionaires, heirs to the Estee Lauder cosmetic fortune. The similarities end there. Leonard, 76, is the solid, thoughtful Lauder. When his father Joseph died in 1983, Leonard took over the company and took it to the moon. Ronald Lauder, 65, is less accomplished, emotional, and prone to excesses. He has unsuccessfully run for mayor of New York and unsuccessfully attempted to corner the television market in Eastern Europe. Both are ardent collectors and have been active in the cultural life of New York. Leonard's reign at the Whitney has been mostly positive, but Ronald's actions at MOMA have raised eyebrows.

How has MOMA been run since 1995 when Ronald Lauder was elected president? In 2004, the museum raised its (required) admission fee to $20 when it reopened after an expansion that cost almost $1,000,000,000. Director Glenn Lowry claims that he personally decided on the $20 fee, which makes MOMA the most expensive museum in New York. (The Met's $20 admission fee is recommended but not required.) Perhaps he is protecting president Lauder, who had to approve the whopping fee or perhaps his claim was meant to divert attention from Lowry's secret slush fund. The 53-year-old Lowry has been the highest paid museum official in the country with a salary (plus benefits and bonuses) of almost $1,500,000 in 2005. But that's the least of it.

Lowry received almost $5,500,000 in secret payments between 1995, the year he was hired, and 2005, the year the scam was exposed. The amounts Lowry received under the table varied from a low of just under

$36,000 per year to a high of $3,500,000. That's an average of almost $700,000 each and every year. Trustees David and Lawrence Rockefeller, Agnes Gund, and Ronald Lauder, made tax deductible gifts to a front they named the New York Fine Arts Support Trust. While both MOMA and the New York Fine Arts Support Trust are tax-exempt charitable organization, they are nevertheless governed by various IRS rules. These rules include the requirement that nonprofit's declare executive compensation (and grants in the case of the Trust) in a truthful and complete manner, without material omissions.

According to Senator Charles Grassley, the reason for the requirement is that, "Disclosure helps keep everyone honest . . . [and] there is a public interest in transparency and accountability from tax-exempt organizations to the public." The New York Fine Arts Support Trust described its payments to Lowry in its IRS filings as charitable contributions. MOMA made no mention of the monies in its filings. Tax experts say the museum is hiding the additional compensation to Lowry because it would undoubtedly exceed reasonable pay for an executive of a nonprofit organization. MOMA is trying to have it both ways by claiming on the one hand that the $5,500,000 was not compensation paid to Lowry by the museum, and on the other hand, that the $5,500,000 was not a grant to Lowry from the trust. There's more.

In 1995 (when Lowry negotiated the multi-million dollar slush fund to make the jump from the Art Gallery of Ontario, in Toronto), he got the museum to cover a down payment he made on an apartment and received reimbursement for all of his mortgage payments. There's even more. In 1999, the New York Fine Arts Support Trust bought the apartment from Lowry, who pocketed the $1,300,000 profit. And more. In 2004, the museum purchased an apartment where Lowry now lives rent free. Lowry has uncharacteristically ducked all questions from the press about his income.

Fair enough. But here is the most troubling question of this below-the-radar operation. Why did Lauder, Rockefeller, and Gund conceal the payments? Your guess is as good as mine. The most logical inference is that, for their own reasons, these collectors wanted to make Lowry secretly beholden to them. Bottom line. Glenn Lowry has to be the world's greatest salesman.

The Unscrupulous

HERE'S LOWRY'S COMPETITION

Godfrey von Kopp

Godfrey von Kopp was an art dealer in Paris who owned a gallery that specialized in paintings by the Old Masters. When a customer entered his gallery, von Kopp, and his associates, would surreptitiously discover his or her preference in art. As soon as the customer left, von Kopp would commission one of his forgers to create a painting in that artist's style. He primarily worked with Jacques Villon (1875–1963), a French cubist painter and printmaker who was Marcel Duchamp's brother. (Villon was known as a speed Constable painter from 1899 to 1902.) A few days after the gallery visit, as soon as the paint dried, von Kopp would call his mark and say a painting by that particular artist had just come up from the country.

An irony to this story is that there was an Englishman named Terry Bradley who copied paintings and antiques for a living and sold them to antique shops as fakes, which is perfectly legal. One day, almost as a lark, Bradley decided to forge a Jacques Villon painting and sell it through Sotheby's. Bradley believed the antique shops were selling his works as originals (he called them legalized fraudsters) and he wanted to see if the so-called legitimate art world was anymore honest than the antique shops. The fake Jacque Villon, which was knocked down for 2,750 pounds, breezed through auction and Sotheby's checks and balances. Sotheby's later admitted that several of its experts saw the painting before the sale. The auction house also admitted they had not checked the provenance of the Villon. "At that lowish price, you don't," sniffed one of the worker bees. Afterward, a pleased Bradley said, "It just goes to show you how easy it is to get a fake through."

Why consider bestowing the World's Greatest Salesman title on von Kopp? How else would you describe the man who sold Rome, Italy's Arch of Constantine (the one adjacent to the Colosseum) to John R. Thompson, the multi-millionaire restaurant owner and art collector from Chicago? The man who also sold Trajan's Column in Rome to Charles T. Yerkes, the American railroad magnet. And, almost sold J. P. Morgan the bronze doors of the Florence Baptistry. Whatever you call him, you must admit, to a salesman Godfrey von Kopp was a salesman.

How do you vote? Lowry or von Kopp?

In early 2005, in a shameful display of raw power, Ronald Lauder got art critic David D'Arcy fired from his 20-year-job freelancing on National Public Radio (NPR). Why did Lauder do it? Because he could. Lauder's nose was out of joint because D'Arcy wrote a piece that Lauder interpreted as negative to him (and MOMA). Anyone who listens to the broadcast (which is available on the Internet) will agree it was a balanced report of the struggle between MOMA and the Jewish family that had the Egon Schiele (1890-1918) painting "Portrait of Wally" stolen by the Nazis. Since Ronald Lauder has been publicly active in having art looted by the Nazis returned to its rightful owners, he must feel the report made him look like a hypocrite. Unfortunately, he has been that and more. Even though he has promised, promised, and promised, Ronald Lauder has not provided provenance information for the artworks in the collection of the Neue Galerie or for those in his private collection. (In mid-2006, D'Arcy sued NPR and MOMA for $5,000,000. The case was settled.)

The Neue Galerie

The Neue Galerie, located in the former Vanderbilt mansion, a gorgeous building at 5th Avenue and East 86th Street in Manhattan, was founded in late 2001 and exhibits German and Austrian art. In mid-2006, the Galerie announced a $50.00 admission price for Wednesday afternoons. You read that right. Fifty dollars. How could such a thing happen?

The back story is that the owner of the museum, balding Ronald Lauder, 64, purchased a stunning Klimt painting of Adele Bloch-Bauer for a reported record price of $135,000,000. In announcing the purchase, Lauder said, "This is our Mona Lisa." (With all due respect for Gustav Klimt's talent, that's like saying Oscar Wilde is William Shakespeare. Or Damien Hirst is GianLorenzo Bernini.) The over-the-top price for the painting caused great interest, so billionaire Lauder saw an opportunity to pay for his $135,000,000 acquisition, $50.00 at a time. Less than a week after the scam was announced, in reaction to horrific press and community reaction, the plan was scratched.

Leonard Lauder

Leonard Lauder, Ronald's older brother, has also been under attack for some time for refusing to provide an inventory (or at least issue documentation) of his private art collection, particularly the Austrian and German works which are known to be prominent in his collection. The issue is whether either Lauder owns any paintings or other artworks that belonged to European Jews and were plundered by the Nazis during World War II. What is particularly galling to Leonard and Ronald Lauder's most vociferous critics is the fact that both Lauders have been vocal, public champions of Jewish rights in general and restitution to Jewish heirs of plundered art in particular.

In late 2007, Leonard Lauder was sued by Georges Jorisch, the grandson of Amalie Redlich, who died during the Holocaust. The suit demands the return of the Klimt painting "Blooming Meadow." Jorisch's claim is basically based on two early catalogue entries which attribute the painting to his grandmother. Lauder denies the charge and refuses to return the painting which he purchased in 1983. There are a number of interesting coincidences in this case.

Art dealer, Serge Sabarsky, who sold the "Blooming Meadow" painting to Leonard Lauder in 1983, is the same individual who (until he died in 1996) was Ronald Lauder's partner in the Neue Galerie. Sabarsky was also instrumental in helping Ronald accumulate his collection of German and Austrian art. E. Randall (Randol) Schoenberg, the attorney in the "Blooming Meadow" case, is the attorney who represented Maria Altman in her successful attempt to recover six Klimt paintings that had belonged to her uncle and were confiscated by the Nazis. Here's the weirdest coincidence of all. One of those six Klimt paintings recovered was the "Adele Bloch-Bauer I" that Leonard Lauder's brother Ronald Lauder bought from Maria Altman for the $135,000,000 and hung in his Neue Galerie. Leonard Lauder has been chairman of both the Whitney Museum of American Art and the Estee Lauder Company.

The Whitney

The Whitney Museum of American Art in New York is the poster child of every sort of museum problem imaginable. Founded in 1931 by

Gertrude Vanderbilt Whitney, its mission has been to support contemporary American artists and show their work. Or, to put it more grandly, chairman of the board, Leonard Lauder, says the museum's key mission is, "To champion American art and living artists." With such a noble calling, why has the Whitney, in the last 30+ years, become almost a joke in art circles?

According to top drawer journalist, Calvin Tomkins, the Whitney has been seriously adrift. It has been called dysfunctional, superfluous, reactionary, market-driven, trendy, and unprofessional. Much of this criticism may be due to the Whitney's Biennial exhibitions. These exhibitions are a survey of contemporary art and are known as the shows the art world loves to hate. The Biennials display art not yet accepted, by artists of varying talents. In other words, the Whitney takes the risk of being ridiculed every other year. That's admirable. On the other hand, however, the Whitney's erratic behavior and consequent problems and criticisms may stem from its own history.

Gertrude Whitney, her friends and curators, ran the museum as a benevolent institution, for the benefit of American artists. They would do whatever needed to be done to help them. The would pay for artist's food and supplies, and even their medical bills, for instance. Certainly admirable and laudable actions. (As a consequence, over the years, the Whitney leadership showed little concern for what the public or the critics thought of the art they displayed.) In those early days, the Whitney served a chivalrous, lonely role in the dog-eat-dog world of art. (When the museum was founded, American art was largely ignored.) When the board does take action, it is often wrong-headed. This is because, in the Whitney's case, the museum is cursed with a double-whammy. In addition to the sheer number of board members, the viewpoints of the two factions are constantly at odds.

Factions? The lady paying the bills, Gertrude Whitney, died in 1942. Even though she left the museum a goodly sum ($2,500,000), the money was not nearly enough to cover on-going expenses forever. Gertrude's daughter, Flora Whitney Miller, picked up the torch and financed the museum operation for the next 20 years or so. In 1961, however, the museum under Flora's leadership was faced with serious financial problems. She gave in to the inevitable and brought in seven outside trustees.

The museum was founded by old money (Gertrude Whitney, et al) who, not unreasonably, decided how its money should be spent. It was saved by new money, who also, not unreasonably, want to decide how their money should be spent. The newly appointed trustees were rich businessmen, mostly Jewish, while the original trustees were mostly WASPs. Slowly, the board expanded into its present size, with an improbable forty-two members on its board. As any freshman in any college will tell you, a 42 member board will accomplish little if anything, inevitably falling into the geometric meeting syndrome. That is, lots of meetings where the only action taken is to schedule more meetings. When Leonard Lauder joined the board in 1977, he wanted to put the museum on a more business-like basis and expand the museum's reach to the general public. Also laudable goals. So there it was, Gertrude Whitney's World of Old Money WASPs, versus the Real World New Money Jewish board members.

For a time, there was an uneasy truce. Flora Miller Biddle, Gertrude Whitney's granddaughter moved up from board membership and became president of the board in 1977 (serving in that capacity until 1995). Things had already started slipping away from the old money however. For example, in 1974, for the first time, the board went outside its four walls for a director and hired Tom Armstrong. Two years later, Armstrong fired the museum's star curator, Marcia Tucker. Since then, the Whitney has been the art world's whipping boy. In late 1989, another tipping point occurred. Armstrong was asked to resign. He refused and, with the assistance of Flora Miller Biddle, mounted a serious, multi-faceted public campaign to keep his job. The battle raged for a full year. The public was both amused and appalled at the shenanigans.

In 1990, Tom Armstrong (a product of the old money) finally fell into the chasm. While many reasons were advanced by the trustees for the firing, the reality was, true or not, Tom Armstrong was considered anti-Semitic because he served on a notoriously anti-Semitic co-op board when it turned down Lawrence Tisch's son for residence. Tisch, who was an important member of the Whitney's board resigned. And that was that. (The charismatic Leonard Lauder was elected chairman of the board in 1994.)

Armstrong's successor, David Ross, hung on for seven tumultuous years, but he finally quit in 1998. The critics hated his shows, which they called trendy rather than substantive, The shows reflected Ross's unsuccessful attempt to please both factions. Later in 1998, smooth Maxwell Anderson, with his Harvard Ph.D in art history, fluency in five languages, slicked-back hair, and practiced accent had everything going for him. Anderson wowed both factions. In classic Whitney Museum fashion, both sides were wrong.

First problem: A museum whose mission is to champion American art and living artists hired a man who was a specialist in Greco-Roman antiquities. As a matter of fact they hired a man who had no link to contemporary art and, truth be known, had no passion for it. Worse, the board learned that Anderson lacked common sense (the same trait they were lacking as a board). Within three months as director, all five of the curators involved with contemporary art resigned. Anderson had changed the ground rules under which curators were to operate, so they all fled. The board constantly interfered in curatorial affairs. Anderson commissioned a Hans Haacke work for the 2000 Whitney Biennial. Called "Sanitation," the controversial piece split the board wide open; even the original family members squabbled among themselves. Publicly. (Anderson is the director who installed an electric eye at the employee entrance to hype the Whitney's visitor numbers under his watch.) Gertrude Whitney's granddaughter (Flora Miller Biddle) and her daughter (Fiona Donovan) both finally resigned from the board in frustration.

In 2003, after five tumultuous years, Maxwell Anderson resigned under fire. (He is presently director of the Indianapolis Museum of Art.) Later in 2003, the board hired 49-year-old Adam Weinberg, who had worked at the Whitney for eight years on two previous occasions. Shortly after taking over, Weinberg inexplicably fired a curator who was on leave caring for a desperately ill child. No good ink flowed from that move.

In 2004, Michael Kimmelman, the chief art critic of *The New York Times,* captured the situation almost poetically. "The Whitney—oh, the poor, perennially insecure Whitney, which can never get its act straight—is going through another of its periodic upheavals. Its last director was pushed out, a new one was hired, the old staff gracelessly purged or induced to quit, yet another curatorial crew brought in. The Whitney has become like Stalin's politburo. The only long-term survivors are the people everybody in the art world knows really need to go: the Trustees."

Kimmelman doesn't even mention the on-going battle on the board over whether, and/or how, to expand its iconic structure located at 945 Madison Avenue (at 75th Street) which was designed by Marcel Breuer in 1966. In 1985, the board scrapped architect Michael Graves's design; in 2003, the board scrapped the architect Rem Koolhass's design; and in 2006, the board abandoned architect Renzo Piano's design. That's right. The trustees hired three architects (and fired two) and spent millions of dollars on plans it eventually abandoned. Finally, in late 2006, the board got it right. They signed a contract with New York City to build a Renzo Piano designed satellite institution in downtown New York, due to open in 2012. In addition, they plan to update the uptown facility.

Problems, however, continued to plague the Whitney from all sides. In 2004, the Whitney trustees fought to cover-up the embezzlement of almost $1,000,000 by the Visitor Services Manager and one of her supervisors. The pair was voiding ticket sales and pocketing the cash. The cover-up tactic failed when Manhattan's District Attorney's office announced that it had arrested the two top employees. Chairman Leonard Lauder and president Robert Hurst, were instrumental in bringing a number of unsavory characters onto the Whitney board, including Dennis Kozlowski (convicted of fleecing Tyco), and Jean-Marie Messier (architect of the Vivendi scandal). During a wide-ranging investigation by the New York District Attorney, it was determined that, to avoid taxes, dealers were shipping empty crates to out-of-state addresses and hand-carrying (so to speak) the purchased art to their clients in New York City's best neighborhoods. Board member Dennis Kozlowski was indicted in 2002 for tax evasion. Koslowski agreed to pay over $20,000,000 to settle his case. President Hurst had been purchasing art for his private collection over the years but was illegally dodging New York sales taxes through the double delivery scam. When the indictments started to fly Robert Hurst was stunned. In swift reaction, to avoid indictment, Robert Hurst (along with over 30 other New York collectors), paid the taxes he had been side-stepping for years. Hurst's tab was a hefty $2,000,000. The

Whitney kept him on as president. (Along the same line, in 2003, man-about-town Samuel Waksal, ImClone founder, pled guilty to fraud and conspiracy for evading tax of $1,200,000 on $15,000,000 of art he purchased from dealer Larry Gagosian.)

To Leonard Lauder's everlasting credit, he orchestrated the greatest donation of artworks in the history of the Whitney. Lauder convinced his fellow board members to give an estimated $200,000,000 worth of American artworks to the museum. In 2002, ten trustees donated 86 dynamite paintings, prints, and sculptures, created by some of the biggest name artists of the postwar era. In that singular but difficult move (it took three years), Lauder raised the Whitney out of the shadow of MOMA and the Met and up to world-class status.

Hard to top that, right? Leonard Lauder did. In early 2008 he announced a whopping $131,000,000 gift to the Whitney (by far the largest in its 77-year history), increasing its endowment to $195,000,000. Compared to other major museums (say MOMA's $850,000,000) the Whitney's endowment is not very impressive. But, the historically generous donation certainly goes a long way in helping the Whitney achieve the standing in the artistic community it strives for and deserves. The gift is all the more remarkable because the only condition was not (as one would expect and would have been fair) to have the institution change its name to the Leonard Lauder Museum. No, the only condition to the historical gift was that the museum agree not to sell its signature uptown building. In mid-2008, Leonard Lauder resigned as chairman of the board of the Whitney, a position he held for 14 years, since 1994.

A DEAL ISN'T A DEAL UNTIL IT'S A DEAL

Beaverbrook Art Gallery

The legal wrangles between the Beaverbrook Art Gallery in Fredericton, New Brunswick, Canada, and both the UK Beaverbrook Foundation and the Beaverbrook Foundation in Canada capture the silliness of the art business. Lord Beaverbrook (William Maxwell Aitken), was a controversial English media mogul who lived from 1879 to 1964. He founded the Beaverbrook Art Gallery (really an art museum) in 1959 with his paintings.

Why was His Lordship an avid art collector? When asked, the clever entrepreneur, known for his bon mots, said, "Buy old masters. They bring better prices than young mistresses."

The dispute began in late 2002. The Beaverbrook Canadian Foundation (called Canadian Heirs for clarity) hired Sotheby's to assess the exhibition policies of the museum, and to examine and report on the condition and insurance coverage of its collection. In a classic case of conflict of interest, Sotheby's recommended that the museum return its two most valuable paintings (a J.M.W. Turner and a Lucian Freud) to the Canadian heirs. The Turner alone is worth over $30,000,000. (The reason Sotheby's advised the Canadian heirs that the two masterpieces be returned to them is because the auction house planned to sell the paintings on their behalf.) The Canadian heirs followed Sotheby's lead and claimed that the two paintings had always belonged to them and were merely on loan to the museum.

In 2004, at the urging of Sotheby's, the UK Beaverbrook Foundation (the English heirs) and the Canadian heirs sued the Canadian Gallery in a London court for return of the paintings. Two weeks later, the Canadian Gallery counter-sued the Canadian and English heirs in a Canadian court, claiming ownership of the disputed paintings. In July 2004, the English heirs agreed to submit its case to Canadian arbitration. The Canadians continued to fight with each other.

In August 2004, Canadian heir Timothy Aitken, president of the Beaverbrook Canadian Foundation and grandson of the first Lord Beaverbrook, filed his own lawsuit against the Beaverbrook Art Gallery. Suddenly, the dispute got personal. Aitken not only accused the Gallery of fraud and lying about (or misrepresenting) ownership, he pled for the return of $10,000,000 in funding his foundation provided the museum over the last 30 years. For good measure, he also asked the court for $5,000,000 in punitive damages and costs. If you are following this, yes, Timothy Aitken, Lord Beaverbrook's grandson, who sits on the board of the Beaverbrook Art Gallery, sued the very same Beaverbrook Art Gallery on whose board he sits. As if their weren't enough parties throwing mud at each other, the New Brunswick government jumped into the fray.

In December 2004, the regional government gave the Beaverbrook Art Gallery a $1,000,000 interest-free loan to fight the Canadian heirs. In 2007, the arbitrator in the English case ruled that the majority of the disputed paintings (85 of the 133) should remain with the Beaverbrook Art Gallery. (The 85 paintings were donated by Lord Beaverbrook to establish the museum in 1959 and are the most valuable paintings in dispute.) The English heirs are appealing the ruling. The Canadian lawsuit is still on the sidelines, awaiting the final resolution of the English suit.

Meanwhile, as the case slogs through the court system, the Gallery is holding an exhibition that contains over 200 of the works whose ownership is in dispute. Reflecting the current money-grubbing attitude of museums, the Beaverbrook Art Gallery (also called New Brunswick's Provincial Art Gallery) is hyping the exhibition on its website, trumpeting, "Highlight of the summer exhibitions is sure to be 'Art in Dispute.'" And, yes, there is an admission charge for "Art in Dispute," the first time in its 46-year history the Beaverbrook Art Gallery has charged admission for a specific exhibition.

THE WHORES OF PENNSYLVANIA

The Barnes

Most people think that if you donate artworks to a museum, the museum will comply with your wishes in connection with the donation. The de Groot bequest to the Met, and the Seilern gift to the Courtauld are striking examples of museums totally disregarding donor's wishes. The Barnes story, however, is the worst. It is not only about a donation gone awry, it's about corrupting an entire way of life. The Barnes, in suburban Philadelphia, was established in 1922 by the rich, eccentric patent medicine mogul Doctor Albert Barnes (1872–1951).

Barnes made his fortune marketing a drug named Argyrol, which was invented by a partner, Hermann Hille. In 1908, the litigious doctor wrested exclusive rights to the drug from Hille in a lawsuit, and spent the rest of his life defending those rights, in and out of court. Barnes was a true eccentric, in the best sense of the work. For example, not only was the workday at the factory of his A. C. Barnes Company a mere eight hours a day at a time when sweatshops were the norm, his workforce was racially and sexually integrated.

And listen to this. During two of the eight hours every workday, Barnes presided over a discussion group, which might feature the works of Bertrand Russell one day, and Sigmund Freud the next, and even Santayana. William James (brother of writer Henry James), was featured regularly. John Dewey was Barnes' first educational director.

Describing Barnes, the historian John Lukacs offered my favorite description of any individual of all time, saying Barnes' face was that "Of a first-rate president of a second-rate university." Isn't that wonderful? Lukacs went on to say, "Beneath his eternally wrinkled brows and behind his rimless glasses his eyes glared strong and clear. His preferences were singular; his hatreds were puissant." Barnes' singular preference? Art. His wife Laura's passion was horticulture.

Barnes' collection, which is the most highly regarded private collection of Impressionist and Post-Impressionist paintings in the world, eventually contained (among others) almost 200 Renoirs (the Musee d'Orsay in Paris owns only 94), over 40 Picassos, 14 Modiglianis, 60 Matisses, 11 Degas, 18 Rousseaus, and 69 Cezannes. That's more Cezannes than all of the museums in Paris own, combined.

How powerful were his hatreds? Barnes fought publicly with everyone from Harold Stassen (then president of the University of Pennsylvania), Walter Annenberg, owner of the most powerful newspaper in the state, art critics, and historians. Barnes particularly disliked Bernard Berenson, who, he felt, was making provenance the basis for collecting art, whereas he felt the basis for buying a piece should be the aesthetic merit of the work. More hatreds? Barnes hated snobs in the world of art (particularly those at the Philadelphia Museum of Art) who "sported English accents and believed that just because they were born with money they had the right to art, and things other people shouldn't have."

Barnes, who was white, crusaded against racism, which was rampant at the time. A champion for social justice, he felt art education could help solve the problems of segregation in America. In his will, Barnes even gave eventual control of his foundation to Lincoln University, a small, historically African-American college.

Barnes had a mansion built on the Main Line outside of Philadelphia and housed his art school and collection in a stunning gallery next door that he had built for that specific purpose. He envisioned his collection as a vehicle to provide art education to the masses, particularly underprivileged children. Barnes never, ever, thought of his collection as a museum.

In 1922, Barnes established the Barnes Foundation, and in its by-laws stipulated (among other things) that "the plain people, that is, men and women who gain their livelihood by daily toil in shops, factories, schools, stores, and similar places, shall have free access to the gallery." (During his lifetime, admittance to see the artworks was strictly by invitation, and Barnes routinely turned away the rich and famous when they tried to gain admission.)

In his will, Barnes not only stipulated the collection should always remain in Merion, Pennsylvania, Barnes also insisted that the paintings not only never be sold or travel, he even decreed that the position of the paintings on the walls should never be changed. In 1951, Doctor Albert Barnes died at the age of 78 in a flaming car crash, reportedly on the way to see his mistress. His enemies (particularly Walter Annenberg) went to work and in 1960 got the Barnes Foundation to open its doors to the public, if only a few days a week and strictly by appointment. In 1989, his assistant/mistress Violette de Mazia died: With the death of the world's strictest keeper of the flame, Barnes' dream began to unravel.

In 1990, a Philadelphia attorney named Richard Glanton gained control of the Barnes. Glanton was a trustee of Lincoln University and the school's general counsel. He was a determined player in the Pennsylvania Republican party and was a political appointment. Once Glanton gained control of the Barnes Foundation his every move was to serve his personal interests.

Glanton spent millions of dollars on frivolous lawsuits, traded the foundation's legal business for votes, traveled its collection, tried to sell off paintings, and spent foundation funds on personal emoluments all over the world. Financial irregularities abounded. Glanton, who once crowed, "I am the Barnes Foundation," operated like the Barnes was his personal fiefdom, hiring key personal and filing lawsuits without consulting the board. If members of the board complained, Glanton had them summarily removed from office or just ignored them. Glanton even filed a lawsuit under the federal Ku Klux Klan Act (the Civil Rights

Act of 1871, which was passed to protect blacks from the Klan), claiming the neighbors were blocking the construction of a parking lot at the Barnes because of racial prejudice. The case was thrown out, with prejudice, as "groundless," and "frivolous," and the Barnes was ordered to pay the defendant's costs. But the roughly $6,000,000 Glanton ran up in questionable legal fees between 1992 and 1998 were real enough, and ultimately caused the Barnes to go broke. The worse sin Glanton committed was changing the focus of the Barnes from that of an educational institution to that of a museum. This had far-reaching and disastrous effects: The educational enrollment skidded to half under Glanton's reign. Richard Glanton was ousted as president of the Barnes Foundation in 1998.

In 2004, in a final slap at Doctor Barnes, the very people he hated gained control of his dream. The court granted permission for the museum to leave the Barnes mansion in Merion in suburban Philadelphia and move to a pedestrian unfriendly location on Ben Franklin Parkway in downtown Philadelphia. The will-busting move was approved in the name of tourism (read money), with the money for the move and a new building coming from the state and three local foundations (The Pew Foundation, the Lenfest Foundation, and the Annenberg Foundation), all of whom had been drooling for years to get control of the Barnes collection. Here's a surprise. The quid-pro-quo for the money was control of the Barnes Foundation. Ironically, to repeat, these are the very people and institutions Doctor Barnes railed against all of his life.

In 2006, Governor Ed Rendell announced a $25,000,000 grant of state money to facilitate the move. This was $10,000,000 more than the entire state budget for arts. How could something like this happen? Politics, pure and simple. Rendell, the quintessential politician, was paying back a number of his wealthy political contributors who wanted to break Doctor Barnes' indenture. These individuals had donated some $1,000,000 to politician Rendell.

There is (very slight) hope on the horizon that the wishes of Doctor Barnes will still be honored. A group of dedicated and concerned citizens, including many neighbors, is waging a serious fight to block the move. Their position is that moving the contents of the gallery would positively kill the cultural and academic experience that Doctor Barnes intended to pass on to future generations. Do you like irony? Here it is in its ugliest form. The neighbors, the pathetic people who for years had violently opposed the Barnes on every level and are now fighting to save it for their neighborhood, are the people most responsible for the impending move.

In mid-2007, Montgomery County (in which the Barnes is located), in an effort to keep the Barnes in Merion, made an offer to buy the foundation and lease it back to the trustees on sweetheart terms. The Barnes Foundation board rejected the gold plated offer out of hand. Determined to move, the Barnes trustees hired architects Tsien and Williams to design a new facility and, in mid-2007 signed a lease with the City of Philadelphia. Controversy continues to plague the Barnes. Later in 2007 Montgomery County fired the attorney it had hired to file a lawsuit blocking the move, claiming the attorney, Mark Swartz, had a conflict of interest. Highly respected critics from around the country continue to weigh in. When the Court denied an application to reopen the case in mid 2008, Edmund Sazanski, art critic of the *Philadelphia Inquirer* (courageously bucking his paper's shameless promotion of the move), called the deal to move the Barnes "The most audacious art heist in American history."

Meantime, Richard Glanton, who was a partner in the Philadelphia law firm of Reed Smith, from 1986 to 2003, in addition to being ousted as president of the Barnes Foundation was hit by a damaging sexual harassment suit. After leaving the presidency of the Barnes, in 2001, Glanton's ally turned nemesis, Niara Sudarkasa (former president of Lincoln University and a trustee of the Barnes Foundation), filed a highly charged lawsuit against Glanton and others. The judge eventually dismissed Sudarkasa's case, and in 2003, the litigious, self-serving Glanton left Philadelphia.

NAÏVE & DYSFUNCTIONAL MUSEUM BOARDS OF TRUSTEES

The Museum of Nothern Arizona

The Museum of Northern Arizona in Flagstaff was founded in 1928 and has had a sterling reputation as a repository of Native American artifacts and items of natural history, particularly as they relate to northern Arizona. At the turn of the century, however, things turned sour. In 2002, the museum was facing a financial crisis with some estimates pegging funds available to cover its expenses at less than one month. How could a key member of the cultural community, with over 3,000 members from throughout the area, fall into this state? There were several reasons, all bad. First, the board of trustees was not paying attention to what was going on. What was going on was that since becoming director in 2000, Arthur Wolf had failed miserably in his fund raising, and the museum had no endowment to fall back on. Then, instead of calling on its membership for help, which is one of the basic roles for members of any community organization, the 16 member board of trustees told no one about the financial disaster facing the museum. What they did was pressure Wolf to resign and instructed the deputy director, Edwin Wade, to select items to sell from its permanent collection. In this highly charged atmosphere, Wade turned to Santa Fe art dealer Steve Diamant, who was a friend. Diamant had not only sold Wade numerous artifacts for his personal collection over the years, he (Diamant) was also married to Wade's secretary.

Diamant, with Wade's help, selected 21 key pieces from the collection, including priceless and irreplaceable Navajo ceremonial weavings (three over 100 years old) and half-a-dozen Hosteen Klah rugs from the 1930s, which are rare and irreplaceable. In his presentation to the board, Diamant made numerous outrageous claims about the museum's storage facilities and about the items he selected. Among other things, Diamant told the board that the items he selected would be sold to one party, and when that party died, they would go to a university. Oh yes, and part of your collection is in jeopardy because of lack of heat, humidity controls, poor wiring, and so on. So you better raise lots of money fast. Very fast. The trusting and naive trustees took the art dealer's word as gospel. Within days of signing the purchase agreement, Diamant, who had secretly pre-sold the artworks, delivered almost $1,000,000 in cash to the museum. The board was thrilled to receive the money, but the 21 paintings and textiles were worth substantially more. When the deaccessioning became public later in 2002, the entire board of trustees and the director resigned.

In early 2005, the new board filed a lawsuit against Steve Diamant alleging a breach of fiduciary duty and fraud. The lawsuit was settled in late 2005, but the terms of the settlement are secret. The attorney for the museum, however, said that he doubts any of the 21 treasures will ever be returned to the museum. Because of the extraordinary and unethical secret deaccessioning, the museum lost its accreditation from the American Association of Museums. Steve Diamant continues to deal, changing the name of his company from Direct Art, Inc. to Fine Arts of the Southwest, Inc.

Bellevue Arts Museum

The Bellevue Arts Museum, located in the eastside suburb of Seattle of the same name, is an outgrowth of the wildly successful annual Bellevue Arts and Crafts Fair, which has been held in the high-end community for over 60 years, drawing over a third of a million visitors each year. The museum's first home consisted of modest rooms in a defunct funeral home. In a cautious step up, the museum moved into a set of modest third floor rooms in the Bellevue Square Mall, which is situated in downtown Bellevue, that is if Bellevue had a downtown. Even though the museum was, yes, modest, it was a worthy cultural asset in the community.

In 1991, when Diane Douglas became director, however, the museum lost its compass and its mission became muddled. The first mistake was to donate its permanent collection to the Tacoma Art Museum in exchange for borrowing rights to the Tacoma museum's permanent collection. The result of this action (besides turning the museum's role upside down) was to lose a decent collection that had taken years to assemble in exchange for meager pickings from a minor museum. Could Douglas and the trustees have possibly believed that the Tacoma Museum was going to lend its choice works, such as they were?

This action symbolized Bellevue's basic problem. The museum had decided to abandon its distinctive crafts, design, and Northwest art heritage, and send a message to the entire Seattle area that it, and therefore the community of Bellevue, were finally big time. Take that Seattle Art Museum. (Seattle is located across Lake Washington from Bellevue.)

Instead of focusing on how it could better serve its constituency as a significant arts and crafts museum, the museum, which lacked an endowment, decided to assume the role of community cheerleader and be the flashpoint for the city's grandiose ambitions. To accomplish this impossible dream, the trustees hired Steven Holl (a trophy New York architect) to design a dramatic, unorthodox, anything but modest 36,000 square-foot building. The litany of mistakes encased within that decision are staggering. The $23,000,000 building is designed to serve more as a community center than art museum. Because of this orientation, the long skinny galleries designed into the building were not conducive to displaying art for exhibitions, or for good viewing conditions. The building's design turned off the museum's core. Even before the building opened, a fake wall was positioned between the two main galleries to make the viewing rooms a bit more user friendly. And the cracks that soon developed in the floor of the main galleries didn't help. The museum's business plan was also flawed. It projected an unrealistic number of visitors to the new building and an impossible amount of income from the art school and museum gift shop. These mistakes caused the museum to borrow heavily to meet operating expenses. Worse, staff and board members failed to continue romancing the donors who made the new facility possible, feeling the dramatic new building would overcome all possible operating expenses, and then some. This meant that the museum continued to operate with no endowment.

These elements produced a perfect storm that engulfed the museum and the city of Bellevue: The Bellevue Art Museum abruptly closed its doors in September 2003, less than three years after its gala opening. To quote the *Seattle Times,* "The museum's unexpected closure left Bellevue leaders stunned and arts patrons baffled that a cultural institution serving some of the country's wealthiest communities could fold for lack of money." The paper went on to say, "Even the timing of the closure was bizarre, announced just two days before a new exhibit opened." *The New York Times* weighed in; "The very public failure in Bellevue has sent a shudder through the museum world."

After the closing the trustees began paying close attention, meeting almost every week to figure out how to get the museum reopened and back on track. Here's what they did: Regarding the building, $3,000,000 was spent on interior renovations; regarding its mission, the trustees voted to return to the original concept of crafts and design; regarding finances, the board raised several million dollars to be used for operating expenses. The planning and hard work that occurred during the period the museum was closed paid off. The Bellevue Art Museum reopened in June 2005, rededicated to serve the community as the area's arbiter and exhibitor of the creative arts rather than trying to beat the Seattle Art Museum in the fine arts game.

Within three months of reopening after the disastrous closing, however, another disaster, albeit smaller, occurred under the noses of the board and staff. A crime was discovered. In late 2007 its chief financial officer, 53-year-old Janet Ellinger was charged with embezzling some $300,000 from the museum between October 2005 and April 2007. Incredibly, museum officials say they did not conduct a background check before hiring Ellinger, its chief financial officer.

The Corcoran

Then there is the Corcoran Gallery of Art. Founded in 1871, it's the first Washington DC museum of art. It has had serious money and perception problems. Budget deficits and a stalled capital campaign were brought on by poorly received exhibitions and ill-conceived expansion plans. An inattentive board of trustees was at the core of the problems, which included the need for some $40,000,000 in maintenance of the museum. Even the curatorial program has been the laughing stock of the art world. David Levy was forced out after 14 years as director and president after the expansion project he championed and focused on was scuttled. (A Frank Gehry addition was cancelled in 2005.)

The museum seems to have recovered. An art college, which is part of the museum, is again being focused upon, with an emphasis on increasing student enrollment and raising the level of instruction. To this end, the museum has purchased a vacant building which will give it additional studio, classroom and exhibition space.

The Milwaukee Public Museum

The Milwaukee Public Museum (founded in 1888), which today sports a spectacular modern building by Santiago Calatrava, has had a checkered past. The Board of Trustees was not paying attention. This inattention encouraged the top financial officer to embezzle museum funds. When the museum tried to cover-up the situation, conflicts of interest were exposed, and wild spending sprees using museum funds were uncovered. The result? As of 2005 the museum was $29,000,000 in debt, most of the staff was laid off, and chaos reigned.

Moderna Museet

The Bellevue Arts Museum is not the only museum with new building problems. The rebuilt Moderna Museet, Stockholm's national museum of modern art (founded in 1958) was open less than three years when had to close in January 2002. The trustees had accepted a building infected with what is called Sick Building Syndrome. The staff was getting sick from mold in the minimalist facility designed by Spanish architect Rafael Moneo. During the two years the museum was closed for repairs, the first-class collection of twentieth-century art was exhibited in various venues in Sweden and around the world. The museum reopened in 2004.

Prior to the museum's building problem, it had an embarrassing problem with fakes. Embarrassing because the scam centered on the internationally venerated Pontus Hulton (1924–2006). In 1990, Pontus Hulten, who was the museum's director in the 1960s, had Swedish carpenters build about 100 fake Warhol wooden Brillo soap pad boxes for an exhibition in Russia. (This was three years after Warhol died.) Pontus then sold these fakes with certificates of authenticity he created, stating that the boxes were made for a Warhol exhibit in Stockholm in 1968 (when he was director), which made them authentic. (What is interesting is that even though the experts agree that Warhol didn't need to touch a work for it to be considered authentic, the pieces do need to be manufactured with the artist's permission during his lifetime.) In 1995, Hulten donated six of the fakes to the Moderna Museet. The other hundred or so remain in circulation worldwide. The scam was first uncovered by the Swedish daily newspaper *Expressen.* Following the expose by the tabloid, an internal investigation was conducted by the museum that confirmed the charges that the sculptures were fakes.

The museum wrote to the Andy Warhol Art Authentication Board that its Brillo boxes were not authorized by the artist and should be removed from the official list of Brillo boxes in the Warhol catalogue raisonné. The Moderna Museet will rewrite their documents to indicate that the six Brillo boxes they own are copies. The tragedy is that the reputation of their beloved ex-director will forever be besmirched.

The Norton Museum of Art

The Norton Museum of Art in West Palm Beach, Florida (founded in 1941), is suffering from low morale due to unfair gaps in salaries and humongous employee turnover. In 2005, the Norton lost 57 employees, including a number of key personnel, somewhere between 30 and 60% of its staff, depending upon who is counting. According to Jose Lambiet, writing in the *Palm Beach Post,* the president of the museum, Harry Johnston, wasn't quite sure of the numbers but felt that, in any case, the attrition was normal and not excessively high.

If the president of the board was right, the museum world is in serious trouble. If he was wrong, the comment shows how out of touch trustees can be. One can only guess at the truth because the renovated museum is small and secretive. Aping one of the Met's most odious policies, employees are forbidden by contract to speak to the press.

JUDGE ME BY MY INTENTIONS, NOT MY ACTIONS

Harvard

Harvard University, which houses a number of museums, admits that it has demanded donations from the owners of items to be exhibited: If you want a show at one of Harvard's museums, the quid-pro-quo is that you make an accompanying donation. Over the years, Harvard has acquired so many fakes it has a closet full of them. In 1943, Edward Forbes admitted that the museum's so-called bronze statues are painted plaster of Paris. De Hory sold a Matisse fake to the Fogg Museum at Harvard. When the school realized their experts had been duped, it began using the drawing as a teaching aide. Forger John Decker's "Bust of Christ" has been labeled and displayed as a Rembrandt since 1964. (In the mid-1990s, a hoard of Greek fragments were acquired; if not fakes, they are surely looted.)

University of Oregon

The Jordan Schnitzer Museum of Art at the University of Oregon is 75 years old. In 2007, its reporting obligation was moved from the provost to the vice-president for advancement. Here's a surprise: The vice-president for advancement is the main university fundraiser. Goodbye educational mission, hello piggy bank. The university's faculty senate opposed the switch.

Oriental Institute of the University of Chicago

Iran lent the Oriental Institute of the University of Chicago a number of historical artifacts for study for a three-year period. Over 40 years later the items have yet to be returned.

Penn State University

In 2001, the Palmer Museum at Penn State University was enmeshed in a controversy when a Memling painting (a Madonna and Child triptych) was declared to be a fake. After an emotional flurry of denial by the museum, the painting was quietly withdrawn from display two months after the controversy began.

Princeton

In late 2007, the Princeton University Art Museum joined the Getty, the Met, and Boston's MFA in agreeing to return to Italy priceless antiquities that had been looted and smuggled out of that culture-rich country. The accord, which comes after years of negotiations, covers eight ancient artworks; four to be returned at signing, and four placed on loan status and to be returned to Italy in 2011. The agreement grants the Princeton Museum the ability to access other equally significant works of art from Italy and gives students access to archeological excavations in Italy for research purposes. Maurizio Fiorilli, who represented Italy in the negotiations, said the agreement was unique because "It is calibrated to favor cultural exchanges. It's the right accord for a university."

University of Virginia

The University of Virginia returned two sixth-century BC marble sculptures to Italy. Maurice Templesman had donated the antiquities.

Wellesley

In 1904, Richard Norton, an art dealer who was also director of the American School of Classical Studies in Rome, detached the head and body of a classical statute before shipping it to Wellesley College, his client. Why? "So that it would not look too perfect to the officers at the export office." Wellesley brags about this.

The Davis Museum and Cultural Center at the college loaned one of its prized paintings, a Fernand Leger, to the Oklahoma City Museum. The Leger was donated to the museum by Eleanor DeLorme, who joined the faculty in 1984. Today, Ms. DeLorme is a senior lecturer in the school's art department and an adjunct curator of the museum. After the Leger was returned to Wellesley, the painting disappeared. Ms. De Lorme was devastated. Ace reporter Geoff Edgers caught her frustration in the *Boston Globe*: "It's a bad place to give any art objects to and I want all of them back." (She had donated other pieces.)

Yale

In about 1912, the Peruvian government gave permission to Yale to keep, until 1916, 5,000 works its representatives had taken from Machu Picchu for scientific study. The Yale University Art Museum refused to return the artifacts in spite of repeated demands. The artifacts (including human bones) were removed from Peru by American explorer Hiram Bingham during three trips to Peru in the early 1900s. Numerous requests for return of the pieces, or just negotiation, have been stonewalled by the Ivy League school. When the university would give Peru the courtesy of an answer (which was seldom) they would give excuses like "we need more time to evaluate the pieces" or "we're analyzing the request." Emboldened by the persistence and successes of the Italians, Peru sued.

In 2007, after almost a century of stonewalling, Yale admitted the crime. In the agreement, the Ivy league school (home to several United States presidents and other political types), admitted that Peru was the rightful owner of the priceless artifacts and the thousands of fragments. (Fragments are important to researchers.) In addition, the agreement calls for Yale to contribute a significant amount of money (amount not revealed) to fund scholarly exchanges with Peru.

Why did Yale fold after 91 years of living a lie? A good guess is that doing hard time in a Peruvian jail is just as unappealing as doing hard time in an Italian jail. Maybe more so.

In a surprise move, in December 2008, Peru found it's voice and sued Yale again, effectively killing the 2007 agreement.

HUMOROUS (OR SCARY) MUSEUM STORIES, DEPENDING ON YOUR MOOD

Austria's National Gallery of Art

In 1912, Paul Poiret, the famous fashion designer, bequeathed Austria's National Gallery of Art in Vienna a 52 piece collection of paintings and drawings. The collection, which includes 14 works by Egon Schiele, is worth untold millions. The collection was last seen at the museum in 1983.

After stonewalling the press and the public for almost 20 years, the museum admitted that it couldn't find any of the artworks. Before acknowledging the horrible truth, the museum authorities came up with several creative excuses which they fed to the press and public. Here's the one I like best: "We never received the pieces in the first place."

The Albertina

Founded in 1776 by Duke Albert von Sachen-Teschen, the Albertina in Vienna sits on the south end of the Imperial Palace in the historic center of Vienna. The museum houses one of the largest and best collections of drawings in the world. It is located in an updated version of what was once the most prominent of the Habsburg living quarters. Sounds good, right? So what's the problem?

The problem is, although the museum's officials don't tell the public, of the Albertina's 60,000 drawings no original drawings are ever displayed on its walls. Got it? The exhibition aspect of the vaunted Albertina consists entirely of fakes.

The Pompidou Center

Two works of California artists, that were borrowed by the Georges Pompidou Center in Paris and hung in an exhibit called "Los Angeles:

1955–1985," were destroyed while on view in 2006. The museum vehemently denied that anything had happened to the pieces, until the *Los Angeles Times* reported the tragedy. After the cover-up was exposed, Bruno Racine, the Center's president, said that in the future the Center would make public without delay any serious damage to a work, and will publish annual statistics on all incidents.

Reina-Sofia Modern Art Museum

A 38-ton sculpture by Richard Serra was reported lost by Madrid's Reina-Sofia Modern Art Museum. As well as anyone can remember, the 38-ton piece was last seen in 1990. In 2004, the museum realized its blunder. In other words, the 38-ton sculpture was not missed for 14 years. Serra gave the museum a newly-struck copy.

The San Francisco Museum of Modern Art

The San Francisco Museum of Modern Art sued the heirs of long time patron Madeleine Hass claiming they had a deal to buy a Picasso for $44,000,000 and suffered damages of $18,000,000 when the heirs put the work on auction instead of selling it to them. A judge threw out the suit.

SNAPSHOTS

Art Institute of Chicago

Two managers of the finances of the Art Institute diverted some $2,000,000 of the museum's money into their personal software company. (One of the richest museums in America, the Art Institute of Chicago has an endowment of almost $700,000,000.) In 2001, the pair was also responsible for a hedge-fund loss of $43,000,000.

The National Art Gallery of Scotland

In 1933, the National Art Gallery of Scotland used its last dime (literally) to purchase what it thought was a Botticelli entitled "Portrait of a Youth." The acquisition was trumpeted with the usual fanfare; Stanley Cursiter, the director, hailed the painting's purchase (for over $1,000,000 in today's money) as a coup for the museum. In 1952, however, not coincidentally after Cursiter retired, chemical tests were applied and a cover-up of a damning document was discovered. The fake painting was withdrawn and stored in basement hell. Incidentally, the fake, which looks as much like a Botticelli as I look like Robert Redford, was painted by Albert Philippot, who was a relative of restorer/forger Jef van der Veken and often collaborated with the master.

Scottish Art Galleries

In 2002, Julian Spalding, then director of the UK's Glasgow Art Galleries, told the press that all of the Scottish museum collections were riddled with fakes. Spalding famously publicly trumpeted that the Scottish museums should have signs at the entrances that say, "Doubt all you who enter here."

The Kunsthistorisches

This famous Viennese museum received a bronze of a life-size nude man in 1806. It claimed the piece ("Youth from Mount Magdalene") was Roman in origin and so labeled it. The imposing sculpture was featured as the centerpiece of its classical collection for 180 years. In 1986, however, the work was exposed as a sixteenth-century copy. The museum continues to display the piece but now acknowledges its masterpiece has lost some 1,400 years of existence and history.

LACMA

The Los Angeles County Museum (known as LACMA), which opened in early 1965, acquired what they thought was a Van Dyke painting called "Andromeda Chained to the Rock" in 1985 and displayed the painting as a masterpiece by the Dutch master. Doubts about the painting's authenticity quickly surfaced, but the museum stonewalled and continued to display the painting as the work of Van Dyke.

In 1998, 13 years later, the museum re-attributed the painting to an imitator of Van Dyke and without announcement removed the work from its walls and put it in storage, where it remains to this day. Does the museum regret it was displaying a fake for over a decade? J. Patrice Marandel, the curator of European paintings, told ace *Los Angeles Times* staff writer Christopher Reynolds loftily, "Perhaps we're sorry, but I wouldn't even go that far."

The National Gallery of Australia

In mid-2006, the museum's prize exhibit, a painting by van Gogh, was exposed as a fake. Michael Daley, director of Art Watch UK, determined that there were numerous inconsistencies in the work and that it could not have been painted by van Gogh.

The Oslo National Gallery

Norway's National Gallery has numerous fakes, including its highly viewed self-portrait of van Gogh with the missing ear.

Peru's Museum of Gold

Most of the 20,000 piece gold collection in Peru's Museum of Gold, which is the most popular museum in Peru, have been determined to be fakes. Of the museum's 4,300 prize holdings, over 4,200 were determined to be fakes and the other hundred are considered suspicious. In a rare example of museum candor toward the public, a Peruvian government agency ordered the museum to post signs informing the visitors that the works can no longer be considered as predating the Inca civilization. The museum's collection only came under scrutiny after a visitor challenged the authenticity of the items and a politically prominent founder died. Peruvian officials fear this discovery of fakes is merely the tip of the iceberg.

The Phoenix Art Museum

In the early 1960s, the museum began to aggressively expand its collection. In the art world, the well meaning but naïve institution became a laughing stock for acquiring numerous fakes. To its credit, the museum moved aggressively to correct the problem. The fakes now rest in the basement.

The Sofia Imber Contemporary Art Museum

In 2003, the museum in Caracas, Venezuela, realized that Matisse's painting "Odalisque in Red Pants," which had hung in the museum for 20 years, had been stolen and replaced with a fake. This is not such an unusual scam; it has occurred in the world's museums numerous times over the years. What makes this case sort of special is that the fake hung on the museum's walls a full three years until the switch was discovered.

The Turkey National Museum

Half of the paintings attributed to Picasso in Turkey's National Museum are fakes. Ironically, the Turkish government acquired the fakes after their own undercover agents (posed as buyers) infiltrated an art smuggling ring.

Usak Museum

In 2001, at this archeological museum located in Western Turkey, three employees (who were art experts) complained to the government that the security was lax at the museum and that the operation was corrupt. Did the government move aggressively? Absolutely. First it rebuked the trio. Then it transferred the three scholars to other museums.

In 2005, the Turkish government learned that several gold and silver items from the "Lydian Hoard," which were on display after being retrieved from the Met, had been replaced with fakes. Finally, in 2006, seven suspects were indicted and charged with smuggling historical artifacts, and failure to give information regarding embezzlement and evidence of a crime. The scammers turned out to be a highly organized gang, operating in 30 of the 93 state-owned Turkish museums.

The Uffizi Gallery

Fakes are so pervasive, even the illustrious Uffizi in Florence, Italy is not immune. One example: The museum has been displaying "The Adoration of the Magi" as a masterpiece by Leonardo da Vinci, and trumpeting the work as one of its grandest holdings. In 2002, however, Maurizio Seracini, a renowned art expert, proved conclusively that the work is not by da Vinci and is a fake.

The Walker Art Center

The museum in Minneapolis traces its roots to 1874 when timber baron Tom Walker began collecting art and antiquities for his mansion. Walker, an amateur art collector, personally decided on the attribution of all of the artworks. A mirror image of Walter Chrysler.

We all know where that leads. In the early 1940s, a new staff was hired for the museum. They reattributed the entire collection, saving the numerous fakes for study purposes. (Called study collections, they are a valuable teaching tool and exist at many universities.)

Wallraf-Richartz Museum and Foundation Corboud

In 1954, Cologne, Germany's oldest museum received a donation of what it believed was an important Monet painting. The work, entitled "On the Banks of the Seine by Port Villez," raised a certain amount of suspicion about its authenticity, but not enough to move the City of Cologne, the museum's owner, to take action.

Fast forward over 50 years later to the early 2000s. The museum, in preparing an exhibition on the impressionist period, technically examined some 70 paintings in its collection, including the Monet. It used infrared light, X-rays, and specialized microscopes, among other tools. The examination proved that the Monet was a fake because of several discoveries. First, the forger started with a preliminary sketch, not a Monet technique. Second, the forger applied a glaze meant to indicate aging. Third, the forger signed Monet's name and then retraced it to make it darker; again, something an artist would never do. In 2008, the museum admitted its mistake in a most unusual press release.

The spokesman, Stefan Swertz, said the museum was philosophical about the discovery. "We are laughing and crying at the same time," he said, quoting what he explained was an old German saying. Andreas Bluehm, the museum director, was also philosophical, but his take on the situation was a bit more logical. "Of course it is sad to lose a significant and valuable original," he said, "But one can also see it as a gain for science and as evidence of the high quality of our restoration department."

The museum owns five authentic Monets. The forgery will be part of the exhibition and remain in the permanent collection, but it will be labeled as a fake. It was refreshing to see a museum voluntarily admit they had been showcasing a fake for five decades.

CHAPTER TWELVE
KING OF UNSCRUPULOUS MUSEUMS

The Strasbourg (France) Museum of Decorative Arts

In 1986, Marie-Madeleine Falbisaner needed money to supplement her meager retirement income so she reluctantly decided to sell a family heirloom, a painting by Simon Vouet. (Vouet was the official court painter of king Louis XIII.) Mrs. Falbisaner, a member of a respected Strasbourg family, wanted to keep the masterpiece in Strasbourg, even though she could have sold it by auction and realized more money. Through an agent, she approached the city of Strasbourg about purchasing the painting for its museum. At this point, the museum's chief curator, Jean-Daniel Ludman, asked to borrow the painting to check on its provenance. Ludman gave Mrs. Falbisaner a personal note promising to return the artwork. Ludman then sent the painting to the Louvre in Paris where the tests confirmed Ludman's opinion that the painting was indeed a Vouet. The curator, Ludman, reported to the city of Strasbourg that there was not the least doubt about its attribution to Vouet. The sale was immediately consummated. When the city and the museum made the purchase from Mrs. Falbisaner, however, they lied to her, alleging the painting was not a Vouet. Yes, they paid her a pittance, based on their lie. But then, the unscrupulous city and museum officials made a fatal mistake.

They reported with glee (in a house promotional newspaper no less) that they had acquired a masterpiece, a Vouet. When Mrs. Falbisaner read the article she was crushed. After getting over the shock of the deceit, she sued. The court agreed with her lawsuit, ruling that the city and the museum had acted fraudulently and in bad faith.

Here's where things get even more ugly, if that's possible. First the city and the museum appealed. Second, they changed their story and now maintained that the painting was not a Vouet. To top things off, believe it or not, Ludman the curator refused to return the painting even though he had signed a personal agreement to do so. This was too much for the judge. He indicted Jean-Daniel Ludman for breach of trust. The Strasbourg Museum of Decorative Arts and the City of Strasbourg, France, which owns the museum, have been found guilty of a blatant fraud against a 73-year-old widow.

CHAPTER THIRTEEN
UNSCRUPULOUS SQUARED

The special privileges that the intellectual and social hierarchy,
represented by the Cambridge and Oxford graduates [Blunt, et al],
were able to bring to the administration of Government in England
proved disastrous to both Britain and America.

MI5 and MI6 and the British Foreign Office
were incapable of distrusting four men who
"were their own kind."

— Russell Aiuto

Anthony Blunt

Anthony Blunt was born in Bournemouth, England in 1907 and died in London in 1983. Blunt's grandfather was an Anglican bishop and his father was a vicar in the Church of England, which qualified the family to be close to that country's upper crust. Or, at least, close enough to get young Anthony into Cambridge University. Blunt ingratiated himself into the ultra-hip, liberal-thinking Bloomsbury group. Plus, he was a brilliant student and quick study. The cerebral Blunt excelled at Cambridge, and in 1932 he was granted a four-year research fellowship.

It was at Cambridge that Blunt began a life-long love affair with Guy Burgess, an unkempt, bear of a young man. Burgess had a horrific effect on Blunt's life, but that never stopped Blunt from loving him. In 1935, Blunt visited Russia, and in 1937 Blunt gave in to Burgess's pleadings and became a spy for the Soviet Union. Like whatever the brilliant Blunt did in his professional life, his efforts on behalf of the KGB were spectacular. Blunt recruited individuals at Cambridge who joined the notorious Cambridge Four (Kim Philby, Donald Maclean, Guy Burgess and our man Anthony Blunt) who were responsible for the most devastating breach of security in England's history

In June 1940, Blunt wormed his way into England's MI5, which is the country's security service (sort of like the FBI.) Throughout World War II, in that sensitive position, Blunt was able to obtain highly classified secret material. The position made it easy for him to pass thousands of sensitive documents to Moscow. Not satisfied with passing on routine classified documents, Blunt biographer Miranda Carter says that "Blunt went to great lengths to arrange for a huge range of secret information to come to his attention."

Here is a summary of papers Blunt passed to the Soviets: MI5 internal documents, personal files on people targeted for cultivation [by the Russians], wireless intercepts, diplomatic telegrams, German intelligence reports from the Eastern Front and elsewhere, military intelligence summaries, MI5 reports on immigrants, surveillance information, personality profiles of key figures in MI5, the name of every MI5 officer, descriptions of procedures and methods of MI5, including how they inserted bugs, how they ran investigations and how they debriefed defectors. Blunt continued his recruiting and document leaking for some 30 years. Experts disagree about how many deaths were the result of Blunt's spying, but a case can be made that it was hundreds, if not thousands, depending on how you count.

Blunt's career received a major boost in 1937, when, thanks to the intervention of the distinguished art scholar, Rudolf Wittkower, he was granted a position at the Warburg Institute. During this time, Blunt also taught classes at the Courtauld Institute. After the war, in 1945, while still working as a Russian spy, Blunt was appointed Surveyor (curator) of the Queen's pictures, and in 1947, he was made director of the Courtauld Institute. In 1951, while still active for the Soviets, Blunt was instrumental in arranging for fellow spies Burgess and Maclean to defect to Moscow. It was about this time that MI5 and the FBI began to have suspicions that Anthony Blunt was a Soviet spy. He began to be questioned. Between 1951 and 1964, Blunt was formally interrogated by MI5 a total of eleven times. Blunt denied everything.

Here's one for the ages. In the face of (and in the middle of) this official suspicion, Russian spy Anthony Blunt was knighted by the Queen in 1956, ironically, in recognition for his services to the Crown. About 1963, the same year Kim Philby defected to Russia, Michael Straight, whom Blunt had unsuccessfully recruited, told MI5 and the FBI about Blunt's treachery. Anthony Blunt confessed.

Now, if you believe that one of the gang that perpetrated the most devastating breach of security in England's long and storied history was exposed and punished, I have 400,000 acres of swampland in New Jersey I'd like to sell you. No, after reading this book, I'm sure you have figured out that the insular world of art and the upper reaches of English society would take care of its own.

In 1964, MI5, after keeping his confession secret for over one year, made a deal with confessed spy Anthony Blunt, granting him immunity from prosecution in return for critical information about the KGB. The British secret service actually believed that Blunt would give them important information. For the next 15 years, while dogging rumors he was the sought after fourth man of the Cambridge Group, Blunt reigned as the king of Britain's art establishment, with unlimited access to the royal family.

How did Blunt do it? Easy, for him. Blunt never upheld his end of the bargain: He consistently fed useless information to his naive deprogrammers. Why was the investigation of Blunt handled in such a pathetic manner? The British upper-class was in the key positions of MI5, MI6, and, indeed, the government itself. They just couldn't get their hands around the fact that Blunt betrayed his class.

In 1974, after 25 years at the Courtauld, Blunt retired as director, having made the Institute a major player in the world of art. At this time, Blunt was appointed Advisor to the Royal Collection (an honorary post) thereby keeping him within the palace walls a full six more years. In late 1978, after learning he was about to be exposed as a Soviet spy, Blunt resigned this position. Finally, in 1979, beating the British press by a length, because of a thinly disguised Blunt in Andrew Boyle's book "The Climate of Treason," the Iron Lady, Prime Minister Margaret Thatcher, told the House of Commons that the traitor, the notorious fourth man, was indeed Anthony Blunt. At this point, reacting to a media frenzy, the Queen stripped Blunt of his position and knighthood. The public also turned against him, stripping him of his various memberships, titles, fellowships and recognitions. Anthony Blunt died a few years later (in 1983) a broken shell of a man.

So what else (besides spying for England's enemies) did this tall, fairly handsome, arrogant, bloodless, emotionally rigid person do to earn his exalted unscrupulous ranking? Blunt was never remotely remorseful that he had betrayed his country. Can there possibly be more? There can be and there is.

But before moving on, remember, we're not talking about a guy named Joe here. Blunt is considered the most powerful man in British art history. At the Courtauld he focused on teaching connoisseurship when nobody else did. The effect of that was to graduate museum directors, art historians and scholars in record numbers. If Americans wanted to authenticate a work of art in the 1960s, they took it to the Courtauld. Also, remember, Blunt was an intimate of the royal family who enjoyed unlimited access to its palaces before and for 15 years after he was exposed as a Russian spy. Besides leading a double life as a Soviet spy and an art historian (head of the Courtauld Institute and curator of the Queen's paintings), believe it or not Blunt had a third secret life.

Anthony Blunt was gay. He and his associates would troll the pubs and taverns in the toughest part of town and pick up what is known as rough trade. In addition, throughout his life Blunt had hundreds of male lovers. Nothing wrong with that; it was his personal life style choice. The problem is that during Blunt's salad days homosexuality was a crime in England. Consequently, Blunt had to work as hard concealing his homosexuality as he did in concealing the fact that he was a spy for the Soviet Union. So, if you're following this, Blunt didn't lead a double life, he led a triple double life. Could Blunt have led a fourple (is that a word?) double life?

He could and he did. Blunt became a closet unscrupulous art dealer, authenticating and handling fakes. In 1959 (while he was still head of the Courtauld Institute of Art and Surveyor of the Queen's pictures and drawings), Blunt met Eric Hebborn in Rome, where Hebborn was studying art at the British School. Hebborn, you will recall, was one of the most proficient art forgers in history. The Blunt/Hebborn relationship was made in heaven. They were both intelligent, widely read, immersed in the art world, leading secret lives, and homosexual. The two men became close, personal friends. In 1963, Hebborn moved permanently to Rome, so when Blunt went to Rome (which he loved) he stayed with Hebborn, and when Hebborn went to London he stayed with Blunt.

All their lives, Blunt and Hebborn denied they were lovers but logic says otherwise. (What's interesting is because both men denied that they engaged in a sexual relationship, otherwise reliable researchers believe these two men whose entire lives were built on lies.) Blunt, from his position on high, helped Hebborn establish himself as a dealer, which gave Hebborn a front for selling his brilliant fakes. Blunt not only authenticated Hebborn's fakes, he became a dealer, subtlety hawking Hebborn's forgeries to unsuspecting dealers, collectors, and auction houses. Because the relationship was carried on in typical Blunt fashion, that is to say secretly, Blunt was highly successful selling Hebborn fakes. In return for authenticating and selling his forgeries, Hebborn paid Blunt finder's fees (read money) and supplied him other goodies (read boys).

Preposterous as it sounds, for all of Anthony Blunt's life-long treachery, heinous duplicity, and traitorous and criminal activity, he didn't spend one single night in prison.

CHAPTER FOURTEEN
UNSCRUPULOUS EMPEROR

SINGLE-HANDEDLY UNDERMINING THE MUSEUM SYSTEM
AS WE KNOW IT

Philip Anschutz

This 69-year-old Denver billionaire, who lives on a large ranch in Colorado, has one of the largest collections of western art in the world. *Fortune Magazine* named Anschutz the Greediest Executive in 2002, and the BBC called him a corporate vulture. Business-wise, while accruing his billions, the highly secretive Anschutz has been involved with, among other things, making and taking bribes, accounting fraud to exaggerate profits, tax avoidance, and other questionable, money-making schemes.

One example. Early in 2000, he urged the employees of Qwest (a company he founded) to hang on to their Qwest stock while he sold over 6,000,000 shares. Anschutz made roughly a quarter of a billion dollars while watching the workers get wiped out. Where did Anschutz, 69, make his money? He inherited a land and oil-drilling business from his father. He segued into more oil, uranium and coal mines, cattle ranches, railroads, communications, newspapers, entertainment, movies, sports, arenas, and anything else not nailed down. You guessed it. The man is smart.

While he may or may not be the greediest, Philip Anschutz is certainly one of the richest, one of the most bigoted, and one of the least public-spirited individuals to ever walk the face of the earth. Bigoted?

Anschutz professes to be an ultra right-wing Christian conservative. What does that mean he stands for? Apparently nothing specifically positive; just generalizations like wanting to change "decadence" in Hollywood, and believing in "family values." The label appears to translate into strictly negative beliefs, such as being anti-gay, anti-single parenting, and anti-abortion. Even anti-social security. In other words, it appears Anschutz is against anything that relates to the real world and real people's needs. Anschutz is a major donor to Christian causes and to the Republican party and its candidates.

So he's rapacious and extreme in his religious beliefs. Does that mean Philip Anschutz is not public-spirited? More important, what does all of that have to do with tampering with a nation's (or world's) book of art?

Let's examine the question. Are museums important to the world's book of art? Here's one clue. Over 30,000,000 people annually visit the world's top five museums (the Louvre, British Museum, Pompidou Center, Tate Modern, and Met). And that's only the top five. How is Philip Anschutz threatening this?

In early 2008, the Denver Art Museum, with the help of Anschutz's donation, purchased from the Philadelphia Museum of Art an 1892 painting by famed American artist Thomas Eakins (1844–1916) named, "Cowboy Singing." (While the amount paid, in typical museum secrecy, has not been disclosed, experts put the price somewhere between $8,000,000 and $15,000,000.) In return for a relatively modest donation, Anschutz negotiated a joint 50% ownership of the Thomas Eakins painting the Denver Art Museum bought, and won the right to display the artwork in his private home six months of every year. In perpetuity.

If you think that's unbelievable, listen to this. Tied to this same donation, Anschutz also negotiated a joint 50% ownership interest in the Denver Art Museum's prize holding, a painting by Charles Deas (1818–1867) named, "Long Jakes (The Rocky Mountain Man)." The Denver Art Museum, which acquired the painting in 1999, naturally owned 100% of the masterpiece upon purchasing it. Since acquiring the Deas masterpiece, the museum has trumpeted on its website that the Deas painting is the crown jewel of its collection; that the Deas painting is the single most influential image in Rocky Mountain iconography; and that, in the painting, Deas established the mountain man as an icon. Anschutz now can enjoy this crown jewel in his private home for six months of every year. In perpetuity.

In addition, as part of the same negotiation, in 2008 Anschutz had the Denver Art Museum sell certain of its works to acquire for him an Eakins sketch and study for an Eakins painting he already owned. Would thousands believe this? The deal raises numerous questions, not the least of which are the ethical ones, which the so-called watchdog, the American Association of Museum Directors (AAMDA) claims to be investigating. Don't hold your breath.

Here are a few logical questions. What do the director and board of the museum tell the 14+ individuals and organizations who raised the funds in 1999 to acquire the Charles Deas crown jewel in memory of Bob Magness. They'll probably say, "Screw Bob Magness, he's dead." How safe can it be to transport valuable paintings to and fro, twice every year? In perpetuity. They'll probably say, "What problem? We'll use bubble wrap." What does the Denver Art Museum tell the visitors who travel great distances to see their crown jewel and/or their latest blockbuster acquisition? They'll probably say, "Come back in six months." Should the museum give its visitors a discount during the six months their crown jewel and their Eakins masterwork are missing in action? They'll probably say, "Don't miss our gift shop." What's next? Can donors make a gift to a museum and therefore acquire a 50% interest in the museum's entire Impressionist or Old Master paintings, and keep the artworks in their homes for six months every year? In perpetuity. Or, maybe they can make a deal for an entire wing and keep the pieces in their home. In perpetuity. Or, maybe, with a smaller museum, a donor can co-opt the entire museum and visit it in total privacy for six months of every year. In perpetuity.

The possibilities are endless and boggle the mind. Philip Anschutz can undoubtedly come up with dozens, even hundreds, maybe thousands of additional possibilities. And then act on them with his cleaver. This scandalous agreement is another case that would never have seen the light of day if alert journalists hadn't uncovered it. When the *Denver Post* announced the arrangement in a routine story, blogger Tyler Green dug in. Based on his postings, the paper's follow-up story was now headlined, "Museum's art deal with Anschutz raises eyebrows." One last question. Where the hell was the board of trustees of the Denver Art Museum?

The Denver Art Museum

The Denver Art Museum, founded in 1893, has had nothing but problems under director Lewis Sharp's "leadership" in the last 20 years. In the early 1990s, Sharp, shortly after having been hired in 1989, made a deal with notorious art dealer Gerald Peters. Peters arranged secret swaps with certain of his friends. The museum sold these private citizens a number of valuable paintings at fire-sale prices in two secret transactions. When the deals were uncovered, the museum found itself engulfed in a major public scandal. When the deals were finally examined, it was obvious they were structured by Peters for his personal gain at the expense of the museum. Peters kept his fees. In 1995, the Denver Art Museum subsequently sold off some 1,500 articles, but this time, smarting from the horrific press, the sale was an auction and announced in advance. In 2006, the Denver Art Museum opened its new addition, with a roof that began to leak. Sharp believed the new structure would in itself draw hordes of visitors; the build it and they will come syndrome. *The Denver Post* reported that Lewis Sharp (who, remember, had been director for the last 20 years and should have known the territory), projected 1,000,000 people would visit the museum the first year. It didn't happen. Not only did the board accept delivery of an addition with a leaky roof, about half of Sharp's irresponsible projected visitor count showed up. In early 2007, the museum was forced to cut staff to reduce expenses. Shortly thereafter, in early 2008, Lewis Sharp, the pathetic director of the beleaguered Denver Art Museum, made his desperate deal with Philip Anschutz.

After entering into the single worse agreement in museum history, Lewis Sharp sunk into complete denial. "I'd do it again tomorrow if I had the opportunity," he said. Let's make no mistake what Sharp was talking about. He was talking about the deal with Philip Anschutz that could be the beginning of the end of 255 years of worldwide museum-going as we know it.

So there you have it. Philip Anschutz, Unscrupulous Emperor. Can the crown can ever be snatched from him? It's doubtful. But remember what they say in sports. Records are made to be broken.

SELECT BIBLIOGRAPHY

Anderson, John. *Art Held Hostage: The Battle over the Barnes Collection.* USA, 2003.

Arnau, Frank. *The Art of the Faker: Three Thousand Years of Deception in Art and Antiques.* Germany, 1959. Translated from the German by John Brown, J. Maxwell. Boston, 1961.

Barnes Catalogue. *Great French Paintings from the Barnes Foundation: Impressionism, Post-Impressionism, and Early Modern,* Italy, 1993; New York, 2005.

Beck, James. *From Duccio to Raphael. Connoisseurship in Crisis.* Italy, 2006.

Behrman, S.N. *Duveen.* USA, 1951, 1952.

Berenson, Bernard. *Sketch for a Self-Portrait.* New York, 1949.

Burnham, Sophy. *The Art Crowd.* New York, 1973.

Carey, Peter. *Theft: A Love Story.* Australia & UK, 2006.

Carter, Miranda. *Anthony Blunt: His Lives.* USA, 2001.

Catterall, Lee. *The Great Dali Art Fraud and Other Deceptions,* USA, 1992.

Clark, Kenneth. *Another Part of the Wood: A Self-Portrait.* New York, 1974.

Cuno, James, ed. *Whose Muse? Art Museums and the Public Trust.* China, 2006.

___. *Who Owns Antiquity? Museums and the Battle Over Our Ancient Heritage.* Princeton, NJ, 2008

Dutton, Denis, ed. *The Forger's Art: Forgery and the Philosophy of Art.* USA, 1984

Duveen, James Henry. *The Rise of the House of Duveen.* New York, 1957.

Gaddis, William. *The Recognitions.* USA, 1952, 1955.

Goodrich, David. *Art Fakes in America.* USA, 1973.

Gladwell, Malcolm. *Blink: The Power of Thinking Without Thinking.* USA, 2005.

Hamilton, Charles. *Auction Madness.* New York and Canada, 1981.

Hansen, Suzanne. *You'll Never Nanny in This Town Again.* New York, 2005.

Haywood, Ian. *Faking It: Art and the Politics of Forgery.* USA, 1987.

Hebborn, Eric. *Drawn to Trouble: Confessions of a Master Forger.* UK & New York, 1991 & 1997.

___. *The Art Forger's Handbook.* New York, 1997

Hess, John. *The Grand Acquisitors.* USA, 1974.

Hofstadter, Dan. *Goldberg's Angel. An Adventure in the Antiquities Trade.* USA and Canada, 1994.

Hoving, Thomas. *Making the Mummies Dance: Inside the Metropolitan Museum of Art.* New York, 1993.

___. *False Impressions: The Hunt for Big Time Art Fakes.* New York, 1996.

Hyde, Stephen, and Geno Zanetti, eds. *Players: Con Men, Hustlers, Gamblers, and Scam Artists.* New York, 2002.

Innes, Brian. *Fakes & Forgeries.* Singapore, 2005.

Irving, Clifford. *Fake: The Story of Elmyr de Hory, the Greatest Art Forger of Our Time.* USA, 1969.

Jackman, Ian, ed. *Con Men. Fascinating Profiles of Swindlers and Rogues from the Files of the Most Successful Broadcast in Television History.* New York, 2003.

Joni, Icilio Federico. *Le Memorie di un pittore di Quadri Antichi, a fronte la versione in inglese, Affairs of a Painter.* Siena, Italy, 2004.

Keating, Tom, Geraldine Norman, Frank Norman. *The Fakes Progress.* London, 1977.

Kurz, Otto. *Fakes.* New York, 1967.

Lacey, Robert. *Sotheby's: Bidding for Class.* USA, 1998.

Magnusson, Magnus. *Fakers, Forgers & Phoneys: Famous Scams and Scamps.* UK, 2006.

Mendax, Fritz. *Art Fakes & Forgeries.* New York, 1956. Translated from the German by H. S. Whitman.

Marion, John. *The Best of Everything: The Insider's Guide to Collecting for Every Taste and for Every Budget.* New York, 1989.

Mason, Christopher. *The Art of the Steal.* New York, 2004.

Maurer, David. *The Big Con: The Story of the Confidence Man.* USA, 1999.

Meyer, Karl. *The Plundered Past.* London, 1973.

Mills, John FitzMaurice, and John M. Mansfield. *The Genuine Article.* London, 1979.

Minneapolis Institute of Arts. *Fakes and Forgeries.* USA, 1973. Exhibition Catalogue.

Moeller, Achim. *In Good Hands.* New York, 1997.

Moffitt, John. *Art Forgery: The Case of the Lady of Elche.* USA, 1995.

Muchnic, Suzanne. *Odd Man in: Norton Simon and the Pursuit of Culture.* USA, 1998.

Muscarella, Oscar White. *The Lie Became Great: The Forgery of Ancient Near Eastern Cultures.* The Netherlands, 2000.

Petropoulos, Jonathan. *The Faustian Bargain: The Art World in Nazi Germany.* New York, 2000.

Radnoti, Sandor. *The Fake: Forgery and Its Place in Art.* USA, 1999.

Reit, Seymour. *The Day They Stole the Mona Lisa.* USA, 1981

Richardson, John. *Sacred Monsters, Sacred Masters.* USA & Canada, 2001.

Samuels, Ernest, with the collaboration of Jayne Samuels Newcomer. *Bernard Berenson: The Making of a Connoisseur.* Cambridge, Mass. & London, 1979.

___. *Bernard Berenson: The Making of a Legend.* Cambridge, Mass. & London, 1987

Schuller, Sepp. *Forgers, Dealers, Experts: Strange Chapters in The History of Art, Germany, 1959.* English translation, UK, 1960.

Secrest, Meryle. *Being Bernard Berenson.* New York, 1979.

___. *Duveen: A Life in Art.* New York, 2004.

Seldes, Lee. *The Legacy of Mark Rothko: An Expose of the Greatest Art Scandal of Our Century.* London, 1978.

Sifakis, Carl. *Frauds, Deceptions and Swindles.* USA, 2001.

Simpson, Colin. *Artful Partners: Bernard Berenson and Joseph Duveen.* New York, 1986.

Sox, David. *Unmasking the Forger: The Dossena Deception.* New York, 1988.

Stein, Anne-Marie, as told to George Carpozi, Jr. *Three Picassos Before Breakfast: Memoirs of an Art Forger's Wife.* New York, 1973.

Stourton, James. *Great Collectors of Our Time: Art Collecting Since 1945.* China, 2007.

Towner, Wesley. *The Elegant Auctioneers.* New York, 1970.

Van Dyke, John. *Rembrandt and His School.* New York, 1923.

Vasari, Giorgio. *The Lives of the Artists.* Translated and with an Introduction and Notes by Julia Conaway Bondanella and Peter Bondanella. Great Britain, 1998.

Volpe, Tod. *Framed: Tales of the Art Underworld.* Canada, 2003.

Vrettos, Theodore. *The Elgin Affair: The Abduction of Antiquities Greatest Treasures and the Passions It Aroused.* New York, 1997.

Waldron, Ann. *True or False: Amazing Art Forgeries.* USA, 1983.

Walker, John. *Self-Portrait with Donors: Confessions of an Art Collector.* UK, 1974.

Walton, Kenneth. *Fake: Forgery, Lies, and eBAY.* USA, 2006.

Watson, Peter. *From Manet to Manhattan: The Rise of the Modern Art Market.* USA & Canada, 1992.

___. *Sotheby's: The Inside Story.* New York, 1997.

___, with Cecilia Todeschini. *The Medici Conspiracy: The Illicit Journey of Looted Antiquities, from Italy's Tomb Raiders to the World's Greatest Museums.* USA, 2006.

Waxman, Sharon. *Loot: The Battle over the Stolen Treasures of The Ancient World.* New York, 2008.

Werner, Paul. *Museums, Inc.: Inside the Global Art World.* USA, 2005.

Wright, Christopher. *The Art of the Forger.* New York, 1985.

Wright, Robert. *The Art Game.* New York, 1965.

INDEX

Also by Nick J. Mileti

CLOSET ITALIANS: A Dazzling Collection of Illustrious Italians with Non-Italian Names

BEYOND MICHELANGELO: The Deadly Rivalry between Borromini and Bernini

www.ingramcontent.com/pod-product-compliance
Lightning Source LLC
Chambersburg PA
CBHW071357170526
45165CB00001B/82